JOSEPH CROSBY LINCOLN (1870 - 1944)

From the painting by Harold Brett finished in 1943.

The Prolific Pencil

a biography of
Joseph Crosby Lincoln, Litt.D.

By

Percy Fielitz Rex

Edited by

Fredrika A. Burrows

with

A Descriptive Bibliography
of First Editions Edited by

Stephen W. Sullwold

William S. Sullwold Publishing, Inc.
Taunton, Massachusetts
1980

LCCCN — 80-51482
ISBN — 0-88492-037-2

FIRST EDITION

PRINTED IN THE UNITED STATES OF AMERICA

Dedicated
to my Cape Cod wife
Ruth Irwin Rex

Preface

The writer of this biography has no intention of splitting Joe Lincoln from head to toe in order to dissect his motives and impulses, his personal likes and dislikes, or his judgements or differences. Rather he has sought to present the story of a man who worked hard at his writing, exercising a prolific pencil to portray those times and places of which he was a part, for the pleasure and profit of hundreds of thousands of people all over America, England, Canada and Australia.

Joe Lincoln kept no journal of his life and thoughts; not even an annual diary of appointments exists to make the preparation of a chronology easy. The author has had to have the help of many people, especially in those places where Joe lived during his 27,054 days on this earth.

Introduction

The dear old Cape! I love it! I love its hills of sand,
The sea wind singing over it, the seaweed on its strand;
The bright blue ocean round it, the clear blue sky o'erhead;
The fishing boats, the dripping nets, the white sails
    filled and spread —
For each heart has its picture, and each its own home song,
The sights and sounds which move it when Youth's fair
    memories throng;
And when down dreamland pathways a boy, I stroll once more,
I hear the mighty music of the surf along the shore.

          (from *Cape Cod Ballads* by Joseph C. Lincoln)

Joseph C. Lincoln was a Cape Codder, not only by birth but by inheritance and association. In a conversation with the late poet Joyce Kilmer, Lincoln said, "I am a Cape Codder. My people have been Cape Codders for generations. They have lived at Cape Cod when they were at home, but most of the time, of course, they were out at sea. I was born at Cape Cod and spent my summers there. I cannot imagine myself tiring of Cape Cod."

Thus we find Mr. Lincoln writing about times, places and people with which he was thoroughly familiar. "In writing of a Cape Cod town or village," he continued, "although I purposely refrained from describing it as any one town in particular, I have tried conscientiously to give it the characteristics of the Cape Cod towns I am acquainted with. The promontories and inlets and hills and marshes in 'my' Cape Cod may not be found where I have located them, but I have tried very hard to make them like those which are, or were, to be found on the Cape.

"And so with Cape Codders in my stories. I have never knowingly drawn the exact recognizable portrait of an individual. — I have endeavored always to be true to type."

Although Lincoln claimed that his characters were not actual people, but composites of several different individuals, readers will recognize in his books many people and events which were part of young Joe's life on the Cape. He didn't need to study types, — he was one himself, even at times lapsing into the old Cape Cod vernacular of pronouncing "hev" for have, "hed" for had, or "e-yuh" in agreement.

And so, like all successful authors, Joe Lincoln wrote about those things which he knew best. "I like the Cape marshes with their different greens, the cranberry bogs with their lavender shades, the stillness of the woods when I ride through at night, the beauty of Cape ponds and lakes, of which we have so many.

"There is a serenity of life there, particularly in the Fall of the year, that would be hard to duplicate — a quietness that is appreciated more and more as we grow older and a friendliness that is nurtured by the peaceful surroundings. I love Cape Cod."

What is this land that Lincoln loved so dearly, where his fictional people lived? It is a land where, as *Time* magazine once wrote, "If a hurricane blew everybody off Cape Cod, it could be re-populated overnight by the fictional offspring of Joseph C. Lincoln."

It is an island "East of America", confronting four "seas", namely, Cape Cod Bay, the Atlantic Ocean, Vineyard Sound, and Buzzards Bay, and cut off from the mainland by the building of the Cape Cod Canal in 1914. It extends from the Cohasset Narrows to Race Point.

Here, on the glacial moraines, amidst pitch pine trees and around fresh-water ponds, members of the Plymouth Colony built villages with white church spires rising above the trees and snug grey-shingled cottages nestled behind the dunes, and founded families whose offspring are now scattered across the nation.

As he wrote about the people of Cape Cod, did Joe Lincoln intend to say something to his readers? It seems to me that in an increasingly computerized world, he reminds us that we too are human, by making his fictional characters human in turn. In a world constantly torn by the sorrows of war and strife, he reminds us that joy is just as much a reality as sorrow. In a world that insists on debunking everything, he reminds us that there is that which is wholesome and good and is to be desired. Joe Lincoln reminds us of our heritage and tells us to keep it intact.

P. F. R.

Acknowledgments

Without the cooperation and contributions of time and materials by many people, this book could not have been published in its present form. We are most grateful to Mrs. Percy Fielitz Rex for entrusting us with her late husband's manuscript and voluminous notes. Her decision was understandably complicated, not only emotionally, but also by a strong desire to see the finished book presenting Joe Lincoln as her author husband saw him.

To Freddie Burrows for having the courage to tackle the difficult task of editing, made even more trying by the shifts in direction by me.

To Virginia Lincoln, (Mrs. Joseph Freeman Lincoln) for the use of valued family pictures, information, and the disruption of her normal routine, all of which helped us immeasurably.

To Josephine B. Ivanoff, who ran interference, encouraged, and pointed out the right direction when courses became clouded.

To Walter E. Babbitt, who saved much needed time by clarifying conditions and suggesting alternative solutions.

To Nancy Titcomb, who shared her book knowledge and extensive Lincoln collection with us. We would be remiss if we failed to mention the interruptions we inflicted on Nancy. Be assured we are grateful.

Because the book was offered in pre-publication, book stores and benevolent groups participated in its sale. All of your efforts are appreciated and we hope were mutually rewarding.

In this regard, there are two people who did outstanding work, and whom we wish to single out for special recognition.

To Mildred Chamberlin, who did an extensive mailing and accounted for a major portion of our pre-publication sales, this along with lending us the use of her extensive collection of books and memorabilia.

To Gladys M. Burgess, who piloted our program through acceptance by the Bourne Historical Society, and who along with her daughter implemented a successful mailing program. For this and favors in the past, many thanks.

We were offered numerous suggestions by well-intentioned friends and advisors as to the form this book should take, from cover design to literary form. We appreciate your concern and regret that all your ideas could not be used.

The bibliography is expanded beyond what the author had originally intended. This was decided upon to make the book a more valuable tool for collectors and students. My son Stephen accepted the responsibility for editing this material, and his considerable contribution beyond what might be considered normal is here acknowledged.

William S. Sullwold

Contents

PART I

Chapter 1

Brewster — A Cape Cod Village

Brewster, Massachusetts, was one of four villages in the Town (township) of Brewster in 1870. The other three villages were East Brewster, West Brewster, and South Brewster, each of which had its own post office and store amidst scattered dwelling houses. Brewster was one of thirteen towns along with the District of Mashpee which made up Barnstable County, the political unit and geographical area known as Cape Cod.

That part of Cape Cod known to the native Indians as "Sawkatuckett" was the north precinct of the Town of Harwich, incorporated on the 14th of September, 1694, by the Plymouth Colony. Brewster was set off by the General Court of Massachusetts as a separate Town on February 19, 1803 with a population of 1353 persons.

These lands of the Town of Harwich were purchased from Indians such as Nepoyeton, his daughters and their husbands, the Quasons, the Sipsons, and others. The ancestors of Joe Lincoln, the Lincolns and the Crosbys, settled on some of these lands before Brewster was separated from old Harwich. Therefore it is said that they settled in Harwich.

There are several fresh water ponds in the Brewster-Harwich area. The Mill pond, the source of Herring River which flows north into Cape Cod Bay, furnished the water power for the settlers' mills. Herring River has been beautifully described by John Hay in his book, *The Run.* Cliff Pond, which was the adult Joe Lincoln's

1

favorite fishing spot, is one of the deepest ponds on the Cape and is now a part of the Nickerson State Park.

In most of the two hundred and fifty some-odd houses in Brewster in 1870 there resided mariners, many of them captains still in active service. Joseph Lincoln's father was one of these. There were blue water, coastal and fishing men. Steam was beginning to replace the great merchant sailing fleet of the eastern coast of the United States (In her letters home Emily Lincoln often speaks of their sailing ship being towed into harbor by a steamer). J. Henry Sears in his *Brewster Ship Masters* gives a picture of the men who were still active and brief accounts of the many well-known captains who called Brewster home. When these men retired from the sea, they became active in the life of the community — in town affairs, in church affairs, in farming, and especially in the new industry begun in Harwich in the 1850's, namely, cranberry growing.

Many of them could afford to and did build fine colonial homes, many of which adorn the village to this day. As a boy growing up in Brewster, Joe Lincoln walked by these impressive houses each day on his way to school, and was accustomed to seeing and knowing many men for whom the sea had been the highway to success.

Since Joe has a great deal to say about churches, it is important for us to know about the churches in his native village, for he almost always writes out of first-hand knowledge.

In a poem called "Wasted Energy", Joe says there are nine hundred people in South Pocus who are divided between their seven churches. In his boyhood, Brewster had about the same number of people divided between the Unitarian, Universalist, Methodist, Baptist, and perhaps a Come-Outer congregation.

The First Parish Church, Unitarian in Brewster was organized as a Congregationalist Church on October 16, 1700. The Reverend Nathaniel Stone, a graduate of Harvard College, William Merrick, John Freeman, Edward Bangs, Josiah Paine, Simon Crosby and Thomas Crosby were the organizers. Joe Lincoln was related to the Freemans and the Bangs, and the father of the two Crosby boys was an ancestor of Joe's. This ancestor was the Reverend Thomas Crosby. This Congregational Church, like many others, became Unitarian in theology and name in the middle of the nineteenth century, and continues so to this day.

In November of 1824, Joe's grandfather, Captain Isaac Lincoln,

Jr., and his great-grandfather, Captain Isaac, Sr., along with General Elijah Cobb, Freeman Foster, E.D. Winslow, Barnabus Thacher, Heman Griffith and Theophilus Berry organized the Universalist Society of Brewster.

So the Lincolns were Universalists and the Crosbys were Unitarians. Since Joe's mother brought him up, he went to the Unitarian Sunday School and church. As we shall see, however, he was married in a Universalist Church in Chelsea, Massachusetts, and during his twenty-five years in Hackensack, New Jersey, he was a very active member of the Congregational-Unitarian Church in that city.

The Methodist Church in Brewster was organized about 1822, and the Baptist Church in 1824. Among the names associated with these churches are people who were only distantly related to Joseph Lincoln.

West Brewster, where the first Lincolns to come to Harwich settled, became an industrial area called "Factory Village". The Winslows had the first fulling mill in America here and the area was sometimes called "Winslow's Mills". However, by 1870 there was not much manufacturing left. There was a knitted goods factory, and another with an interesting name, "The Button & Harpoon Manufactory" operated by Charles Freeman. (The Freemans were related to the Lincolns by marriage.)

At that time Brewster had no bank as well as no hotel, no restaurant, and no telephone or telegraph service. There was a telegraph office at the depot in Harwich Center where Miss Sarah L. Sears was the telegrapher. Miss Carrie Baker was the telegrapher at South Dennis, and Miss Amelia Snow presided over that instrument at Orleans. At a later time Miss Edith Wright of Pocasset held the very important post of telegrapher at the railroad-ferry-boat station at Woods Hole. In his story "Izzy and The Other", Joe gives Gertie Cummings the job of telegrapher in his depot at Wellmouth. Joe knew that being a telegrapher was one of the good jobs open to women of the time about which he wrote.

Dean Dudley's *Directory and History of Plymouth and Barnstable Counties for 1873-74* reports that in 1873 Dr. Samuel H. Gould was the resident physician in Brewster. It is more than likely that he attended Emily Lincoln when her son was born. Charles S. Foster, the Town Clerk and Treasurer, recorded Joseph Crosby Lincoln's birth in the Town Register. (The Fosters and Lincolns were related through Joe's grandmother).

3

Elisha Crocker sold boots and shoes in his store in Brewster, and his son, Elisha, Jr., was the local undertaker. Benjamin Crocker was a blacksmith, and his son, Benjamin, Jr., sold stoves and such in his store. Another blacksmith was Zoeth Snow, Jr., — horses were power in 1870.

There were six country stores in the Town, one of which was operated by Captain Warren Lincoln, Joe's first cousin twice removed. Joseph Foster had the East Brewster country store, which also contained the Post Office, and Eben F. Ryder, a selectman, had the West Brewster store and Post Office.

Emily Lincoln's sister, Mrs. Martha Crosby Huckins, was the Brewster Postmistress. She kept the Post Office in her millinery shop next door to the house in which Joe Lincoln is said to have been born.

The succession of this Post Office is interesting. Silvanus Stone (1746-1811), grandson of the first minister in Brewster, The Rev. Nathaniel Stone, became the first Town Clerk and Treasurer of Brewster on March 8, 1803, and on July 1, 1804, Mr. Stone became the first Postmaster in Brewster. The Postmasters of the early days of the service kept the post office in their houses, but more often than not in their stores.

Freeman, in his *History of Cape Cod*, gives us an interesting item about postmasters in Brewster. On March 8, 1810, one Edward O'Bryan (O'Brien) was appointed Postmaster of Brewster. The Town Meeting of this year voted "to remonstrate against the appointment of O'Brien as postmaster, he being a foreignor, and in the opinion of the inhabitants, an alien".

Dr. Joseph Samson became postmaster on October 1, 1815. Gen. Jeremiah Mayo had the post office in his house beginning February 11, 1833. Dean Bangs became postmaster May 8, 1849. Ebenezer H. Knowles took over the office on April 3, 1851.

Joseph Clark Crosby, grandfather of Joe Lincoln, followed Ebenezer H. Knowles as postmaster in Brewster. Mr. Crosby kept the post office in his shoemaker's shop next to his house. When he died, his daughter Martha Crosby Huckins became postmistress.

Known in the family as the "house and shop", the property was transferred to Captain Joseph Lincoln on September 15, 1866. Phebe Crosby Crosby, second wife of Joseph Clark Crosby, had inherited it from her husband upon his death. From a comment

4

in a letter written by Captain Joseph Lincoln, it appears that he gave his wife's stepmother a note for the property.

The transfer was reported in the Barnstable County Probate Court Records as follows: "Beginning at the northwest corner of the premises by the public road thence easterly by Sd road Seven Rods and Seventeen Links (126.72 ft.) to a stake by the fence thence southerly by land of Desire Crowell Six Rods and Ten Links (105.6 ft.) to a stake thence southeasterly by land of Sd Crowell Ten Rods and Sixteen Links (181.56 ft.) to a stake by the fence thence northerly by land of the heirs of Jeremiah Mayo Seven Rods and Sixteen Links (126.06 ft.) and thence by other land of Sd Mayo thence northeasterly Seven Rods (115.5 ft.) to first named bound together with the dwelling house and shop standing on the premises."

The Brewster schoolhouse was three-eighths of a mile along the Public Road, west of Joe Lincoln's first home. The First Parish Church which he and his mother attended was one-fourth of a mile east of his home. The shore of Cape Cod Bay was about five-eighths of a mile north of the house and shop. The Ladies' Circulating Library was about halfway between Joe's home and his church on the Public Road. Joe did not have far to go to do the things expected of a child in those days — he could get the mail for his mother from the shop attached to his home, walk to school and church, and pick up groceries at the general store down the road. It was in this setting that Joseph got his first impressions, — impressions that he was to describe so realistically in his writings.

The Lincoln plot in Union cemetery, Chatham, Mass. Two small stones in foreground are Joseph C. Lincoln and his wife Florence S. Lincoln.

6

Chapter 2

The Lincolns of Brewster, Mass.

Lincoln Genealogy

1. Thomas Lincoln, d. 1691 Hingham
   mrd. Miss Annis Lane, d. 1683
2. Benjamin Lincoln (1643-1700)
   mrd. Miss Sarah Fearing (1649-1716)
3. Deacon Thomas Lincoln (1674-1739)
   mrd. Miss Rachel Holmes, d. 1757, b. Rochester, MA.
4. Nathaniel Lincoln (1704-1772)
   mrd. Miss Hannah Astine (1712- ?)
5. Nathaniel Lincoln, Jr. (1738-1785)
   mrd. Miss Mary Crosby Clark (1741-1783)
6. Captain Isaac Lincoln (1773-1829)
   mrd. Miss Deborah Rogers (1774-1840)
7. Captain Isaac Lincoln, Jr. 1797 - lost at sea 1838
   mrd. Miss Desire Freeman Foster, Jr. (1800-1891)
8. Captain Joseph Lincoln (1825-1870)
   mrd. Miss Emily Crosby (1832-1897)
9. Joseph Crosby Lincoln (1870-1944)
   mrd. Miss Florence Elry Sargent (1872-1954)
10. Joseph Freeman Lincoln (1900-1962)
    mrd. Miss Virginia Cross (1906-   )

References

Farmer: *A Genealogical Register of the First Settlers of New England;* Lancaster, Mass. 1829

Mayo: *Mortuary Record from the Gravestones in the Old Burial Ground in Brewster, Mass.;* Yarmouth, Mass., 1898

Bowman: *Vital Records of the Town of Brewster, Mass. to the End of the Year 1849;* Boston, Mass., 1904

From records of the Brewster Congregational Church, 1700-1790, containing Lincoln and Crosby genealogical material (25 copies privately printed).

The Lincolns who settled in Hingham, Mass. about 1636 came from Hingham in Norfolk County, England. There were at least four Thomas Lincolns in Hingham, Mass. in the mid-seventeenth century. One of these migrated southward and became the ancestor of the great Emancipator, Abraham Lincoln. Another Thomas Lincoln of Hingham who died in 1691 had married Miss Annie Lane and was the father of Benjamin Lincoln (1643-1700), who married Miss Sarah Fearing. Benjamin and Sarah were the parents of Thomas Lincoln, who married Miss Rachel Holmes and settled in what is now called West Brewster, Mass. Thomas and Rachel and their son Nathaniel were received into the Brewster Congregational Church in 1708. The church record spells the name "Linckhorn" — this is the way the recorder heard the Englishman say his name and did not ask him to spell it. The same church records also state that "On March 25, 1716 after the death of Deacon Freeman, Mr. Thomas Crosbey and Mr. Thomas Lincoln were chosen by ye Church, with ye concurrence of their Pastor to Succeed in that office." This Thomas Crosby was the brother of an ancestor of Joe Lincoln's mother, but Deacon Thomas Lincoln was a direct ancestor of Joe Lincoln. Deacon Thomas Lincoln was elected a Selectman of Harwich in 1718 and served in that office for eight years. He died in 1739, and his widow, Rachel Holmes Lincoln, married Benjamin Myrick in 1740 and died in 1757.

Nathaniel Lincoln (1704-1772) was the eldest son of Deacon Thomas and Rachel Holmes Lincoln. He was born in Hingham, Mass., and came to Harwich with his parents. He married Miss Hannah Astine and they had nine children, one of whom was Nathaniel Lincoln, Jr. (1738-1785), who married Mary Clark.

Nathaniel, Jr., lived at Sheep Pond in Harwich. His tombstone in the Church Cemetery is inscribed with this humility:

> "O let me hear thy voice divine
> Pronounce the glorious ble'sing mine;
> Enrolled among thy happy poor,
> My leargest wishes ask no more."

Nathaniel Jr. sired three ship captains: Capt. Silvanus Lincoln, who was the father of Captain Warren Lincoln, the cabin boy; Captain Nathaniel Lincoln 3rd, who married Rebecca Cobb; Captain Isaac Lincoln, Sr. who was Joe Lincoln's great-grandfather; and Nathaniel, Jr.'s daughter Mary, who married Captain Benjamin Berry, a name which appears in Joe Lincoln's mother's correspondence.

Captain Joseph Lincoln, father of Joe Lincoln, was born April 17, 1825 in Brewster, Mass. He was the oldest son of Captain Isaac Lincoln, Jr., and Desire Freeman Foster, Jr. Lincoln. Captain Isaac Lincoln, Jr. (1797-1838), was the second of Captain Isaac and Deborah Lincoln's nine children. Isaac Jr. married first Mary Foster, daughter of Captain Benjamin and Desire Freeman Foster. Mary Foster Lincoln died young, and in 1822 Isaac, Jr. married his first wife's sister, Desire Freeman Foster, Jr. (1800-1891). It was she who brought the Freeman name into this branch of the Lincoln family, and became the much loved grandmother of Joe Lincoln. We might point out here that Isaac Lincoln, Sr. (1773-1829) was the first of the ship captains in this Lincoln line, and was Joe's great-grandfather.

Joe's father, Captain Joseph Lincoln, went to sea as a cabin boy when he was fifteen years old, and at twenty-eight years of age was captain of the full-rigged ship "Maria". His first wife was Susan Paine Mayo, who was born August 17, 1828. Very little is known about Susan. It is rumored that she was a very large person. Her size and weight did not prevent her from being blown overboard in a gale while sailing with Captain Joseph on October 17, 1856. Her tombstone in the Brewster Cemetery is inscribed with these epitaphic words:

> "The sea, the dark, the stormy sea,
> drew me beneath its wave,
> but the blest Saviour died for me
> and he my soul doth save."

There were apparently no children born to this marriage.

About a year after the death of his first wife, on October 26, 1857, Captain Joseph Lincoln married Miss Emily Crosby. She was the second of Joseph Clark and Susan Bangs Crosby's four children. There will be more about these parents of Joe Lincoln in a later chapter.

Sometime after the birth of his son and only child, Captain Joseph Lincoln sailed south as master of the bark "Amelia". After a sudden illness, he died on his ship in the harbor of Charleston, South Carolina on December 19, 1870. A copy of the record of his death, obtained by the late Mrs. Ethel C. Entwhistle of North Attleboro, Mass., and graciously sent on to this writer is presented below. This record is from the office of the Registrar, County Health Department, Charleston, S.C.

NAME... Lincoln, Capt. Joseph   SEX......Male
AGE......43 years   MARRIED STATUS......
PLACE OF RESIDENCE...Bark Amelia   OCCUPATION...Marine Captain
PLACE OF BIRTH........?
DISEASE....Spasmodic stricture of intestine
PHYSICIAN....E. H. Kellers
PLACE OF INTERMENT ....sent to New York
DATE OF DEATH.....December 19, 1870
REMARKS ....out of town

Captain Joseph Lincoln's body was buried in the Brewster Cemetery and his tombstone merely records his name, date of death and his age. Joe Lincoln was only ten months old when his father died, so he had no recollection of his male parent — what he knew of him he would have had to learn from his mother in later years.

Captain Joseph Lincoln was master of the following ships:
    1853-1859: The bark "Maria"
    1860-1862: The bark "Wyman" (Emily Crosby Lincoln
                 with her Captain)
    1863-1866: The bark "Kleber"   "
    1867-1869: The bark "Mist"   "
    1870:   The bark "Aurelia" (The ship on which
                 Capt. Joseph Lincoln died)

Ship model of the "Mist" commissioned by Joseph C. Lincoln.
Courtesy Mrs. J. Freeman Lincoln

The Bark "Mist"

The bark "Mist" was first enrolled at Boston on May 3, 1865. Enrollments were a Custom House document indicating that a vessel was engaged in coastwise shipping, whereas a Register indicated deepwater or foreign trade. The enrollment shows she was built at Pembroke, Maine, in 1864. She measured 513-35/100 tons, 136-3/10 feet in length, and 30 feet in breadth, with 17-6/10 feet in depth of hold. "Mist" was described as having two decks, three masts, a square stern, and a billet head. Her master was Joseph Lincoln. Owners were Pliney Nickerson of Boston and Thomas Nickerson of Newton. The previous document issued before this enrollment was a register at Passamaquoddy, dated January 30, 1864. "Mist" was then registered at Boston on October 31, 1865, with the same captain and owners as above. She was destroyed by fire at Valparaiso on the 7th of December, 1869, while discharging coal.

The above information was acquired from Philip Chadwick Foster Smith, Curator of Maritime History in the Peabody Museum, Salem, Mass.

One of Joe Lincoln's treasured possessions was a model of his father's favorite ship, "The Mist", which Joe had made by a ship-model maker in Boston. This model is still in the family.

The Brewster home where Joseph C. Lincoln was born and raised. This is the Crosby "house and shop" referred to in the story.

Chapter 3

The Crosbys of Brewster, Mass.

1. Simon Crosby (1608-1639)
   mrd. Miss Anne Brigham
2. (Rev.) Thomas Crosby (1634-1702)
   mrd. Miss Sarah Fitch 1662
3. William Crosby (1672-?)
   mrd. Miss Mercy Hinckley, widow of Tho. Hinckley
4. Tully Crosby (1715-1760)
   mrd. Miss Hannah Hall
5. Edmund Crosby
   mrd. Miss Thankful Myrick
6. Captain Solomon Crosby (1776-1811)
   mrd. Miss Phebe   ?   (1778-1819)
7. Joseph Clark Crosby (1805-1865)
   mrd. Susan Bangs (1807-1836)
8. Emily Crosby (1832-1897)
   mrd. Captain Joseph Lincoln (1825-1870)
9. Joseph Crosby Lincoln (1870-1944)
   mrd. Miss Florence Elry Sargent (1872-1954)
10. Joseph Freeman Lincoln (1900-1962)
    mrd. Miss Virginia Cross (1906-   )

References

Mayo: *Mortuary Record from the Gravestones in the Old Burial Ground in Brewster, Mass.;* Yarmouth, Mass., 1898

Bowman: *Vital Records of the Town of Brewster, Mass., to the End of the Year 1849;* Boston, Mass., 1904

Crosby: *John Crosby of Yorkshire and Some of His Descendants 1440-1940;* privately printed, Hartford, Conn., 1940

The name "Crosby" is of Danish origin and is variously spelled. It signifies "the place of the cross". In 1205, an Odo de Crosby lived in Yorkshire, and in 1220 a Simon de Crosseby was in Lancashire. This Crosseby was the ancestor of the Crosbys of New England.

Simon Crosby (1608-1639) was born at Holme-on-Spaulding-Moor in York County, England. On the 18th of April, 1635, Simon, with his wife Anne Brigham and their three-month-old son, Thomas, embarked on the "Susan and Ellen" for America. Joe Lincoln's Aunt Martha and her husband, Nelson Huckins, named their first child Susan Ellen. One wonders if they knew that Susan's ancestor Simon Crosby came to America on the "Susan and Ellen". More about Susan later.

Simon Crosby settled in Cambridge, Mass., where he was admitted a "freeman" on March 3, 1636. His son, Thomas, who had been baptised at Holme-on-Spaulding-Moor in Yorkshire, graduated from Harvard College in 1653. In 1655 we find him in Eastham on Cape Cod, where he is the un-ordained teacher of the Church. The (Rev.) Thomas, as he was known, married a Sarah (last name unknown), who bore him twelve children, including one set of twins and one set of triplets. When the (Rev.) Thomas died suddenly in 1702, Sarah married a John Miller of Yarmouth, but, we think, bore him no children.

The (Rev.) Thomas Crosby, with his sons Thomas and Simon, was an organizer of the Church in Harwich (now Brewster). The (Rev.) Thomas had left Eastham about 1670 and settled in Harwich as a merchant. His son, Thomas, was elected a Deacon on March 25, 1716, the same day that Joe Lincoln's ancestor, Thomas Lincoln, was elected a Deacon, as noted in the chapter on the Lincolns of Brewster.

Another son of the (Rev.) Thomas Crosby was William Crosby. William Crosby was born in 1672 and married Mercy Hinckley. One of their sons was Tully Crosby (1715-1760), who married

14

Hannah Hall. They had a son Edmund Crosby, who married Thankful Myrick, and they became the parents of Captain Solomon Crosby.

Captain Solomon Crosby (1776-1811), Joe Lincoln's mother's grandfather, was a contemporary of Captain Isaac Lincoln, who was Joe Lincoln's father's grandfather, making both great-grandfathers men of the sea. Only one of Captain Solomon's sons went to sea, and he was drowned at fourteen years of age. The other son, Joseph Clark Crosby, was born on the 15th of December, 1805 in Brewster.

When he was twenty-one years of age, Joseph Clark Crosby was living and working in South Boston. The following is hardly a love letter, but he sent it to his future wife, Susannah "Susan" Bangs, who then lived in Brewster.

Boston 22 Jan 1826

Beloved Susan

I now improve this opertunity of writing a fiew lines which wil informe you of my good helth and hope this wil find you enjoying the same. I now you hav long expected to here from me but it has ben impossible for me to write before this opertunity as it is a large family where I work and I hev not ben here but once before now therefore I hope you wil forgiv my long silense for I shel alders remember you the same altho my opertunitys for writing are very fiew - the plase where I work is 6 miles from here it is quite a lonesom plase as there is not enny young men which I hev formed an acquaintanse with. Enaly hes recoverd her helth and spirits she apperse like a new creture from what she was when I was here before David sailed the furst of this month. I hev not hed the pleasure of seing Pedy sense I came from Home - I cannot write you enny news as there is not enny here but I shel expect to here a grate delie from you sone giv my respects to youre brother and sister and all inquiring friends

Tell Marthy Crocker I shell write to hur the furst opertunity— I must bid adieu after beging you to write sone after receiving this

Believe me to be very truly and affictionatily yours Joseph C. Crosby P.S. Please to dirrect your letters to boston

Susannah "Susan" Bangs was the sixth of the ten children of Elkanah and Sally Crosby Bangs. Two of her brothers were mariners; Captain Elisha Bangs was master of the ships "Rajah", "Denmark", "Faneuil Hall", and "Crimea"; Captain Freeman H. Bangs was master of the ships "Roxana", "Joseph Holmes", "Celeste Clark", and "Faneuil Hall". He was lost with his last ship off the coast of Brazil, bound for Calcutta in January, 1866. Susannah and Joseph Clark Crosby were married in Brewster February 19, 1829, and the couple went to South Boston where Joseph was employed. They had four children born in South Boston: first, Martha Bangs Crosby, who married Nelson Huckins of Barnstable when she was eighteen years of age; second, Emily Crosby who married Captain Joseph Lincoln and was the mother of Joe Lincoln; third, Sarah Crosby, about whom we know nothing; and fourth, Joseph Crosby, who at nineteen years of age was "lost at sea" in a gale in the North Atlantic. We quote the following letter from young Joseph's captain as an illustration of what the words "lost at sea" meant on so many tombstones in cemeteries on Cape Cod:

Havre 2nd Feby 1856

Mr. Joseph C Crosby
     Brewster
       My dear Sir
     I fear you may think me without proper feelings in not having addressed you before, but I assure you that it is not the case. On my arrival at Plymouth I was disabled and could not write without much pain, and since leaving that port I have been beset with trouble and care and it seems that everything has gone wrong since he left me.
     You have already been made acquainted with the loss of your son and permit me my dear sir without many words to give you the details of this unhappy occurrence which caused his early fate deprived a father of his only and dear son and sisters of an amiable brother.
     It was on the 22nd December in a dreadful Gale from the west south west. We had been scudding or running the ship during the previous night. At daylight the gale increased with such fury that I was obliged to heave the ship to. This we succeeded in doing and had everything furled but the Main Top Sail and Fore Topmast Stay Sail when I considered all safe We lay this way until nine A. M. And as we had got a great deal of water in the Cabin your son was with me in the Cabin bailing water as happy as ever I saw him and when I complained of so

much water in the Cabin, he said that it was nothing and that he had seen as much water in the "Wild Ranger" Cabin and went on bailing cheerfully. After we had got the heft of the water out of the Cabin I commenced to change my wet clothes and had succeeded only in getting on dry underclothes and he had not left me more than fifteen or twenty minutes when we shipped a dreadful sea which threw the ship on her beam ends and on righting the mate sung out for me that Mr. Crosby was overboard. I sprung for the door and in rushing on deck nearly lost myself. When I recovered myself nothing was seen of him. Nor do I believe that he was even seen after he went overboard. Two other seamen were lost with him at the same time. My carpenter was knocked down much the same as I was but his case was more serious, he broke his skull, while I only was bruised. Another man had his spine of his back broken by a fall. The Carpenter has died, the other man lived by last accounts. And now my dear sir what can I say. It was impossible to render him any assistance in the situation of the ship even if he had been seen. The ship was completely buried in water and what sail I had set blew away together with main Top Sail Mast, and had she not been the best ship in the world we should none of us probably seen the end of that dreadful storm. I do truly feel for you and would offer you my sympathy but well do I know that words are idle and unavailing and that nothing short of divine aid can reach the depth of your sorrow and heal your wounded Spirit. I will leave you with him who knoweth all things in heaven and earth and although we are sometimes grieved by his dispensations yet we must believe that if we view them rightly they all turn to our good.

He was a remarkable boy. I never saw him out of humor and amidst all the clamour taking in and making sail I never heard him utter an oath or call a man out of his name — he was always cheerful and calm and I need not tell you how much I miss him for he was my mainstay and since I have lost him everything has gone wrong.

I have packed everything of his in his chest and in case I should not come home myself will send them to you by the first opportunity. I have no convenience for writing and feel assured that you will consider it. Regards to your Wife, your children and friends and assure them of my sympathy on this most sorrowful occasion. I remain my dear sir very truly yours

Freeman Crosby

"Susan" Bangs Crosby, Joe Lincoln's mother's mother, died in South Boston on October 19, 1836, sixteen days after the birth of her fourth child. Sometime thereafter, Joseph Clark Crosby returned to Brewster and bought the property known as "The House and Shop". He supported his family as a shoemaker and as the postmaster in Brewster. At the time of Martha's marriage at eighteen years of age, the marriage register lists her as a "mantua maker". She and her father used the same shop.

On August 30, 1846, Joseph Clark Crosby married for his second wife Phebe Crosby, daughter of Abijah and Desire Crosby of Brewster. Joe Lincoln was to know her as his step-grandmother. Joseph Clark Crosby died December 14, 1865, leaving the home, property and shop to Phebe.

Martha and her husband had had two children, a girl and a boy. The boy, named for his father, Nelson Huckins, only lived about a year; the girl, known as "Susie", grew to womanhood. Nelson Huckins deserted his family. Since Emily Crosby, married to Captain Joseph Lincoln, was at sea a great deal of the time, the household consisted of Martha, "Susie", and "mother" Crosby.

In order to help out financially, Phebe Crosby Crosby deeded "The House and Shop" to Captain Joseph Lincoln on September 15, 1866. In this manner the birthplace of Joe Lincoln came into the possession of his parents. Phebe died on September 27, 1876, at which time Joe was six years old.

The tax assessor's Atlas of Barnstable County for 1880 shows the outline of "The House and Shop" on the lot marked as belonging to Emily Crosby Lincoln.

Chapter 4
Captain Joseph and Emily (Crosby) Lincoln

In order to understand Joe Lincoln, we need to know what kind of people his mother and father were. No one remains alive who knew them, and aside from the letters which they wrote to those at home when they were abroad, there is almost nothing else to answer our question. But there are the letters, so we turned to a handwriting analyst, Mr. Raymond A. Rider of Wareham, Mass. The following is our account of his analysis of the handwriting of Captain Joseph and Mrs. Emily Crosby Lincoln:

The Captain was a strongly motivated man who was aggressive, determined, and wanted his own way — he could be called stubborn. But he was very frank and above-board, and was essentially open-minded and altruistic with a strong love for others. He took over the ownership of "the house and shop" after the death of Emily's father so as to protect the home and business of Emily's step-mother and sister, Martha, and assured them that as long as he and Emily lived they would not be in want.

He was full of enthusiasm and enjoyed life, being sexually well-motivated. He was outgoing and very sure of himself — he was greatly influenced by his mother (the much-loved Desire Freeman Foster Jr., Lincoln Thacher). Capt. Joe loved to talk, and when he talked, he used enthusiastic but smooth-flowing gestures with his hands. He could stretch a story and add to it, just as his son was to do so well in later years. However, when he tired of a conversation, more than likely he would end it and walk away.

Capt. Joe was a man with dignity and a touch of vanity. The color in his writing shows that he liked the good things of life, good food and good clothes: he probably dressed well and in the latest fashion. There are signs of intuition, and he may have enjoyed music and dancing (Emily reports in her letters about the parties they attended when their ship was in a harbor).

He had depth of feeling, and everything hit his emotions hard. He was loyal to what in his mind was important, and he could carry a grudge (He had a severe attitude toward the husband of Emily's sister, Martha, who deserted his wife and child). His philosophy of life could be considered restricted, and in religion and morals his ideas were fixed. (He and Emily would go to church ashore when they were in a harbor with a Protestant Church).

Captain Joe had an excellent memory and was curious, wanting to know all the answers — he would not only want to know your name, but also what you did for a living and what you owned, and he strongly resented any encroachment on his own private affairs.

He had skillful hands and could make many things, as he shows a mild creative ability. The rhythms and fluidity of his writing indicate that he walked with a smooth gait.

Captain Joe was a very restless person — he liked to travel and was always wanting to go places (which not only sent him to sea but kept him there). He liked to have order wherever he was, at home or aboard his ship, and insisted on it. He was a man who knew what he was doing, and had considerable organizational ability, which indicates he was a good captain. He was good at mathematics and kept his accounts in good order. He was a little stern, and was not to be argued with, especially on his ship. His goals in life were very high, and having analyzed a situation, he moved forward to the accomplishment of what he set out to do.

Many of the qualities which show up in the hand-writing of Captain Joe will be found in a character created by Joe Lincoln, Cap'n Ezra Titcomb in *Partners of the Tide.* Joe did not intend Cap'n Ezra to be a picture of his father, but the similarities are very interesting. Young Joe must have listened very carefully to his mother's account of the Captain, and remembered when he created Cap'n Ezra.

Emily Crosby Lincoln's personality was quite different from Captain Joe's. She had high ideals, very strict morals, and was very proud. She was defiant, but had ways of using her defiance gently. She liked color and appreciated good things (she was pleased when her captain bought flowers and brought them to their cabin on shipboard). She kept a neat house and cabin, which was proper in the light of the Captain's demand for order in all things. She was independent and had excellent control of her speech and ways of life. Once in a while she flared up and would kick things around — she had a temper but was careful not to show it when Captain Joe was around.

She was more objective than her husband in her analysis of a situation. She had no interest at all in idle chit-chat, would never gossip, and could keep a secret. She would tackle one thing at a time, which might have been a source of conflict with Captain Joe.

Emily liked other people but was essentially a loner, and more moderate than the Captain. (She seems to be quite content to sit under her awning and read or write when she is alone on the ship). She was good at details: every "t" in her handwriting is crossed, every "i" is dotted. She has a good memory, although not as good as Captain Joe's. She shows that she was influenced much more by her mother than by her father.

Emily had a great deal of skill with her hands. The color in her handwriting shows pure originality and artistic ability. She had a natural talent for arts and crafts, and considerable ability in organization (hat making, knitting and dressmaking would have been naturals for her). She was a "string-saver" — she saved anything that might be saved, and she was a good listener, which helped make her marriage a success.

She wore attractive clothes but dressed in moderation. She had a way of keeping her husband guessing. She knew how to get around him so that he would never know her completely.

Emily was well satisfied with her station in life. She was very direct in her approach to life, and practical and simple without any complications, and a perfect lady at all times. She describes the long and monotonous trip from Glasgow, Scotland to Cocanada, India, in a very simple, direct way, but without the kinds of complaints many lone women on a ship might make. On their return, she writes to her family to have her "velvet cape ready for her in Boston" when she arrives.

Joe Lincoln's father and mother sailed together many times to the far off places of the earth. They and their ancestors came to know foreign cities and their harbors almost as well as they knew their home port. On these voyages Emily was the correspondent, writing quite regularly to her family in Brewster. Letters were given to ship masters who were bound for Boston, and letters were received by the Lincolns from ships which came into the harbors where they were at anchor or at the offices of the American Consuls.

Emily's letters tell about their trips, describe the scenery, tell about the food and people of the place, and of their visits ashore. Fortunately, many of Emily's letters survive — some belonging to her granddaughter Anne.

Paramaribo July 3rd 1861

My dear parents and sister —

Here we are safely arrived in South America one week ago yesterday after a pleasant voyage of twenty eight days. I was not sick at all but enjoyed the passage very much not keeping away from the table but twice all the way out. I was burned up pretty black I can tell you when I got here for I used to sit on deck under the awning nearly all the time and sew and read. We are stopping at a Mr. Ments house and enjoy myself very much. They are so pleasant and Mrs. Ments does everything she can for me. I wish you could look at me and all my surroundings at this time. I think you would be amused, everything is so strange and different from what we have at home. This house is a large wooden one (as they all are) very high in the walls without plastering no carpets on the floors as they can't have them down in this country. Then we have plenty of Black servants to wait upon us so that we have nothing to do.

As I look out of my window I can see all kinds of strange sights, not a chimney to be seen anywhere but large white wooden houses and such beautiful trees, the Palm, Tamerind, Orange, Almond, and many others that I do not know the name of. Then you will see the slaves going along with loads of Pineapples, Plantins, Oranges, and Oh lots of other fruits and vegetables which they carry along on the tops of their heads , for they carry everything in that manner and such heavy loads as they have sometimes, you would not think it possible they could carry them on their heads without touching a hand to it.

*Paramaribo is a seaport city on the Surinam River, Surinam, South America.

Then we have a fine view of the river from this house and can see all the vessels coming in and going out and I see the boats coming from and going to the plantations and hear the negroes on them singing or at least what they call singing but I must say I don't hear much music in it, but a gentleman told me the other day if I could understand them I should be very much amused as they compose all as they go along and then all their dresses look so strange, but I think that many of the negroes dress with a great deal of taste. I am treated with a great deal of kindness and hospitality. Every day I have some new kind of fruit to try, nearly all of them I like very much and I can truly say I never knew how pineapples and oranges tasted before, they are delisicous. I am very careful and only eat a little of these things at a time for fear of getting sick.

This morning I had a large handsome boquet sent to me by a lady here. I have been out to walk but once since I have been here as it is the rainy season here and is wet the most of the time. I am hoping to have an opportunity to go on to a plantation before I leave here. Joseph's cargo is nearly all discharged and we shall probably be away from here in about three weeks, but can tell you better when I write again and that I think will be in a few days. Tomorrow is Fourth of July and Mrs. Ments has invited all the American Captains here to dinner and we are to dine on roast turkey, chicken pie +c +c. I would like to know what you will all be doing. I am afraid I shall not have letters from you while I am here as I do not know of any vessels coming from Boston.

I want very much to hear how they are getting along in the war. I shall have a great deal to talk about when I get home. I will try to remember all I can and tell you of what I see.

July 5th I must tell you now how I spent my Fourth. In the morning Mrs. Ments and myself went to make a call, then came back and dressed for company. There was a Captain Stafford here and several ladies. Captain Higgins was expected but did not come. About one o'clock we sat down to dinner. We had Roast Turkey, Chicken Pie, Boiled Ham, Vegetable Soup, Lemon Custard Tarts made of Pineapple, Beer, Champaigne, +c. For desert we had Pineapples, Oranges and a kind of fruit called Shaducks, they look something like an orange only much larger, we drank toasts and had a very nice time I can assure you. Last evening we had an invitation to the American Consul's but there was company here and I thought I would not go. Joseph and the other gentlemen went for a few minutes, then came back and we had supper, and we finished the evening with singing, talking +c. Went to bed at twelve o'clock, so ended this Fourth of July and a very pleasant one it was to me I can assure you.

Joseph finished discharging cargo yesterday and we ought to be away from here in three weeks but I don't know how long they will keep him waiting cargo. I believe they are to put in only enough for ballast. I

23

suppose Father has the Postoffice by this time. Joseph sends love to you all and we will write by the first vessel which leaves for Boston which I think will be next week and I shall write at the same time, now I will bid you all good bye for this time as I want to write Ella a few lines.

From Emily with love to all

New Orleans, July 10th, 1863

Dear Father, Mother, and Sister

At last we have arrived all well and safe. but we have had a long tedious passage and I am fearful you will all get anxious about us before you hear of our safe arrival. All the way we have had head winds and calms. not much heavy weather but we all got almost discouraged before we got here. I was well all the voyage. was not sick at all and enjoyed the voyage very much. had nice accomodations, etc. We saw nothing of the Alabama or any of the other Pirates although once I got quite frightened. Joseph and myself were down in the Cabin reading when the mate came down and said there was a Steamer in sight. We went up and in a few minutes she changed course and came towards us. I thought sure we were gone then and went down and commenced picking up my things but I did not know what to do first so concluded to leave everything till I found out whether they were friends or foes. We did not have to wait very long as they came up to us pretty rapidly and ran up the Stars and Stripes but I did not feel quite safe until they sent a boat along side and I saw the uniform of Uncle Sam then I breathed freely again. We were spoken by one other of our boats after that but I was not so much excited as at first.

One week we were lying at anchor off a small Island waiting for a fair wind, there was nothing to be seen there. We took a Pilot off of the 5th of July and was from that until the 10th trying to get in to South West Pass where we took a steamboat to tow us up the river. Coming up the river we had to stop over one night at the quarintine ground as it was so late when we got there the Doctor would not come off to us and we were nearly devoured by Musquitoes (but am not troubled with them here as there is none to be seen through the day and at night we have a good Musquito bar). we passed the forts (Jackson and Philip) that we read so much about at the time New Orleans was taken and I also saw the wreck of the Perona, the boat you will remember did so much execusion and fired a broadside just as she was sinking. there was also the wrecks of a good many boats all on the river that the rebels set fire when our fleet came up to prevent them falling into their hands. There is a

24

great deal of destruction to be seen everywhere here. property destroyed by the rebels. the city is full of Soldiers and Gunboats almost without number are all around us so I feel as if we were well protected. I can not realize I am in New Orleans and so near our enemies. I suppose you will have heard ere this of the surrender of Vicksburg and Port Hudson. They are now taken without doubt as boats arrived here last Friday night bringing the report direct from there and on Saturday evening they had a grand illumination and procession in this city but unfortunately we was not here to see it as we did not arrive here till yesterday (Sunday) Morning. The Bark Hannah Crocker of New York was towed up the river by the same boat as took us. we were lying close along side. on Saturday evening we were all sitting talking on deck when the alarm was given that other Bark was on fire. everyone jumped and sprang on board of her from the Steamer and our vessel. In a few minutes the hose from the Steamer was got ready and holes were cut in the deck and through the Cabin floor and water poured down. the fire was down the lower hold but nothing could be done and in a very short time she had to be cut adrift and she burnt to the Waters edge and then sunk. I never saw anything done so quick after the fire was discovered. The Captain of her only saved a few of his clothes and his Chronometer and Spy Glass . a few of his charts, etc.. It is supposed that the fire caught in the hole from the heat of the hay. she was laded with Hay and Coal and she must have been on fire some time or she would not have burned up so quick. The vessel nor Cargo was insured so she is a total loss. I can assure you I was sadly frightened.

I wish you could look in on me now and see the splendid Boquet Joseph bought for me for five cents that is setting on the table by the side of me. It is very healthy here there has not been one case of yellow fever and no other sickness. I went to take a walk with Joseph yesterday afternoon. had a pleasant time but saw nothing worth writing about. We got four letters from home today, one from Lucinda one from Augusta, and two from you Martha also one from Susie which I am going to answer. but there was a steamer came in today from New York and I think we ought to have got letters by her. but have got none yet. the others had been here waiting for us. I shall send these letters by the Steamer that leaves on Wednesday and shall send more by the one that leaves on Saturday. I think there is no doubt we shall come directly back to Boston in Balast as there is no freights and no prospects of any at present. so we shall have a shorter passage than we had coming out. Joseph joins in love to all and now good bye for a few days when if nothing happens I shall write again.

Yours with love

Emily

My Dear Sister

As there is a steamer to leave tomorrow for New York I improve the opertunity to send you a few lines although I have nothing new to say. We are both very well and it still continues very healthy here and old residents say there will be no sickness here this season or it have commenced before this time. but it is as healthy here as it is in New York or Boston. We have got nearly all the cargo discharged and I think they will begin taking in Ballast for Boston on Monday. if so we shall probably not be here more than a week or ten days longer, so if the privateers do not get us and nothing else happens we shall hope to see you all very soon.

Since I wrote you last there has been great excitement here on account of the arrival of Rebel prisoners from Port Hudson and Vicksburg. there were 91 officers among them and five of them were brothers, the oldest not yet 23 years. it makes the secessionists in this city rather down in the mouth and I hope we shall have good news from the North by tomorrows mail. the last we had was very favorable. I do wish we could get letters by this Steamer but I am afraid we shall not. as we did not get any the last and you probably think we are away from here before this time. I hope you have got through with your work before this and are now having a good time resting and visiting. I think Brewster will begin now to be very lively as it is about time for the company to commence coming from Boston. I should have liked to have been at home when the volunteers arrived home. I hope they are all there well by this time. We received a call this afternoon from one of the Orleans volunteers. he is in the same company that Gardner Weatherbee was. his name is Walker. he has a wife and two children at home. he has been sick and is still unable to do active duty. he looked miserable. Joseph knew him very well, he used to be in a clothing store in Boston. his regiment is going home soon but he thinks of stoppin here this Winter as he is afraid our Winter would be too much for him.

When you see Abbie give my love to her and I will try to write her the next Steamer but shall not have time now as I have written two letters already. one for Mother Thacher and one for Augusta. I think a great deal about Uncle Freeman and the children and I wish I could be at home when he gets there but am afraid I shall not. I have thought so much about Nancy Freeman, the way she died. I think it was awful how much she must have suffered. I was also very sorry indeed to hear such sad news of Bela Berry. I do hope that they may yet hear from him. but I suppose that is hardly to be hoped for.

I believe there are two other American Captains have their wives here but I have not seen them yet but don't know but one of them may call on me this evening I think if it is pleasant tomorrow we may go out to some place either to take a walk or ride and perhaps the next letter I shall have something new to tell you.

Yesterday there was a Steamboat left here for St. Louis, the first one for a long time and there was a great cheering when she left. I hope she will get through all right. Joseph is away now. he is out most of the day attending to business and trying to hear of some cargo to take home aboard - he has not as yet - and I don't think he will now. Most of the vessels are going home in Ballast - People think that business will be good for ships in two or three months when they commence getting the produce down from up river.

Oh how glad I shall be if this war will only be ended soon, still I don't say "peace at any price" as some do but I want to see the right triumph as I think it will at last. Give my love to Father, Mother, and Susie. Joseph joins with me in sending love to you and all others and now good bye for one more week when I shall write again if nothing happens

Yours truly

Em

Leghorn Dec 19th 1864

My Dear Sister

I suppose that you will have heard from Mother Thacher of our safe arrival here and that we were both well etc. We are both still the same with the exception of slight colds which we have. I think is owing to the wet weather we are having for it has rained every day for nearly a week so that I could not go on shore much. There are no other American vessels here, but several English Captains who seem to be very nice people. One of them is from Nova Scotia has his wife and two children with him. A week ago yesterday we all went ashore and went to church to the Scotch Prespyterean and heard an excellent sermon. it was such a treat to go to church once more. After church we went to a hotel and got dinner then took carriages and rode out to a place called "Montennara" about six miles from here. We went out to see a Catholic Church. It was very beautiful, Marble Gilt-work paintings etc . but I could not help but think of how many in these countries are kept poor just by having such splendid churches and supporting so many lazy Priests, for let you go where you will you are always troubled by the beggars, they know very quick when they see any strangers. Yesterday, we all went to the Scotch church again in the morning. We were very happy to get a long (letter) from you and Susie last Thursday and you may be sure it was well read. I read it over four or five times before we slept that night. Oh! there is nothing like letters when you are away from dear friends and to hear the good news all are well. I hope I am thankful for all the blessings which are given to me and while enjoying the gifts I hope I shall not forget the Giver. I would liked to have heard the sermon you speak of in your letter. I often think of your lot, dear sister, and be assured I am well aware of the difference there seems to be between us the way we are situated but who can tell how long it may be so. I hope you may yet see brighter days, and my lot may not always be of the same happiness as now.

You will see by Mother Thacher's letter that we have been out to Pisa. It was indeed a sight worth seeing and so was the other buildings I wrote about. The Baptiste is very handsome and there is a fine echo in it. The guide hollered two or three times and I never heard anything so nice. It was just like the notes of an organ. tell Susie I have a photograph of the Tower also one of the Baptiste and one of the Cathedral for her album. I have got her all the stamps of this country which I think I shall send in this letter. Joseph went to the post office in Genoa and got one of every kind that is used.

I don't think we shall get away from here before the first of January. this Rainy weather is putting us back. I must say I have not seen much of the "Sunny skies of Italy" you read so much of but I suppose it is not the right season. You must allow us a long passage home for the Bark will be deep loaded and not coppered so that we expect that she will move rather slowly.

I wish you would have my Cloak and Velvet Bonnet in Boston, if we live to get there I shall need them. I am looking for another letter from you every day now. Mr. Crocker is well. he got a letter from Clara at the same time I got yours. He ought to write but I don't believe he will. I have spoken to him about it two or three times.

You did not mention anything in your letter about George Bangs but I was glad to hear from Clara's letter that they had heard from him and that they were all alive and well. We were very sorry to hear Lucinda had been sick again. I am very much afraid those attacks of Pleurisy will some time throw her into the Consumption. I hope they will keep the new Minister till we get home for I want to see and hear him. I expect the days will seem long on the passage home. I want to see you all so much. I dream of you nearly every night. Tell Father I dreamed of him so plainly Saturday night that it almost seemed as if I had seen him. Tell Susie that I thought and spoke of her on her Birthday. I hope she had a good time to her party. It does not seem possible that she can be fourteen years old. our only baby. soon we shall have none. I don't believe Martha you love Susie much more than I do. it don't seem to me I could love a Child of my own much better. I hope she will be "cured of her Catarh". I suppose you have almost just got through your breakfast while we have been to dinner and Joseph has gone ashore again and I am sitting here alone. Once in a while going up on deck to see what is going on there. I wish you could look in and see me don't you? Tuesday morn. When Joseph came aboard last evening he brought another letter from you written 27th November. I was very glad to get it but sorry to hear that you was troubled with that pain again. do see some Doctor about it and not let it go until it is too late. This is a beautiful morning. the pleasantest we have had for more than a week.. this afternoon I am going on shore to have a walk about Leghorn and look at some little Alabaster ornaments to bring home. I don't think you are imposing on me at all asking me to get you these things. I was intending to get some. I only wish we had the money to spare there are many things I could spend it for. I would have liked to have been with you to the Ordination and wish I could be with you Christmas but suppose we shall be in Leghorn. Those English Captains want we should go ashore with them and get a Christmas dinner. I suppose we shall go but I don't care much to go for it is Sunday. We shall all go to church together in the morn then go to a Hotel and get dinner. last Night we were all on board the "Brasillian". The Captain has his wife. had a pleasant time. they don't any of them seem like English.

J oseph sends much love to you all. I shall write again next week. and I think that will be the last one before we get away from here. if we only have good weather Joseph says he thinks we may be loaded this week, I hope so, I long to be on the passage home. Give my love to all our friends and take a good share for yourself. Now good bye for another week

Your loving sister

Emily

Glasgow Oct 4th / 67

Dear Sister Martha

I suppose that ere this you have heard from me several times since I arrived here through Emily. which I suppose is well on her way by this time and if nothing happens I hope to meet in a week from today in this place. And I am in hopes to hear tomorrow that she left in the boat of the 28th direct for this place. according to telegram to that affect which left here the 18th of last month. shall be ready for sea the last of next week. wind and weather permitting so that she will not have much time to spare on her arrival here. hope that she got my telegram also the letter I wrote on arrival. I am very well at present and have been most of the time since I left home. am sorry to say that I am going on another long voyage from this place. will probably be 10 or 11 months before I get back to this part of the world again if nothing happens to me on the voyage. am bound to Cocanada with coals from thence to Rangoon or Bassein for rice. back to the United Kingdom or continent. am very sorry that I could not come home. as I long to see you all very much. but could see no business for the vessel that would pay her to come that way. do hope that Em got my telegram and is on her way now. for I shall be very much dissappointed if I do not see her next

29

week. Would not have gone on this voyage without her. if there is anything to keep her at home. but cannot think but what I shall see her soon. if she has come I want you to do as you have for years past. make yourself comfortable in the house and shop. and I hope that you will do well in your shop. am only sorry that I am not able to help you in any way. hope that I may see better days yet. tell Mother Crosby that on Em's arrival here I will send her an order on the owners for some money which she can draw at any time. Would like her to draw it as soon as convenient after she gets it and endorse on the back of the note which she holds the amount received. With much love to you and Susie and all friends I close.

Your brother Joseph

Tell Susie I should be much pleased to hear from her. also yourself.

J. L.

Oct. 5 have just received a line from Em saying that she would leave N. Y. on the boat of the 28th which is pleasing to me. J. L.

Cocanada April 17th (1868)

My dear Sister And Susie

At length we have arrived safely at this place after a long tedious passage of 177 days. just think what a time to be on the water and then not to get one line from home on our arrival. I can assure you I feel disapointed and anxious enough to hear from you for I don't know now when we shall get letters as I am very much afraid we shall get none at our next port. I have not a doubt you have written us a number of letters but they are not to be found in this place. We wrote you to send in care of the American consul and you probably did and there is none here. We are both well and have been most of the time since we left Glasgow. Joseph had two quite ill turns just before we got in but I think it was owing in a great measure to care and worrying because we did not get along any faster and was having such a long passage. I know you have all felt very anxious about us and I am afraid will almost have given us up before this reaches you. We had no gales or rough weather on our passage but calms and head winds plenty of them and to cap the climax our Chronometer was over 90 miles out so that when we made the land we were over 70 miles farther up the bay than we should have been. we had to go in and stop a few hours as we were nearly out of fresh water, and then make another start. it took us ten days to get from that place back here for there was such a strong head current. This is not much of a place. we lay about five miles from the shore and there is not much to be seen excepting the natives that come off in the Lighters. I am quite amused in watching them. Their dress does not cost them much for they (are) almost entirely naked. all the most of them wear is just a little piece of cloth and they are almost as black as the coal they are taking out of the ship. then they wear their hair done up behind their heads in a kind of bob. they have rings

30

in their ears, through their noses and on their fingers and toes, also plenty of silver and brass bands around their wrists and ankles and then they keep up such a chattering they are like a parcel of monkeys. Susie I just wish you could be here for a short time if no more but I suppose you would be terribly shocked. however you would soon get used to seeing naked men. by the way how is all our friends in Chatham. how is it Martha do you have to have the parlor warmed every little while? Oh what I would give for a good long letter from you. I want so much to hear what you both have been doing this long cold winter. Whether you went to school in Middleboro Susie and if she did how Martha got along without her. I suppose you have been very lonesome. many times I think of you very often I can assure you and wish we did not have to be so widely seperated but I hope we shall all be spared to meet again in a few months more and then how happy we shall be - we will look forward and pray for this and the time will soon slip away.

It is very warm in this place but perfectly healthy, no kind of sickness. We have been here one week today and am in hopes to get away again in two weeks more. this is the first opertunity there has been to send letters. I wish we were coming home from Rangoon instead of going back to Europe. I should like to hear how Aunt Desire is and mother Crosby. Oh dear! there is so much I should like to hear from home. what you did Thanksgiving. what Susie did in the evening etc. we thought of home on that day. and knew you was all thinking of us. we had a chicken pie and plum pudding for dinner but it did not seem much like Thanksgiving it was too warm. I wish you were both here this morning sitting with me. Joseph has gone ashore. I am alone sitting on deck under the awning trying to keep cool. once in a while going to look at the Coolies and occasionally eating a Bannana. There is not much fruit here now as it is not the season for Oranges and Mangoes are not quite ripe. I shall send a letter to Mother Thacher today with this. I would like to hear whether Lucinda is still on the earth or whether she has left us. I shall send you another letter by the next mail. Does it seem possible that it has been seven months since I bad you good bye. Joseph joins with me in sending lots of love and you must keep up good courage and don't work hard but take it easy. You can now Martha for Susie is a young lady now. I suppose she is a first rate cook by this time. I shall have to take a few lessons of her when I get home. I wish I could have a nice piece of apple pie and some good yeast Bread and Butter for my dinner. I would not ask for any meat this warm weather. I have been ashore and spent one day since I have been here. but was glad to get on board again. it was so much warmer there and not much to be seen. I don't know as I shall go again while I am here. I am in hopes we shall go to Rangoon from here as that is quite a place I believe and we shall lay nearer the shore. But I must now draw this letter to a close and say good bye till another week when I shall write again if nothing happens. Give our love to Mother Crosby and all our other friends.

Yours with much love

Emily C. Lincoln

P.S. We have just received word this morning we are to go to Bassein direct from this place. Em

Jan 24th (1869)

My Dear Sister

We left London Friday evening and Gravesend Saturday morning and today Sunday we have had a fair wind and beautiful weather and if it continues hope to be at the "Isle of Wight" so as to land the Pilot early in the morning when I shall feel as if we were fairly started on our passage home and God grant we may reach there in safety and find all our friends alive and well to receive us. You must not look for us too soon. don't begin to look till we have been out forty days and if we should be sixty even eighty days you need not be alarmed so Joseph says. but I hope we shall not have so long a passage as this.

Tell Susie if she is up to Boston about the time we may be there to look out for us and leave word into Mr. Anthony Crosbys where she may be found. Joseph sends love to all he is almost sick with a cold. Joseph remitted to you from Barring & Co. a draft for 57/ fifty seven pounds if Mother Crosby or you wish any of the money to use you can get it cashed, if not keep it till he gets home.

(in Joseph's hand)

Em writes that I have sent you a draft on Baring & bros for 57 I will say L 57 Sterling. if you need it or any part of it use it. if not keep it till we return. Tell Susie not to be married till we get home. as I should like to dance at the wedding.

Dear Sister don't let N writing you trouble you at all. don't give it a thought but go on as you have done and I don't think you will want for any of the comforts of life as long as Em and myself lives.

I hope that he, the aforesaid N H will never meet with me for I can't say what I would do to him. now Martha keep a stiff upper lip and we will soon be with you if nothing happens to us on the passage which I hope and trust they will not

Your brother

Joe

(in Emily's hand)

Joseph has filled up this sheet — so I will only say, good night and I hope we will soon meet

With much love

Emily

This was Emily's last trip with her husband. She returned to their home in Brewster to await the birth of her baby.

32

Chapter 5

The Birth and Boyhood of Joe Lincoln

Two hundred and fifty years after the landing of the "Saints and Strangers" on Cape Cod and the signing of the Mayflower Compact, and while the ship was anchored in Provincetown Harbor: Victoria being in the thirty-third year of her long reign over the British Empire: General Ulysses Simpson Grant being the eighteenth President of the United States of America: five years after the Central Cape Cod Railroad reached the village of Brewster on "the bended right arm of Massachusetts": the Sun being in the constellation called Aquarius: one day after Abraham Lincoln's sixty-first birthday, had he lived: one day before St. Valentine's Day, had it been celebrated: on the Sunday of the Christian Year called Septuagesima, the 13th day of February 1870, Joseph Crosby Lincoln, Cape Cod author, was born.

February, the month that begins with Ground Hog Day's weather predictions, is not the best month for visitors to Cape Cod — it tends to be damp and cold and bleak — perhaps that is why the calendar makers make it the shortest month. But it is the month of St. Valentine's Day, which changes the atmosphere for old maids with hope chests, girls with prospects, and wives with futures when their husbands remember.

February must be a good month in which to be born, for it is the birth month of George Washington (22), Abraham Lincoln (12), of Charles Dickens (7), Henry Wadsworth Longfellow (27), Jules Verne (8), Thomas Alva Edison (11), of Louis Braille (4), Susan B.

33

Anthony (15), Victor Hugo (26), of Horace Greeley (3), Enrico Caruso (25), and "Babe" Ruth (26); also, of Florence Sargent (15) who became Mrs. Joseph C. Lincoln, and of Virginia Cross (9) who became Mrs. J. Freeman Lincoln.

In *The Outermost House,* Henry Beston tells of finding " a soppy pink paper" on a wreck on the Great Beach of Cape Cod. It was a booklet entitled *If You Were Born In February* which included these comments:

"Those who were born in the month of February have a particular affection for home", and also, "They will go through fire and water for their loved ones". Certainly "affection for home" was a characteristic of Joe Lincoln, and one of the chapters in his first novel is called *"Through Fire and Water".* My, my, how things get interwoven!

On February 13, 1870, one day before Valentine's Day, Joseph Crosby Lincoln was born in a small house next door to the Post Office in Brewster on Cape Cod, Massachusetts. Captain Joseph Lincoln and his wife, Emily, were 45 and 38 years old, respectively, and so the safe arrival of their first child, a son, on this cold and wintry day was welcomed with joy and relief.

He was a strong and healthy baby and the Captain foresaw a cabin boy from his own family on his own ship in the near future. Joe's mother, however, had reservations. And it was not to be. Before the child was a year old, his father died aboard ship on a voyage south, and Joe was left to be brought up in a home in which there were no men. The household consisted of his mother, Emily (Crosby) Lincoln; his mother's sister, Martha Bangs (Crosby) Huckins; and his step-grandmother, Phebe (Crosby) Crosby.

Although there was little money, Joe's childhood was happy and care free. A chubby, blonde, freckle-faced boy, he joined other children his age in swimming in the cold waters of Cape Cod Bay, of playing "Run, Sheep, Run" behind the house in the evening dusk, and eagerly climbing the sandy dunes in anticipation of the return slide. He picked wild blueberries and cranberries for the delectable pies his mother made, and fished in the nearby fresh water lakes.

In summer Joe ran barefoot over the dusty roads on errands to the general store, located a short distance away, and often strayed down to the harbor, where he watched the fishermen painting their boats and mending their nets or the lobstermen repairing their traps. Here the impressionable youngster heard accounts of adventure and tragedy at sea. In the winter Joe lingered in the Post Office to listen to the tales of the oldsters gathered around the heat-radiating pot-bellied stove.

When he was five years old Joe began his education in the village school. Like most boys he disliked school and only went because he had to. In his book of remembrances, *Our Village*, he tells us something of what school was like in his youth .

He was not an outstanding scholar, but did learn to read, and in his *Cape Cod Yesterdays* he recalls the books for boys in the Ladies' Select Circulating Library in Brewster. Joe became a voracious reader and continued so throughout his life. As a boy he read books by Oliver Optic, Harry Castleman, Mayne Reid and Horatio Alger, and no doubt many others.

One of the verses Joe put into his first book, *Cape Cod Ballads and Other Verse,* was called "The School-Committee Man", and it ends with this stanza:

"We have ter listen awful hard ter every word of his
  And watch him jest like kittens do a rat,
And Laugh at every joke he makes, don't care how old it is,
  'Cause he can boss the teecher — think of that!
I uster say, when I growed up I'd be a circus chap
  And drive two lions hitched up like a span;
But, honest, more I think of it, I b'lieve the bestest snap
  Is jest to be a school-committee man."

Joe never got to drive a pair of lions in a circus, but he did become a school-committee man in Hackensack, New Jersey, as we shall see later.

Cap'n Warren Lincoln's general store was located across the road from the school in Brewster when Joe was a boy. When he writes his memory sketch about it, the school is across the street from Cap'n Daniels' store, and "Besides candy, Cap'n Daniels sold slates and pencils and penholders and sponges and T.D. pipes - fine for hayseed and sweet fern - and elastic for sling shots, and marbles, and goodness knows how many other necessities of boy life. Therefore it was a graceful, though rather obvious act of kindness to build the schoolhouse directly opposite a depot of supplies."

In his early poems Lincoln wrote about the many activities of a boy's life — "The Cooky Jar ", "The Dark Closet", "Goin' Swimmin' ", "His New Brother", "Hookin' Melons", "Our First Fire-Crackers",

35

"Sermon Time", "Sister's Best Feller", "The Sweet Fern Cigarette", "When Papa's Sick", "The Woodbox", and "The Winter Nights at Home", to name a few. Many of his subjects were from observation in other homes that he visited, or perhaps wishful thinking. We know that Joe had no new brother, he was an only child, and he had no sister to have a 'feller'. His father died before Joe knew him so his winter nights were with womenfolk only. And since these three women had strong ideas on how a boy should be brought up, there is considerable doubt that Joe knew much about 'hookin' melons' or 'smoking sweet fern cigarettes' from personal experience. There is that dark closet, however, a likely punishment for an erring boy who was being brought up nicely.

He often visited his father's mother, who lived in West Brewster near where the first Lincolns in the area had settled. Widowed when her husband, Captain Isaac Lincoln, Jr. was lost at sea, Desire Freeman (Foster, Jr.) Lincoln had remarried Captain Jonathan Thacher, who died before Joe was born. "Mother Thacher", as his grandmother was known, lived until Joe was twenty-one years old.

The adult Joe remembered the times he had visited this Thacher home and tells us something about it in two poems, "Grandfather's Summer Sweets" (apples, you know) and "Summer Nights at Grandpa's". There was no grandfather in the Thacher place when Joe was a boy, but in his poems he had all of the relatives any child had, and here is how he writes of the home:

"Summer nights at Grandpa's — ain't it fun to lay
In the early mornin' when it's getting day —
When the sun is risin' and it's fresh and cool,
And you're feelin' happy coz there ain't no school?
When you hear the crowin' as the rooster wakes,
And you think of breakfast and the buckwheat cakes;
Sleepin' in the city's too much fuss and noise;
Summer nights at Grandpa's are the things for boys."

Chapter 6
The Chelsea, Mass. Years (1883-1899)
and the *Bulletin*

When Joe was thirteen years old Emily decided to move to Chelsea, Massachusetts, where she could find employment as a dress or hat maker. Up until this time she had been keeping house for her step-mother-in-law (Phebe died in 1876) and her sister Martha, who was the Postmistress.

Emily and Joe shared the inheritance from Captain Joseph Lincoln, which was his equity in "The House and Shop". Emily had had herself appointed guardian of the boy so that she could apply to the court for permission to sell his half share in the family property. According to the Probate Court papers dealing with the matter, she received $300.00 for his share at a private auction held in Chatham, Massachusetts, on December 28, 1883.

Mother and son moved into an apartment at 145 Walnut Street, and Joe was enrolled in the Williams Grammar School, located about a block away at 5th and Walnut Streets.

The city of Chelsea, situated north east of Boston between the Chelsea and Mystic Rivers, had a population of 25,709, as recorded in the census taken in 1885. This was a far cry from the life that the young boy had known in a small village on Cape Cod, but he soon adjusted, making friends with other young people in the neighborhood and entering into activities at the school.

It was during these 'teen years that Joe became interested in the theater, possibly taking part in school plays. We do know that he built a toy theater at home and operated it in the lonely hours after school before his mother returned home from work.

Joe was in Chelsea during the school year but, because of his fondness for Cape Cod and his love for his cousin, Susan Huckins Howard (Mrs. Marcus W. Howard) of Chatham, he spent the summers with her and her family, finding a job to help out with finances.

In discussing the life of Joseph C. Lincoln, Lowell Ames Norris of the old Boston Herald told his son, Curtis B. Norris, Medical-Science Editor at Boston University, that when Joe was fourteen years old he worked in a fish market in Chatham. He was such a compulsive writer that he would tear off sheets of the heavy brown paper used for wrapping the fish and seclude himself while he wrote down his thoughts. Mr. Norris, a distant relative, said that some of Joe's earliest stories were written in this manner and that Joe lost at least one job due to it.

At this time Joe Lincoln was editor of the school paper and perhaps writing verses and yarns to take back to school in the Fall.

School records which would have given us facts and dates of Joe's attendance and activities were all destroyed in the great Chelsea fire of April 12, 1908. The fire covered an area one and one half miles long and three-quarters of a mile across the center of the city and destroyed the house in which the Lincolns lived and the Williams Grammar School.

At a time when the majority of Cape Cod boys went to sea as "cabin boys", as their fathers had done before them, it was decided by Joe's relatives that he should enter the business world. How he envied those boys who were heading for the life of a sailor and adventure, stories similar to those he had heard during all his boyhood years.

It was not to be. When Joe graduated from grammar school he went to work as a runner for George T. Sears, Wholesale Salt Dealer at 228 State and 81 Commercial Sts., Boston. The following letter tells something of him at this time:

Office of
George T. Sears
WHOLESALE SALT DEALER
228 State & 81 Commerce Sts.
Boston, Mar. 31st 1886

Dear Aggie:

I received your nice letter and liked it very much. Nigger got her letter too and sends letter to Beauty. Tomorrow is April Fool's day, you must fool all the folks. Shall you put any cotton in papa's biscuit this year. I wish I was going to be with you as I was last April but I hope to see you in the summer. I guess you have nice times now down there at Chatham, you and Florence. Ask Beauty if she goes swimming in that back yard much. I guess she doesn't like to wet her feet. They caught a big rat upstairs at the store here. He was so big, that although they got seven cats (every body around lugged in his cat) not one would dare to touch him. Finally the big dog next door came and finished it with one shake. Before he was killed though they had him outdoors on a flour barrel with a big sign on the trap "the only living African Skunk, has already killed three keepers, keep your hands off the bars". Every body who came past would stop and look at him, and then go away laughing. How are all the dolls now. Has Dandy Jim still survived. Your papa was up to see us for a day last week. I wish you was with him. Last Sunday another boy and myself went up to the horse car stables for a walk. I guess you would have liked to have been there. There was between three and four hundred horses. We saw them fed. They put the stuff they eat in a big cart with wheels and push it along. Every horse has a pitchfork full of the stuff for his dinner or supper or whatever it is. When you come up to see me I will take you up there if you want to go. You tell Grandma to write me when she gets the time and give my love to everybody. Now I must close for Nigger wants to write.

So Good Bye from Joe

We asked Mr. Rider, the handwriting analyst, to do an analysis of this letter of the sixteen-year-old Joe Lincoln, and here is our account of his report.

The writing is very mature and the flare for lifting the last stroke of a word shows his optimism — "I am going to be somebody, I have enthusiasm and high goals and plans". He has a sharp, keen mentality, but will take his own time to reach his goals, and not be pushed around or disturbed by other people. He likes to retire to a quiet place, preferring to be alone and not annoyed.

There is a lot of color in his hand-writing, showing that he is a vain young man, a man of ideas who knows what he is going to do. He has a great deal of pride and tends to perfection. He is extremely persistent with an excellent memory. He is a very healthy individual with excellent muscular control and could spend long hours at work without being upset.

Joe understands the use of and has good projection of space, his margins in his letter are nearly perfectly straight. He has a lot of natural and pure creativity, and considerable intuitiveness. He is a very conservative type of individual who applies himself diligently to his project, and is a "string-saver" — seldom discards a useful item — saving ideas to be used later. The rhythm of his writing speeds up his thinking. He is very careful and cautious and has a restricted philosophy of life, but once he gets an idea, nothing can stop him. He has a sixth sense which aids him in his writing. Joe being a conservative person will tend to write in a modest style and choose "homey" plots.

In 1887 Joe changed jobs and became a clerk in a brokerage house at 88 State Street, Boston. He held this position for about six years, when he became a "clerk at 30 Sudbury St., Boston". In 1895 he became a bookkeeper for the Swift Desk Company, located at 53 Portland St., Boston. There is no evidence that he did any writing during these years.

In order to increase their income, Emily took on a couple of boarders. These young men came from Barnstable and had jobs in Boston. Their names were Francis L. Maraspin and Charles Matthews.

To show you how young and high-spirited these youths were, here is a little anecdote that has been passed along to us. Next door to the Lincoln apartment there lived a spinster who put her parrot's cage in the open window every day for an airing. Using a bean shooter Joe and the two boarders would "shoot" this bird with beans. The parrot would express his feelings about the bombardment by cussing like an angry sailor, having, no doubt, belonged to a sailor formerly. The harrassment and the language used by the parrot annoyed the spinster. She would partially close the blinds to protect her parrot but the young men became more expert and shot through the openings. There is no known ending to this story.

Charles Matthews left after a while and went out West, but the friendship between Joe and Frank Maraspin went on throughout Joe's life. In his later years Frank Maraspin was a very solemn person: "One should never laugh because one will pay for it in tears", was one of his sayings. But that did not disturb his friendship with Joe Lincoln, who could not be a solemn person if he tried: serious perhaps, but never solemn.

During the years 1894-96, Joe had become a pupil of Henry Sandham, the artist, with studios at 152 Boylston Street, Boston. Sandham who signed his work "Hy", was a well-known painter of historical essays on canvas, such as "The Dawn of Liberty" which hangs in the town hall of Lexington, Massachusetts. His 12 x 21 ft. canvas, called "The March of Time", hangs in the National Gallery of Art in Washington, D.C. "Hy" came to Boston from Montreal, Canada, where he was born and where he had been a founder of the Royal Canadian Academy of Arts. He began in Boston as an illustrator — Edgar Allen Poe's *Lenore* in 1896, Helen Hunt Jackson's *Ramona* in 1900, and many others.

In 1896, Joe decided that he had no liking and no talent for bookkeeping, gave up his job, and determined to become a full-time artist. In later years he told a friend "I have always felt that they were as glad to get rid of me as I was to leave." In his *Galusha the Magnificent,* Lincoln exemplifies his own feelings of frustration and inadequacy in a calling not to his liking through the experiences of the temperamental Galusha.

Joe and a fellow student at Sandham's, Howard Reynolds, set up a commercial art studio in Room 19 of 18 Pemberton Square, Boston. The two collaborated on a short story, "The Studio Puzzle", which was published in a Boston ten-cent magazine called *The Owl.* They also collaborated on some verses and sketches sold to a bicycle magazine. At the end of 1895 the partners decided to go their separate ways. Reynolds stayed at the studios and Lincoln moved to a studio at 12 Pearl Street, where he hung his sign out as a commercial artist and illustrator. At this time he was still making his home with his mother at 113 Walnut Street in Chelsea. Joe and Emily had moved several times over the years, which leads one to wonder whether or not their financial situation had deteriorated.

The commercial art venture was not a great success. We have been unable to find any of the 'work' that Joe did during this time at his studio. When Sterling Elliott, editor and publisher of the *League of American Wheelmen Bulletin & Good Roads,* invited Joe to come on his staff as illustrator, Joe readily accepted. He went to work in the office of the *Bulletin* in the Russia Building at 530 Atlantic Avenue, Boston.

Charles Edward Pratt (1845-1898) was the founder and first president of the League of American Wheelmen, the first bicycle club in America. "The Father of the League" founded the Bulletin in July of 1885. A magazine called *Good Roads* was started in January, 1892. The first issue of the combination of these two magazines, called *The League of American Wheelmen Bulletin & Good Roads* came out on April 5, 1895. The editor and publisher was Sterling Elliott. A magazine started in 1895 called *"The Wheelman"* was published in Boston and edited by Mary Sargent Hopkins.

The first piece of Joe's work that Elliott bought was a poem and a sketch entitled *"A Query"*, a "girl-watchers complaint", although Joe did not call it that. The poet complains about the dress of the Victorian girls and women who were making a fad of bicycle-riding. But a "girl watcher's complaint" in 1896? Of course, there is nothing new in that complaint, except perhaps that there is more to cover the girls and thus more to complain about.

A Query
Oh, all ye learned ones who know
The ways of woman-kind,
Pray answer me a question that
Doth much perplex my mind.

Why does the maid with dainty form,
When ere she goes awheel,
Bedeck her lovely limbs with skirts
That reach down to the heel;

While she whose form is thinner far
Than maiden's e're should be,
A cycling skirt will always wear
That ends just at the knee?

During 1896 Joe wrote several nostalgic poems which indicate that his thoughts were often turned to his boyhood in Brewster. One in particular, published in the October 9, 1896 *Bulletin,* was reminiscent of Aunt Martha's hat shop.

The Ballade of Polly's Hat
From *(League of American Wheelmen Bulletin, Oct. 9, 1896)*

Frame that was fashioned in France,
    Straw from a Tuscany hill,
Bent in a shape to entrance,
    Or, as the ladies say, "kill";
    Decked at the milliner's will,
Ribbon and bow and all that,
    Lace never made in a mill, —
This is Miss Polly's new hat.

Ostrich plumes nodding a dance
    As the spring breezes blow shrill,
Plucked from the biped, perchance,
    Near some South African rill;
    Graceful in plumage and quill,
Arched like the back of a cat,
    Curled with the cunningest skill, —
This is Miss Polly's new hat.

Satin of glossy expanse,
    Colors the rainbow might spill,
Hat-pin of gold to enhance
    Charms that these beauties instill;
    Silver-frost buckles to fill, —
Just the one place that is flat,
    Georgeous ensemble to thrill, —
This is Miss Polly's new hat.

Envoy.
Doctor, her father is ill,
    Fainting-away on the mat;
He has just glanced at the bill, —
    This is Miss Polly's new hat.

In "Waiting for the Mail", Joe fondly recalls the pleasant evenings spent in the grocery store waiting for the arrival of the mail.

Waiting for the Mail
(League of American Bulletin, May 14, 1897, p. 540)

After supper, of an evenin'
'long 'bout ha'f past six o'clock,
When I've fetched termorrer's wood in,
'n I've milked 'n seen t' the stock.
It's 'most gin'rally my custom, or my habit, you may say,
To stroll down to the groc'ry, where the "Office" is an' stay
An' meet the other fellers 'round the stove an' set an' smoke,
That is, smoke or chaw or sunthin', an' jest laff an' crack a joke
With the rest the crowd, I tell yer, it's clean comfort to the core
Waitin' for the mail er evenin's, down t' Bingham's groc'ry store.

Course, I don't expect a letter, every time the mail comes in,
'though my son Elnathan writes me, an' Maria, now'n agin,
An' the Barnhill Weekly Bugle comes 'round every once a week,
But it's more the social sperrit that I'm after, so to speak.
Why, you can't help feelin' woke up when old Capt'n Salt 'll tell
'Bout the cur'us flyin' fishes that he seen t' sea an' — Well!
When Rube Pettigrew gits goin', gosh, we nigh bust through the floor.
Waitin' for the mail er evenin's, down to Bingham's groc'ry store.

Male an' female. See the p'int now? Wan't that great? I tell yer what
Never stopped to think nor nothin', but jest give it good an' hot,
An' when he see how 't was takin', course, he said it over then,
An' jest emphasized a little, where it needed it, an' when,
"Gosh!" I sez to Rube, "I'm thinkin'," s' I, "I'd like to bet a hat
'T will be quite a spell, by Judas! 'fore Sam hears the last of that".
Talk about your wit an' humor, I git all I want an' more
Waitin' for the mail er evenin's, down to Bingham's groc'ry store.

The year 1897 was marked by three major changes in Joe Lincoln's life. First, his mother, Emily Crosby Lincoln, who had provided him with a home and been his companion for the first twenty-seven years of his life, died of pneumonia on the 28th of February at their home in Chelsea. Joe had her body buried near his father's grave in the Brewster cemetery.

Second, Joe married Florence Elry Sargent on the 12th of May and she became his companion for the rest of his life, forty-seven years. They were married by the Reverend H. Perry Bush, D.D., in Chelsea, according to marriage records in that city.

Florence was a reserved, quiet young woman. Her mother, who was a native of Maine, died when she was young and her father, Charles Sargent, was a picture-frame dealer in Chelsea. He died before Joe and Florence were married. Florence was employed as a bookkeeper and lived alone at 105 Orange Street.

It has been said that Joe Lincoln and Florence Sargent were engaged for several years before they were married. The long engagement may have been due to many or any one of a number of reasons — Joe had been the sole support of his mother for several years, and to take on a wife on his meager income was not possible: perhaps the women did not care to live together, or there was not adequate space. It is also possible that Joe was not ready for marriage. However, when his mother died, and after a proper interval of time, he and Florence were married.

Their wedding announcement stated, "At home after May twentieth, 131 Washington Avenue". Married on the 12th, at home on the twentieth — they did not go very far in eight days. If Joe had his way they probably went to Cape Cod. He had relatives there who would have wanted to meet his wife.

Joe had no published piece in the *LAW* magazine issue of May 21, but in the issue of May 28, the piece "Home Agin'" appeared, and in the next issue, June 4, what was the title? — "Bird's Nesting Time". The third important event in Joe's life in 1897 happened on September 17, when the name Joseph C. Lincoln appeared for the first time on the masthead of the *Bulletin* — he was one of three Associate Editors. In an interview with Arnold Patrick he was to say "Everyone except myself, was riding a bicycle in those days — so, knowing nothing about bicycling, I found myself Associate Editor of the *League of American Wheelmen Bulletin*. I did the illustrations for the magazine", and he added under his breath, "they were pretty dreadful pictures, too."

While Joe Lincoln was shifting from commercial art to writing, the verses called "Life Paths" were published in the *Bulletin* of October 8, 1897. Here he appears to be thinking out loud about the course of his life, as he explains to his wife and himself:

"But narrow our path may be, my dear,
    And simple the scenes we view,
A heart like thine, and a love like mine,
    Will carry us bravely through.
With a happy song we'll trudge along,
    And smile in the shine or showers,
And we'll ease the pack on a brother's back
    By this workaday life of ours."

In contrast to what is published as 'poetry' today, Joe's verses are transparent — the picture, the person, the season, the subject, comes through clearly. His themes are too simple to be important and are understood on the first reading. He writes of the familiar and the commonplace, but watch out! — this is a sly fellow who hides something more than fun under his humor. For instance, in the verses labeled "And There Are Others", published in the *Bulletin* of September 11, 1896, he pointed up a problem that afflicted organized labor, a problem unresolved to the present day.

AND THERE ARE OTHERS

By Joe Lincoln

Every day, for ten year or more,
Joe Hawley's come down to the grocery store,
And sot on a barrel and argified
That the rich was tannin' the poor man's hide.
"We can't earn the price of a decent meal,
We're ground beneath Capital's iron heel,
We workin' men don't stand no show
For an honest livin', by Gosh!" says Joe.

46

There ain't a thing that he don't know
About the "Laborin' Class's" woe;
And he'll sit all day and lay down the law,
And only stop to "borrer a chaw,"
While his wife at home, she takes in sewin'
Or goes out washin' to keep things goin'
For the only work, I ever saw
Joe Hawley do, was to work his jaw.

Joe's verses, and that's what he preferred to call them, were written for people who were not loaded down with literary or critical apparatus. His readers, like the people who listened to the itinerant ballad singers in the days before books were common, were able to be surprised and pleased when the story unfolded in rhyme. They had no sophisticated, automatic, judgmental categories of good and bad verse. How many people do you think managed to read each copy of the thousands of copies of the magazine published each week?

Joe wrote jingles, rhymes, verses, and some poems during his writing life. To the very end, in his last novel, *The Bradshaws of Harniss,* Joe loved a jingle, and included this one —

"If I could pick my earthly lot
I wouldn't be a worm,
To burrow in a garden plot
And squirm and squirm and squirm.
But yet, I'll say this for that worm:
No matter how he feels,
He does his job — which is to squirm —
And squirms — but never squeals."

No doubt Joe knew very little about these little animals which Aristotle called "the intestines of the earth", but his small tribute is to be preferred over the announcement on a can of herbicide which proudly proclaims "this same chemical can be used to eradicate earthworms". The writer of that suicidal statement never heard the words of George Sheffield Oliver, " The burrowing earthworm is Nature's own plough, her chemist, her cultivator, her fertilizer, her distributer of plant food. In every way, the earthworm surpasses anything man has yet invented to plough, to cultivate or to fertilize the soil". Joe is very right — the earthworm does his job.

47

Lincoln was twenty-eight years old when the Spanish-American War began on the 21st of March, 1898. He had been married less than a year, and his wife had a job as a bookkeeper but he did not enter the service. He would have made some kind of a soldier. With his temperament and his complete lack of skill with tools and guns, plus his utter abhorrence of a regimented life, the Army was well off without him.

Joe responded to the Spanish-American War by writing several poems. The list includes "The Boys in Blue"; "A Ballade of Blue Jackets"; "War and Mud"; "The Reg'lar Army Man"; "The Army Hardtack" and "Our Country's Dead". All of these poems were published in the *LAW Bulletin* during the war years. They show his high regard for the soldier and his own dread of army life.

To Joe, "killing" is wrong morally, but fighting to protect country and family must justify the means.

The earliest written comment on Joe lincoln's writing known to this author is by Daniel B. Latimer. His comment was published in the *League of American Wheelmen Bulletin* for December 24, 1897. under the heading *Toasts and Roasts*. Using the letters L, A, W, he wrote something about all of the members of the staff, and of Joe he wrote, "Ludicrous, Agreeable, Writings — Joe's". It is interesting that his comment is on Joe's "writings" when Joe was on the staff as an "illustrator".

At the time that Joe Lincoln's first verses and sketches appeared in the *Bulletin*, the weekly magazine had a paid circulation of 59,328 copies. It reached its highest paid circulation with the issue of April 8, 1898 — 104,268 copies weekly, going all over the United States. When Joe wrote his last piece, *A Snow Song*, published December 30, 1898, the paid circulation was down to 73, 294 copies per week. Roads were improving, automobiles were replacing bicycles, and the membership of the *League* was dropping rapidly. Joe left the *League Bulletin* at the end of 1898, and in August of that year, Elliott changed the name of the magazine to *Elliott's Magazine*. In spite of this change, it soon faded away.

Illustration accompanying "War and Mud" in the *League of American Wheelmen Bulletin. Courtesy Mrs. Percy Rex.*

WAR AND MUD
Joe Lincoln

Says the blatant General Weyler, "If they'd give me half a chance
    I would show the 'pigs' a Spaniard's not afraid;
For I wouldn't wait a moment, but my army I'd advance,
    And the cursed Yankee country I'd invade!"
        But he doesn't know the job he'd have to tackle,
           Or he'd never leave the land of his abode;
        He would stay at home and hide, if he'd ever tried to ride
           Through the mess the Yankee people call a road.

'Tis a wondrous combination, and we make it out of clay,
    And of sticks and stones and refuse, and of mud,
And it's trodden down and kneaded in a most ingenious way,
    And we moisten it with water in a flood,
        Till the bottom is as thick as "hasty pudding"
           And the surface is completely overflowed:
        Then we mix it up with glue to a pasty kind of "goo",
           And we find we have a Yankee country road.

So, if Weyler should invade us, why, his armies would be stuck
    In a place where they could neither walk nor swim;
But, alas! our noble soldiers would have just as wretched luck —
    They'd be mired so they could never get at him.
        And the methods that the generals would follow,
          Would be warfare of a most peculiar mode:
        Each would calmly settle down, waiting for his foe to drown
          In the soupy, slippy, sloppy Yankee road.

Oh, the brainy road-constructors have a very rigid rule,
    As the highways that they build us would denote:
'Tis to make the roads too thin to hold a man or horse or mule,
    And a little bit too thick to use a boat;
        No doubt it is a very clever system,
          And they're justified in clinging to the code,
        But it's lucky, seems to me, that the war is on the sea,
          And not upon a Yankee patent road.

Part II

Joseph Lincoln's Point of View

At that time it seemed to every writer that New York City was the publishing center of the world, and to be recognized one must live nearby.

One evening, about a year after their marriage, Joe followed Florence into the living room after the supper dishes were done and told her that he wanted to ask her a question. She sat down in a rocking chair while Joe, head bowed and hands clasped behind his back, paced the floor.

"Flo, have we courage enough to put our furniture into storage, to live in one room, to cut our ties here, to move to New York, — and to see?"

They both knew that it was a gamble and that the rent came due with monotonous regularity, but they decided to take the plunge. Joe gave up his position as Associate Editor at the end of 1898, Florence resigned her bookkeeping position, and they moved to Brooklyn, New York. There, trying to economize, they lived in one room on the third floor of a rooming house, and prepared their meals over a gas burner.

Arnold Patrick, reporting on a long interview with Joe Lincoln, writes this in the *Bookman* for January 1925, quoting Joe, "Knowing little of banking, I found myself in the office of the American Institute of Bankers". Patrick explains, "This institution, in those days starting on a small scale, has since turned into the large and well-known Junior Bankers of America. Mr. Lincoln here acted in the capacity of a secretary, combined with duties which would now be termed, I presume, 'publicity'"

Maybe Joe "found himself" in banking, but we suspect that faced with the necessity of finding a job which would provide him with a steady income, he went out and took what he could find, even though it was not what he wanted most to do.

Thus, we now find Joe employed as an editor of a banking magazine during the day; each night, after supper was cleared away, he worked, bent over a small oak table under a dim electric bulb hanging on a cord from the ceiling, writing verses and poems to be sent to such magazines as *Harper's Bazaar, Ainslee's, Saturday Evening Post,* and, of course the *League of American Wheelmen Bulletin,* for acceptance or refusal.

These were anxious days, filled with anxiety and hope. Would their move be justified? The first writing of Joe Lincoln to be published in *Harper's Bazaar* was a short, short story called "Mrs. Phidgit's System", which appeared January 13, 1900. Mrs. Phidgit, foot-weary and home late from shopping around for lower prices all day, admits to her husband, "I've spent almost a dollar more than I would if I hadn't tried not to be extravagant." Without a moral appendage, this little story tells us that even though the Lincolns had little money, Joe had no intention of being foolish about it.

Three of Joe's short stories were published in the *Saturday Evening Post* in 1900, namely, "Josiah and the Seventh Son", " 'Enry 'Iggins 'Eart Story", and "Solon Pepper's Courtship". The Post also published two of Joe's new Poems that year, "The Winter Nights at Home" which was included in *Cape Cod Ballads,* and "The Little Feller's Stocking", illustrated by Fanny Y. Cory. The latter poem reflects the financial situation in the Lincoln home and Joe's attitude towards it. Here is the last stanza:

> "And the crops may fail and leave us with our plans all gone to
>   smash,
> And the mortgage may hang heavy, and the bills use up the
>   cash,
> But whenever comes the season, jest so long's we've got a dime,
> There'll be something in that stocking — won't there, Mary? —
>   every time

And if, in amongst our sunshine, there's a shower or two of
     rain,
Why, we'll face it bravely smilin', and we'll try not ter complain
Long as Christmas comes and finds us here together, me and you,
With the little feller's stockin' hangin' up beside the flue."

Although "The Cod-Fisher" is the only one of Joe's poems published by *Harper's Weekly* (July 7, 1900), nevertheless it appears that
the Boston *Journal of Civilization* realized the quality of the work.
This poem is clear evidence that Joe Lincoln was capable of more
than the "verses" that he wrote for the less critical readers who knew
him so well. However that may be, this poem "The Cod-Fisher" will
live long after the cod-fish has become an extinct species, if for no
other reason than for the one line "For men must die that men may
live". This line summons up visions of people throughout the ages
who have given up their lives that mankind may benefit thereby.
By its very truth, it immortalizes its author.

The Cod-Fisher

Where leap the long Atlantic swells
     In foam-streaked stretch of hill and dale,
Where shrill the north-wind demon yells,
     And flings the spindrift down the gale;
Where, beaten 'gainst the bending mast,
     The frozen raindrop clings and cleaves,
With steadfast front for calm or blast
     His battered schooner rocks and heaves.

To some the gain, to some the loss,
     To each the chance, the risk, the fight:
For men must die that men may live --
     Lord, may we steer our course aright.

The dripping deck beneath him reels,
     The flooded scuppers spout the brine;
He heeds them not, he only feels
     The tugging of a tightened line.
The grim white sea-fog o'er him throws
     Its clammy curtain, damp and cold;
He minds it not — his work he knows
     'Tis but to fill an empty hold.

Oft, driven through the night's blind wrack,
    He feels the dread berg's ghastly breath,
Or hears draw nigh through walls of black
    A throbbing engine chanting death;
But with a calm, unwrinkled brow
    He fronts them, grim and undismayed,
For storm and ice and liner's bow —
    These are but chances of the trade.

Yet well he knows — where'er it be,
    On low Cape Cod or bluff Cape Ann —
With straining eyes that search the sea
    A watching woman waits her man:
He knows it, and his love is deep,
    But work is work, and bread is bread,
And though men drown and women weep
    The hungry thousands must be fed.

To some the gain, to some the loss
    To each his chance, the game with Fate:
For men must die that men may live —
    Dear Lord, be kind to those who wait.

At a time when Joe could ill afford the time or the cost of commuting to work he was persuaded by his friend, Sewall Ford, also an author, to move out to Hackensack, New Jersey. Hackensack, the County Seat of Bergen County in northern New Jersey, was settled by the Dutch about 1640. Named for an Indian tribe, the Hackensack, this suburban, residential town rose gradually from the banks of the Hackensack River to a ridge commanding panoramic views to the south and east. Sewall Ford and his family lived on this ridge at 283 Summit Avenue. About 1910, after the success of his first novel, Joe would build his first house at 366 Summit Avenue.

But, at the time of their move from New York City, the Lincolns settled on a pleasant street with friendly neighbors. On July 16, 1900, shortly after their arrival, a son and only child, Joseph Freeman Lincoln, was born. Since his father and both his paternal and maternal grandfathers were called Joseph, the youngster came to be known as Freeman.

There is a discrepancy in the record of Freeman's birth in Hackensack. His parents' names in the city records on the date of birth are given as "Joseph Crosby" and "Florence Sargent", so the child's name is given as "Joseph Freeman Lincoln Crosby". A clerk in the city hall, on making this discovery, commented that the father must have "added the Lincoln to his own name later for literary purposes", an interesting explanation of a recorder's mistake.

The name Freeman was brought into the Lincoln family by Joe's paternal grandmother Desire Freeman Foster, Jr. Lincoln Thacher. Her mother was Desire Freeman, daughter of Lemuel and Mary Freeman, who married Captain Benjamin Foster. One of Joe's uncles, Captain Freeman Jackson Lincoln, also carried this old Cape name. He died when Joe was four years old.

There were Freemans in Joe's mother's family, also. One, Captain Freeman Crosby, was master of the ship from the deck of which Emily's brother, Joseph, was swept to his death in a dreadful storm in the north Atlantic. It was he who wrote the compassionate letter to the lad's parents.

The Joe Lincolns and their friends, Mr. and Mrs. Harry B. Harding of 268 Clinton Place, Hackensack, used to employ a young neighbor to take Freeman and the Harding daughter out for an afternoon airing in one baby carriage. This was Priscilla Harding, who became a librarian at the Sandwich, Massachusetts Library. She retired in 1970.

Young Freeman Lincoln attended Miss Harper's Kindergarten and the primary grades of the public school in Hackensack. When he was about eleven years old, he transferred to the Hackley School, a Unitarian Boarding School in Tarrytown, New York, where he prepared for Harvard College. Freeman's father, Joe Lincoln, was very conscious of his own lack of formal schooling and its limitations, and was determined that his son should have the advantage of a college education.

A survey of the published writings, poems, and short stories by Joe Lincoln produced in the years 1900 to 1904 makes it hard to realize that through those years Joe had a regular full-time job and was commuting from Hackensack to New York City every work day. He was also an active member of the Unitarian Congregational Church, serving on its Board of Trustees. He became the father of a son in 1900 and produced his first novel in 1904.

This, a kind of preface to becoming a writer full-time, shows a man of considerable energy. In a lecture to freshmen at Harvard on the subject of becoming an author, Joe, speaking from personal ex-

55

perience, said that in the beginning years the would-be writer would do well to have a job that produced money for house and family, otherwise the writing would be beset with the worry of how to keep alive, and, in any case, would know many "tin-lizzie" days. The sale of writing helped out financially, to be sure, but payments for poems and short stories were meagre, and Joe had to be more concerned with getting published than with becoming rich.

Ainslee's Magazine began publishing Joe Lincoln's short stories in its October, 1900 issue with "A Matter of Twenty Thousand". The atmosphere of this story is not of Cape Cod, but that of a shore town such as Chelsea, Massachusetts. The "Cape Cod sand flea" and the "Cape Ann jellyfish" who vie for the hand of "Mag" Kelly by attempting to win a reward for the capture of a sea-monster are not the kind of people Joe used in his subsequent writing. In its day *Ainslee's* was a popular magazine and published many of Joe's yarns, until it ceased publication in 1912. Two poems appearing in *Ainslee's,* "Fusts", and "The Age of Wisdom" have almost nothing in common in form or style with the verses published in the *Bulletin,* nor did Joe see fit to include either of them in his anthology.

The American Press Association, which sold literary material to newspapers across the nation, published Joe's poem "A Thanksgiving Dream", on their Thanksgiving Page in November of 1900. This poem is included in both *Cape Cod Ballads* and *Rhymes of the Old Cape.*

In their December issues, the Association provided both New Year material and end of the century material. Joe's "Uncle Ezra's New Year Reverie" tells us something of what it was like at the end of the Nineteenth Century. Joe was thirty years old that year and his reactions to the calendar maker's event are in the following lines:

Comes the Twentieth Century

Eleven thirty, New Year's Eve — the Nineteenth Century's dyin!
The clouds are weepin o'er his bed, and sad the wind is sighin;
Old Doctor Time has given him up — there ain't no use in physic,
His breath comes short and wheezy-like, same' mine does with the
    phthisic.
But tho' I know he's booked ter sail on board old Charon's packet,
There'll be no weed upon my hat, no crape upon my jacket,
Fer when I've lived, as he has done, a hundred years, full measure,
I think I'll say ter Death, "Shake hands! I'm proud ter have the
    pleasure!"

And yet he's been a smart old boy — there's been few cycles quicker
Ter see and grab a brand new way ter make our wheels go slicker.
Before he come slow coaches wuz our fastest locomotion,
And cranky winds wuz all we had ter shove us 'crost the ocean.
But now, great Scott! our railroads mark the map of every nation,
And steamers rush our letters round the whole consarned creation;
The telephone and telegraph have come to ease our labors,
And make John Bull and Uncle Sam chat just like next door neighbors.

The X-ray lights a chap's inside and shows the framework of it,
The spry typewriter prints his words a hundred to a minute,
The phonograph repeats his speech in tone that's plain tho' squeakin,
The movin picters show him how he looked when he wuz speakin,
Electric ranges cook his food, electric launches float him,
And through electric lighted streets electric wagons tote him.
And if one of 'em runs him down and does his vitals sever,
The doctors put some new ones in and fix him better'n ever.

Eleven forty-five — I seem ter hear a distant hummin
And lively music in the air — the Twentieth Century's comin!
What does he bring, I wonder now, ter tickle and surprise us?
What magic tricks is up his sleeve ter please and paralyze us?
Will our grandchildren go abroad upon an airship liner,
Or whiz straight through the earth upon the hourly train ter China?
Will we "expand" until the moon's divided 'mongst the nations?
Will war news telegraphed from Mars affect the stock quotations?

Will water burn, I wonder? And will fire be cold and freezy?
Will nothin be impossible and miracles jest easy?
I wonder if — But there! I'll stop; my "wonderer's" gittin tired,
And see! 'tis on the stroke of twelve! The Old Year has expired.
"The Nineteenth Century's dead!" So says the old clock with its
        tickin,
He's dead and gone fer good and all, but I'm alive and kickin.
Ring up the curtain! clear the stage! I'm ready fer the drama,
You're welcome, Mister Twentieth! Now start your panorama!
                                        Joe Lincoln

The American Press Association advertised Joe's long poem,
"Carrier's Address 1901", as follows: "the clever work of a clever
writer. Arranged for newspaper or pamphlet use. Must not be used
before Dec. 15, 1900. Sold to but one paper in a town". This poem

has newspaper people in the place of Canterbury Pilgrims, and newspaper tales in the place of the Tales of a Wayside Inn. We have to wonder how Joe became so familiar with what goes on in a newspaper office.

The Carrier's Address consists of a series of poems relating to newspaper business. It includes the "New Year News", "The Journalistic Pilgrims", "The Editor's Tale", "The Reporter's Tale", "The 'Devil's' Tale", "The Foreman's Tale", and concludes with "The Carrier's Refrain":

The Carrier's Refrain

The editor sits in his sanctum
    And ponders and scribbles away;
The reporter goes down through the streets of the town
    And picks up the events of the day.
The typesetter fills up his galley,
    The pressman his labor pursues,
But I sing not their praise, for this carol I raise
    For the fellow who brings us the news.

The householder rises for breakfast
    And steps to his vestibule door;
The dew of the dawn is still wet on the lawn,
    Yet the Carrier's been there before,
The merchant steps out on the sidewalk
    And longs for the editor's views;
He takes but one stride, and his want is supplied
    By the fellow who brings us the news.

He travels the lone country byways;
    He shouts in the brisk city street
O'er his route he must go, be it rain, sleet or snow
    Or the weltering midsummer heat.
He carries the world to our doorstep.
    Earth's journal makes ours to peruse,
And we'd stagnate and rot in our shells were it not
    For the fellow who brings us the news.
So here's to the Carrier laddies!
    Good luck to their hustling crews!
The newsboy who capers, the man who sells papers,
    The fellows who bring us the news.

Many newspapers and magazines have been started on Cape Cod over the years, and many were short-lived. It is not known what Cape Cod newspapers Joe Lincoln knew and read nor do we know how much these newspapers contributed to his knowledge of the Cape.

One cannot but wonder whether Joe knew any of the newspaper people of the Cape and from which ones he learned what he put into the several newspaper stories which he wrote.

By the close of 1900, Joe's published writings numbered fifteen.

A poem showing Joe's patriotism and love of country is "Columbia's Valentine", published on the Valentine's Day Page issued by the American Press Association for 1901.

Columbia's Valentine

My Dear Columbia:
    Now's the festive season
When all the world goes courtin blithe and gay
When there's much rhyme and mighty little reason
    And Mr. Cupid's postman fer a day.

And as ter my eye nothin can excel you
    I'll kinder spur this haltin muse of mine
And write a little ditty jest ter tell you
    You're still your partner Samuel's valentine.

More than a hundred years have took their transit —
    One twenty-five I think's the right amount —

Sence you and me decided that we'd chance it
    And start housekeepin on our own account;
Sence Marm Brittania tried ter whip her daughter
    And found the job too big fer one ter do.
And old Pa Bull sneaked home across the water,
    And left me paddlin' of my own canoe.

'Twas kinder rugged trav'lin when we started,
    Fer cash was scurse and times was middlin bad,
Few friends was true and they wuz but ha'f hearted,
    And Injuns was the biggest crop we had.
But yet we never grumbled at our ration,
    We worked and dared in spite of Fortune's frown,
Till now there ain't a spot on all creation
    Don't know that Yankee Doodle's come ter town.

Our Yankee engines drag the Russian mail trains,
    Our Yankee bridges span Egyptian streams.
From frozen seas where Greenland's icy gale reigns
    Ter India's strand our Yankee commerce steams.
Our Yankee army keeps the Chinese steady,
    Our Yankee navy floats on every sea,
And eighty million Yankee hearts are ready
    Ter keep this Yankee land ferever free.

And so, Columbia, I have wrote this letter
    As sort of an admirin valentine
That says we're good, but always growin better,
    And great, but climbin up ter superfine.
And, not ter brag, but jest between us two, dear,
    I'll whisper that I'm sartin — yes I am —
The finest land on earth is run by you, dear,
    And

        Your devoted partner,

                Uncle Sam.

    It comes as somewhat of a surprise to find that Joseph Crosby Lincoln was listed in the second edition of *Who's Who in America.* But there he is on page 684 of Volume II, 1901-1902, which a gracious lady Librarian in the New Bedford, Mass., Public Library dug out for me:

    "Lincoln, Joseph Crosby, 62 Maple Ave., Hackensack, N.J." with several lines about this young author. At this time Joe Lincoln had not written a single one of the 39 novels for which most people know him, but his poems in the *League of American Wheelmen Bulletin and Good Roads*, published in Boston, had been going into the homes of a hundred thousand subscribers weekly, across the nation. In the first two years of the Twentieth Century, the American Press Association was selling Joe Lincoln's poems and short stories to newspapers in most of the cities of the United States. *Ainslee's Magazine, the Saturday Evening Post, Harper's Weekly, Harper's Bazar, Life, Punch, Judge, Current Literature,* and *Types* (a typesetters' magazine published in England) had published poems and/or short stories by Joe Lincoln before 1902. Joe himself referred to these writings as "verses", and "yarns". He had no illusions about their literary quality, but he had the great encouragement of a reading public, whose response made his writings saleable.

Joe Lincoln illustrated what Fowler in *Modern English Usage* states: "It is both true and important that a thing that appeals to simple emotions evokes a wonderfully wide response".

Joseph Crosby Lincoln in his garden at Crosstrees in Chatham.
Courtesy Mrs. J. Freeman Lincoln

Chapter 8
Cape Cod Ballads and Other Verse

The first book written by Joe Lincoln was *Cape Cod Ballads and Other Verse.* It was published by Albert Brandt, in Trenton, New Jersey in 1902. This hardbound yellow cloth volume of 78 "verses" was Joe's anthology of his own poetry written between 1896 and 1902. All of the poems had been published in magazines – there appear to be none that were written especially for this book. None can know why a poet selects from his poems this one and omits that one, – someone else might make a different selection, but it is his book and therefore his choice. Since he dedicated the book to his wife, Florence Sargent Lincoln, we might ask whether she helped in making the selections.

Most of the verses in his first book are filled with Joe's recollections of his boyhood on Cape Cod and the vacations that he spent there. They are homely pieces which show what life in his youth was like, and a great deal as well about his own background. In his boyhood, Joe lived in a village full of men who had gone to sea as boys – Brewster was full of working and retired ship captains. Almost all of his male Lincoln relatives and some of his mother's male relatives were mariners – some were "lost at sea". It was natural for Joe to have a hankering for the sea.

What a change in style and phrasing takes place when he writes of the sea and the seashore! In Joe's introduction to *Ships and Water,* by Alfred A. di Lardi, Philadelphia, 1938, he wrote: "To tolerate the sea is ridiculous and to be merely favorably inclined toward it is impertinent. You cannot merely 'like' the sea, but you can love it. Oh, yes, you can do that."

The *And Other Verses* in the title was added because Joe included some off-Cape "verses" in the collection. Some of these pieces were written while the Lincolns were living in Brooklyn, such as "The Fift' Ward J'int Debate", "O'Reilly's Billy-Goat", "The Hand-Organ Ball", "Fireman O'Rafferty", and "The Ballad of McCarty's Trombone". The latter was written for the Saint Patrick's Day Page, issued by the American Press Association in March of 1901, and is one of the many holiday poems that Joe wrote.

Edward Windsor Kemble (1861-1933) did the illustrations for the *Ballads.* Already well known, he had illustrated Mark Twain's *Library of Humor* published by Webster in 1888, and in 1892 he did the illustrations for Houghton Mifflin Co.'s two volume edition of Stowe's *Uncle Tom's Cabin.* In 1908 we found him doing political cartoons for *Everybody's Magazine* when we were searching that magazine for Joe's short stories. In 1923 Kemble illustrated Putnam's two volume edition of Washington Irving's *Knickerbocker's History of New York.* One could wish to know whether Brandt, the publisher, or Joe, the author, was the friend who engaged Kemble to do the illustrations for the *Ballads.* It is a tribute to this illustrator to say that his works are collectible today.

Volumes of poetry usually quickly find their way into used-book stores, but clippings with a Joe Lincoln verse are often found tucked into a well-worn Bible with other printed treasures. Have you attempted to buy a copy of *Cape Cod Ballads and Other Verses* lately? This thin, yellow cloth-clad hard-cover is a collector's item and brings "collector's prices" if you can find one. While this doesn't testify to the so-called literary merit of Joe's verses, what it does say is that there is a large reading public which loved what Joe wrote.

Almost none of Joe's verses have been used in anthologies, except his poems of the sea and sea-going people. Joshua and Florence Crowell included Joe's "The Life-Saver" on p. 155 of their anthology. *Cape Cod in Poetry*, Boston, 1924. William M. Williamson included "The Cod-Fisher" on p. 290 in his anthology, *The Eternal Sea*, New York, 1946. And in 1969, J. V. Hinshaw edited an anthology, *East of America,* published in Chatham, and included "The Cod-Fisher", "The Surf Along the Shore", and for some unknown reason, "Little Bare Feet".

B.O. Fowler of 5 Park Square, Boston, wrote a review of *Cape Cod Ballads* for the July, 1902 issue of the *Arena,* published in Trenton, New Jersey. Since this is the first review of Joe's first book, we quote in part as follows:

"Lovers of popular lays and verses descriptive of the common life will take genuine delight in Joe Lincoln's Cape Cod Ballads, which has just appeared from the Brandt Press; for here will be found almost four-score of those popular rhymes which, originally appearing in Harper's Weekly, the Saturday Evening Post, the Youth's Companion, and other journals, were promptly copied by the daily and weekly press of the land.

Mr. Lincoln is a young man, being born in Brewster, Massachusetts in 1870, but his verse has made his name a household word in thousands of homes. He is the youngest of a coterie of singers of the common life in homely phrase, and of which James Whitcomb Riley stands at the head, with Sam Walter Foss and Will Carleton as well-known representatives.

Many of Mr. Lincoln's verses contain exquisite home pictures and child memories, which, softened and glorified by the lapse of time, possess all the beauty of the distant mountain-peak crowned with glistening snow and robed in purple haze - pictures that are always dear to the normal mind when the materialism of modern life has not crushed out idealism.

The poems, as is usually the case with books of this kind, are of unequal value; a few, I think, are hardly worthy of a place in the volume, but the collection as a whole is excellent."

After the publication of *Cape Cod Ballads,* Joe seems to write less for the year 1903. However, one of those things that happens to poets happened to him. No one knows for sure why a man by the name of Henry Shepherd selected Joe's jingle "Susan Van Doozen" from *Cape Cod Ballads* to be the one and only poem by Joe Lincoln that was set to music. This piece of sheet music was copyrighted by W. Hutchins, and published by A. H. Goetting of Springfield, Massachusetts. We have never heard the music, but we have seen a copy of the sheet music. We believe that the music is in the style of 1903, but the lyric seems to us to be at least equal to much of what was set to music year after year and disappeared as fast as it appeared. This one piece of sheet music remains as a fact of Joe's writing career, whatever else may be said about it.

Since *Cap'n Eri* was published in 1904, and since Joe was writing it at night after work, we are surprised that anything else was published in 1903.

This is not too bad for a fellow who was at work on his first novel. The beginning of a trend takes place here, poems begin to decrease in

Ye children of the mountains,
    sing of your craggy peaks,
Your valleys forest laden,
    your cliffs where Echo speaks:
And ye, who by the prairies
    your childhood's joys have seen
Sing of your waving grasses,
    your velvet miles of green.
But when my memory wanders
    down to the dear old home
I hear, amid my dreaming,
    the seething of the foam,
The wet wild through the pine Trees,
    the sobbing crash and roar,
The mighty surge and thunder of
    the surf along the shore.

Joseph C. Lincoln
"Joe Lincoln"

Inscription on the flyleaf of a presentation copy of *Cape Cod Ballads*.
Note the resemblance to the poem in the introduction, and the use of
"Joe Lincoln" in the signature.   *Courtesy Mrs. Mildred C. Chamberlin*

number, and short stories, at least the number of short stories published, begins to increase.

The poem published in *Ainslee's Magazine* for December, 1903 was "A Voice for Santa Claus". Because it treats of an effort that has never been successful, and does not appear in either of Joe's own anthologies, we quote it here.

A VOICE FOR SANTA CLAUS

Read it last week in the paper, ha'f of a page it had;
Read it out loud to mother; my, but it made her mad!
Somethin' some college feller said in a mile-long speech,
That Santy Claus was a humbug that nobody ought to teach;
That tellin' the children stories of how he comes through the snow
To bring 'em their toys and dollies, was wicked and bad and low;
That him and his prancin' reindeer, his pack and his old red sleigh,
Was nothin' but lyin' nonsense that ought to be thrown away.

Nothin' but lyin' nonsense, teachin' a child deceit?
Nothin' but fairy stories? Maybe, but ain't they sweet?
What would you give, you fellers,—gray-headed grandads all,
Workin' from morn till evenin', over this hard old ball, —
What would you give in money, cash that you work for so,
To b'lieve in the fairy stories you b'lieved in long ago?
What would you sell your past for? How much would close the deal
That brought up your mem'ries' treasures of days when them tales was real?

Christmas without a Santy? 'Member the nights before?
'Member how hard you listened, hearin' the old folks snore,
Hearin' the wind a-whistlin' up in the chimney flue,
There in the place where Santy somehow would wiggle through?
'Member the Christmas mornin's? 'Member the stockin's? What?
Wasn't they filled with glories? Nothin' that cost a lot,
But, 'cause old Santy brought 'em, wonderful things, you bet!
'Member just how you loved him? Some of us love him yet.

Christmas without a Santy? Puddin' without the plums!
Think of the million youngsters waitin' the day he comes,
Countin' the hours and minutes, thinkin' they hear his sleigh,
Jest as their daddies heard it, back in another day.
Nothin' but lyin' nonsense, wicked to spread around?
Then I'm a wicked liar long's I'm above the ground.
Long as I've got a rooftree, while there's a chimney flue,
Santy shall come to my house. How is it, folks, with you?

67

Joe Lincoln wrote about Christmas and Santa Claus with boyish enthusiasm as a young writer. Loving to act, he dressed in the traditional costume and played "Santa Claus". He even sketched himself in that role and gave the sketch to his oldest granddaughter, Anne, in whose possession it remains today.

The sketch by Joe Lincoln of himself as Santa Claus, included in a letter to and now in the possession of his granddaughter, Anne.

Chapter 9
The Way of Life is Writing

Lincoln's first novel, *Cap'n Eri*, was written during the evening hours along with his poems and short stories. One wonders how Joe Lincoln could produce such a quantity of writing, especially since he was commuting to New York City to work during the day. Begun in May, 1903, the novel was finished and published in February, 1904. Like all of his future novels, it was a story of the coast. Three Captains — Cap'n Eri Hedge, Cap'n Percy Ryder and Cap'n Jeremiah Burgess, seek a housekeeper to reduce the chaos in their home. The book was dedicated "to the memory of my mother". She, of course, was Emily Crosby Lincoln.

Cap'n Eri became an almost overnight success, and its author decided to give up his banking job and devote his time and energy solely to writing.

No more writing at night after a full day's work at the office; no more commuting between Hackensack and New York City. Now he would put his full time and strength into his writing. He realized that this new way of life was likely to bring prosperity, something he had never known in the first thirty-four years of his life, and was determined to accomplish it.

Joe set up a time schedule which varied little throughout the remainder of his life. He was an early-to-bedder and an early-riser. After breakfast he read the New York Times and then was off to his study — in Hackensack or Villa Nova, at the "Crosstrees" in Chatham, or wherever he happened to be at the time. Here he dreamed and

69

wrote from 9:00 a.m. until 1:00 p.m., which was lunch time. His goal was to write one chapter a week.

Lincoln's granddaughter, Anne, remembers the host of long, sharp pencils in their containers on his desk ready for his use (he could not stand a dull-pointed pencil). There were pads of ruled, legal-size yellow paper on hand, and original drafts were always written on this kind of paper. If one examines his manuscripts, many of which survive, one will see the sharp thin lines of his writing. The legend of "the short, stubby, soft pencil", supposed to have been originated by Joe, continues; for example, in a newspaper article by Barbara Arno, "Typewriter too Simple so Lincoln used a Stub", published in the *Sunday Standard Cape Cod Times* on August 23, 1970. It's a nice legend and somewhat romantic, but only a legend.

The manuscripts were sent out to be typed, for Joe did not use a typewriter, nor did he learn to dictate his material to a stenographer.

In a letter to his son, Freeman, dated February 11, 1925, Joe writes, "My book progresses with fair steadiness. Today I finished Chapter VII. About a chapter a week is my gait, and I shall try hard to keep it up. That will mean the finish about May 15, or perhaps sooner." The book of which he speaks here is *Queer Judson*, which began to appear serially in the *Ladies Home Journal* in July, 1925.

During his adult life Joe Lincoln read books, newspapers, and magazines regularly. When his granddaughter Anne was in high school and college she found that her grandfather had read aloud to her most of the books on the required reading lists. He often said to people who interviewed him that he had no special favorites, he just read all of the good writers, old and new, and was, in a sense, a self-educated man. He was not a scholar but certainly well-read. He used Webster's Unabridged Dictionary continuously and frequently read subjects that interested him in his *Encyclopedia Brittanica*. He was also quite addicted to *Bartlett's Familiar Quotations*, which he used to find ways of phrasing rather than as a source of direct quotation.

Wherever they lived, the Lincolns went for a drive in their automobile in the afternoon. In several interviews, Mr. Lincoln mentions that driving was one of the pleasures that he enjoyed most. Neither he nor Mrs. Lincoln learned to drive a car and so there were chauffeurs to take them out around the country-side. Their chauffeur in Chatham was Clarence Small. The grandchildren refer to the early autos as "the big black Cadillac period". This period ended when a Cadillac burned up. Then came "the horrible green Nash period" at the beginning of World War II.

No matter where he lived or how far away he travelled, Joe Lincoln always returned to Cape Cod. As a youth he went to Brewster and Chatham from Chelsea, Massachusetts, to visit his grandmother and cousin. He went to Brewster and Harwichport with his family from Hackensack, New Jersey. And from Hackensack and Villa Nova, Pennsylvania, after 1916 and until his death in 1943, he always went to his beloved "Crosstrees" in Chatham for the long summers.

Joe travelled to California, spent some parts of winters in Florida, and went to England and the continent more than once, but throughout his life Cape Cod drew him home as no other place did. He left Cape Cod an immature boy with few coins in his pocket, and he returned to the Cape with a name widely known and no financial worries.

Very little has been written about Mrs. Lincoln, leading one to suspect that she may have kept to herself a great deal. Quiet, unassuming, even shy, she left most decisions to Joe. Never disagreeing verbally, or disapproving, one still knew when someone or something was in disfavor.

There were times that Flo was unable to be very active in church affairs in Hackensack because of "delicate health". She read a great deal and belonged to a reading club. However, she travelled with Joe, and of course was with him on their trips to California and Europe and their migrations from their winter homes to their summers on Cape Cod.

One interest that Mr. and Mrs. Lincoln had in common was a love of antiques. Flo was very much involved with Joe in collecting early American furniture, Sandwich Glass, and whale-bone scrimshaw.

"'Do you know what I had made up my mind to do?'"
[Page 11]

"'I can see a great many things, Mr. Pratt,' says she."
[Page 3]

Pictured above are two frontispiece illustrations by artists who worked on Joe Lincoln's books. The one on the left is by Howard Heath for *Mr. Pratt's Patients*, and the one on the right by J. Henry for *Cap'n Dan's Daughter*.

A problem in writing this biography is that we have been unable to locate very much information about the relationship between Joe Lincoln and the many men and women who illustrated his writings. Many of them were "Fellows of the Society of Illustrators" based in New York City One artist whom Joe particularly admired was Harold M. Brett. It was a big event in 1915 when Brett illustrated Joe's short story, "A Guest from Samaria", which was published by *Everybody's Magazine* in May. This was the first of Lincoln's writings to be illustrated by Brett and it was followed in June by the artist doing the illustrations for Joe's new book, *Thankful's Inheritance*. This collaboration was to begin a close friendship that lasted until Joe's death.

When on Cape Cod, Joe and Flo Lincoln came to the Maraspin home in Barnstable once or twice each summer for dinner at midday.

72

Joe always wanted Quahaug Chowder, made by Mrs. Maraspin, for the main dish of the meal.

The young daughter of the Maraspins', Lois, was very fond of Mr. Lincoln because he took her in his lap and laughed with her. In one instance when the Lincolns were there, Lois insisted on playing ball with the boys before dinner. When it was nearly her turn to bat, the first dinner bell sounded. Here was a three-pronged misery: one, she hated chowder, but she wanted to be with Mr. Lincoln at dinner; two, she wanted to be with Mr. Lincoln, but she just had to bat; three, if she stayed to bat, the house-rule was, late, no dinner, period. She stayed to bat, hit the ball a good whack, and horror of horrors, the ball went through the dining-room window, landing in the chowder all over Mr. Lincoln. Lois had no chowder that day with Mr. Lincoln, but she had proved to the boys that a girl could hit a pitched ball, and that was important to her.

Joe and Mrs. Lincoln usually came to the Maraspin home at the time of the annual Barnstable County Fair. Joe and Frank would go to the Fair, but the ladies would stay at home and talk. Joe loved the fairs with their color and rural atmosphere. His description of the activities at fairs in the short story, "A Pig and a Prodigal", and in the novel, *Mr. Pratt,* shows his interest and pleasure in those country festivals .

One time Maraspin told Joe a story about a person who sat on a musical chair at a funeral while the music box played "The Campbells are Coming" to the startled mourners. Mr. Maraspin's daughter remembers that her school teacher had a musical chair in her parlor which played that tune. When Lois and her mother would go for tea at the teacher's house, the little girl would be allowed to sit on the chair and make it play. She often wondered in later life who her father's story was about and at whose funeral the event occured. She remembers sitting on the chair and hearing it play but she is sure she never sat on it at a funeral.

Joe tells the story of the musical chair near the beginning of his novel, *Mary-'Gusta,* where Mary-'Gusta sits on the chair at her step-father's funeral, and it plays with disastrous results for her.

When Lois Maraspin Perry was a little girl, Joe told her that feather weathervanes were one of the very oldest kinds. Lois, having made quill pens out of large gull feathers, as many a Cape Cod child has done, asked Joe, "Do you have a feather weathervane because it is old or because you are a writer?" Joe smiled, she says, but would

73

not answer the youngster's interesting question.

When "Crosstrees" was sold out of the family after Mrs. Lincoln's death, the feather weathervane was reserved and is a treasured possession of the remaining family.

The Lincolns spent the winter of 1904-05 in an apartment in New York City while Joe wrote his second novel, *Partners of the Tide.*

In 1905, Lincoln had an assignment which was of particular interest to him and which gave him a great deal of pleasure. He was asked to write the Foreword for J. Henry Sears' *Brewster Shipmasters,* published by C. W. Swift of Yarmouthport, Massachusetts in 1906. In that book, Sears mentions Joseph Lincoln (Joe's father) and tells the story of Captain Warren Lincoln, which is titled "The Cabin Boy".

The annual migration from Hackensack to Brewster and back in the fall continued, with Joe completing a novel a year plus numerous poems and short stories.

In 1910 the Lincolns built a house at 366 Summit Avenue, in Hackensack, the first home that they owned. This was a welcome milestone.

Joe Lincoln was very active in the Unitarian Congregational Church on Park Street near Central Avenue in Hackensack (the congregation later moved to another location). The building was constructed in late 1901 for the new Unitarian Society, which had held its first Board of Trustees meeting in January, 1900. Mr. Harry B. Harding presided at that meeting, Mr. Irving Banta was Treasurer, and Mr. Sewall Ford was Secretary. We do not know just when the Lincolns joined this church, but by 1904 Joe was a member of the Board of Trustees and serving on the House and Lecture Committees. Florence was a member of the Hospitality, Fellowship, and Social Entertainment Committee.

No one can fully understand the writings of Joseph Crosby Lincoln without a knowledge of his theological orientation. It is expressed in the preamble to the Constitution of the Unitarian Congregational Church of Hackensack, which is as follows:

"We, the members of the Unitarian Society of Hackensack, accept the religion of Jesus, holding in accordance with His teachings that practical religion is summed up in love to God and love to man, and uniting on this basis, we adopt the following Constitution:

Article I. The name of this society
Article II. The Object of this church is to practice and to spread the religion of Jesus.

Article III. Members — Any person in sympathy with the object of the church may become a member by signing the Constitution.

(Other articles have to do with the details of the organization and the operation of the society.)

Without any attempt to evaluate this statement, let it be said that the Constitution differs from the basis of other churches in that they represent the religion "about" Jesus, while this particular one represents the religion "of" Jesus.

Joe was also an active member of the Men's Club of the Unitarian Society of Hackensack. The 50th Anniversary (1947) brochure of the church says of the Men's Club:

"They work actively on such projects as public play-grounds, a new high school, protection at railroad crossings, arbitration of strikes, and school board elections". This list of projects looks like a list of the hopes of many citizens groups of the late 1960's, but Joe and his associates were working at these things fifty years before.

They were successful in one of these projects at least. On March 19, 1912, at the election held at the Hackensack Armory, Joseph Crosby Lincoln was elected to a three year term on the Board of Education of Hackensack. Joe served from April 1, 1912, to March 31, 1915. In an interview with Adam C. Haeselbarth published in *The Book News Monthly* of May 1, 1914, Joe makes these comments on his experience on the Board of Education; "It is most interesting work and it certainly does have the faculty of making one realize how very little the average citizen knows concerning the workings of his town affairs, and the manner in which his children are educated, and the way in which the public schools are really conducted. Each of us, being an average citizen, is much too likely to criticize carelessly, to condemn without investigation, or to take sides one way or the other in public matters without first learning for himself the rights and wrongs of the subject upon which sides are taken".

In the summer of 1913, Joe Lincoln took his family to England to spend several weeks. Freeman was then thirteen years old and his father thought that he would benefit from the experience of living in a foreign country, as well as the pleasure the whole family would receive. Joe was also anxious to see how people in other countries lived and to study them in relation to his writing.

They rented a house in the country in Buckinghamshire, hired a car and chauffeur and went on daily excursions around the area. Joe

75

and Freeman fished in the nearby streams and visited with neighbors on their walks to the general store. Incidentally, the small town general stores served the same purpose as those with which Joe was familiar on Cape Cod — a gathering place for passing the time of day and story telling.

Adam C. Haeselbarth, in the article cited before, subtitled, "An intimate study of the man who made Cape Cod famous in a series of tenderly human stories", quotes Joe as follows:

"My books have all dealt with the New England character, and my readers, I presume, expect that, but in this story I am taking my Cape Codders far away from their home surroundings. I did much the same thing in my novel *Cap'n Warren's Wards*, although in that case I took the captain merely to New York. Last summer Mrs. Lincoln, my thirteen-year-old boy, Freeman, and I, spent two months in rural England. We hired a delightful old house in Buckinghamshire and spent our summer amid the kindly English people — and they were kindly and most hospitable. After this experience I never shall believe in the cold, reserved, distant Englishman who is never friendly until after a year or so of suspicious watchfulness. If there are such people, they did not live in that part of England."

Many years later, Joe and Flo spent some time in France and Switzerland (1926), and in 1928 the Joe Lincolns and Virginia and Freeman vacationed in Europe.

Joe still had thoughts about plays and play acting. With his usual enthusiasm, he organized a dramatic club under the auspices of the church, and on the 19th of April, 1915, the Unitarian Dramatic Club of the Unitarian Congregational Church produced a play entitled "Uncle Tom's Cabin". This "Soul Stirring Tragi-Comedy Drama" was "Disarranged, Revamped, Half-soled, and Otherwise Assaulted Without Special Permission by Sewall Ford and Joseph C. Lincoln", according to the notice on the playbill for the occasion. Joe played the title role, something he loved to do and did in many of the plays produced at the church, many of which he also wrote. Sewall Ford, the author, played the part of the Lawyer. B. B. Wells, the artist, played the part of Phineas Fletcher. Miss Lydia Banta of Sandwich, Massachusetts was a pickaninny in the production, and it is from her that we have much information about Joe Lincoln's plays written and produced in Hackensack.

After an interview with Joe Lincoln in 1924, Arnold Patrick reported in an article in a series called "Getting into Six Figures", published in *The Bookman* of January, 1925, that in his youth Joe had "built himself a toy theatre. You'll find that from Robert Louis Stevenson, backward and forward, this has been a childhood amusement of authors and playwrights. Lincoln built his miniature structure, painted his scenes and characters, wrote his own plays and put them on. In a darkened room he would raise the small curtain and behold his own stories come to life for him. Long after the proper age for toys, he indulged in this pastime.

" 'You know why I gave up my toy theatre?" he questioned. I nodded, laughing. "Well I guess lots of youngsters have given up things like that because they thought other youngsters or their elders wouldn't understand'."

It can be assumed that this toy theatre activity took place while Joe and his mother were living in Chelsea, Massachusetts, when Joe was between the ages of thirteen and sixteen. Joe was in a strange city. His mother was still at work when he came home from school. His theatre was something he could do and apparently did alone. Although Joe never became a great dramatist, his toy theatre is an indication of his native imagination, and his urge to create drama.

It was not until 1910 that Joe Lincoln first ventured into the field of drama. He and William Danforth wrote and copyrighted a dramatization of his novel, *Cy Whittaker's Place.* The text of this drama has all of the directions for costumes, scenes, properties, etc.. common to published plays. The script exists in mimeographed form but is not available for collectors. For some reason the play was never published, and Joe never mentioned it in interviews he gave later in life.

In a brochure printed for the fiftieth anniversary of the Unitarian Congregational Church of Hackensack in 1947, the following tribute to Joseph C. Lincoln appears in the "Church History" section of the brochure:

"During this period (i.e., following the building of the church in 1902), a very active group was the 'Unitarian Dramatic Club' which was sponsored by Joseph C. Lincoln, the author. Mr. Lincoln was one of the loyal supporters of the church during the years he resided in Hackensack. He wrote and directed many of the productions which played to capacity audiences. Familiar names in the casts of characters included Ben Wells, the artist; Sewell Ford, the author; Allan Jacobson; Harry Harding, father of Miss Priscilla

Harding, retired Librarian of the Sandwich, Mass. Public Library; Irving Banta, father of Miss Lydia Banta of Sandwich, Mass.; Rathbone Williams; Emile Strange; Harry Williamson; Harry Doubrava; and William Stark."

Sewell Ford wrote and Joe Lincoln took the title role in a production of "Ole King Cole" in 1916.

Joe Lincoln also wrote a play entitled "Gladys of the Brick Yards or Plinkity Plunk on the Plank Road", which was produced by the Dramatic Club. An actual Plank Road ran from Hackensack to Little Ferry, N. J., and passed by a brick yard on the way.

On the 10th and 11th of April, 1917, the Unitarian Dramatic Club produced "The Mortgage, The Minister, and The Million or Gracious Heaven, What a Night". The play was written by Joe Lincoln, who also acted the lead, Zabriskie von Plankrhode.

The Rev. James A. Fairley, Mrs. Fairley, and their daughter, Frances, were the cast in a Joe Lincoln farce in two acts called, "Suppressed Desires", produced on the 25th anniversary of the Unitarian Congregational Church, January 14, 1922.

Three plays were produced at the church on the 2nd and 3rd of March, 1922, with the titles, "The Rest Cure, a one act farce"; "Dust of the Road, a dramatic allegory"; and "Commodore Peters, a character sketch", in which Joe played the part of Joe Stiles.

Many of the names and dates of plays written and directed by Joe Lincoln during this period have been lost. They were produced for two or three main purposes. The actors enjoyed the work of production and their role in keeping amateur theater alive. Secondly, the performances played to packed houses; those who attended had an evening of hearty laughter in the midst of whatever occupied their lives otherwise, and if the scripts passed into limbo, at least good things had happened through them. The third purpose of the players was to raise money for their church. Raising money for the church helped the Board of Trustees or other governing body to pay the bills to keep the church running, so that more money could be raised to pay more bills that unfortunately kept piling up.

Chapter 10
Summers in Chatham, Mass. 1916-1943

On May 21, 1915, Mary Frances White (Mrs. Frederick M. White) of Manhattan, deeded land on Boulevard Road in Chatham on Cape Cod to Joseph C. Lincoln. This property is described in the deed as follows: "110 feet on Boulevard Road; Easterly 200 feet; Northerly 110 feet; and Westerly 200 feet". (Barnstable County Registry of Deeds, Grantees — Book 340, page 225). It was on this land that Joe had "Crosstrees", his "summer cottage", built in 1916. Joe had come a long way by his writing in sixteen years. When he left Chelsea at the beginning of 1899, he had relatively nothing. Now he had come back to Massachusetts owning a fine home in Hackensack, and proposing to build a sizeable house in Chatham.

It was to be his pride and joy for the rest of his life.

The village of Chatham is situated at "the funny bone" on the elbow of the "right arm of Massachusetts". It is a place of Light-Houses and Life-saving Stations. It has an ancient windmill which ground grain for the residents. It has a marker designating the place where Samuel de Champlain landed and had a bad time with the Natives in 1602. It has suffered from the charge of being the residence of "mooncussers" and was dubbed "Scrabbletown" for this activity. William Nickerson bought most of it from the Monomoyick Indians, and fought with the authorities at Plymouth over his purchase for the rest of his life. It is filled with retired, notable people. There are artists and authors living quietly in its lovely old houses and enjoying all of the fine things of life.

79

The architect for "Crosstrees" was Mr. Cox. Its builder was George Wing Hopkins; his son, Fred I. Hopkins, was the foreman.

The Lincolns lived near the fourth hole of the Chatham Bars Inn nine hole golf course, which made it handy for Joe. Although he was not a "dedicated" golfer, he enjoyed the exercise and the companionship of other golfers. At that time Cap'n Clark was the caddymaster. The caddies got 25 cents plus a 10 cent tip for nine holes; for eighteen holes they received 75 cents plus the tip.

Two young girls, Nina Hopkins, daughter of Fred I. Hopkins, and Constance Eldredge, whose father owned a livery stable, wanted to be caddies but were afraid to compete with the boys. They approached a Mr. Bachellor and his daughter on the third hole and asked him if they could caddy. He took them on and gave them some pointers. When the course was finished he held out his hand with change in it and asked "How much do you charge"? They said they didn't know, so took 15 cents each. After that the girls were accepted as caddies with the boys and Nina caddied numerous times for Joseph C. Lincoln.

This interesting account was told to me by Nina Hopkins Underhill on March 16, 1973, at an interview with her at her home in Needham.

Many people went to Chatham to see "Crosstrees", the home of the man whose yarns they loved. They bought picture post cards of "Crosstrees", and Jack Frost sketched it and included the sketch in his *A Cape Cod Sketch Book*, published in 1939.

William Cary Duncan spent three days at "Crosstrees" with the Lincolns in the summer of 1940. Duncan wrote a fine account of the Lincolns and their life by the sea, with a description of the garden and

"Crosstrees", the Lincoln home in Chatham. From a postcard of the home.

the house, which was published in *Better Homes and Gardens* in the September issue of 1940. Of course he refers to the Lincoln's son as "Truman"— he apparently thought it was something like that when he wrote the article. He writes that Joe's mother's brother was "an old sea-dog" — Joe's mother's only brother was drowned at sea at age 19. It is by such means that many legends have grown up about Joe Lincoln.

Duncan writes, "Certainly the talented and exceptionally attractive mistress of the 'Crosstrees' must be, like her famous husband, a lover of flowers. No woman with her culture and charm could fail to be sensitive to beauty in any form; and she would be infinitely less the congenial and sympathetic wife and mother she is if she didn't enter wholeheartedly into everything contributing to either the comfort or pleasure of her husband and son."

World War I (April 6, 1917 - November 11, 1918) is very obvious in the background of Lincoln's novel, *Shavings,* and a very real part of the story of *The Portygee,* published in 1920. But Joe did more than write stories about this war. He sold Liberty Bonds in New York City department stores during the noon-hour rush periods. In one of his lectures he reminisced, "Once, in company with other writers and a few actors and illustrators, I was taking subscriptions for Liberty Bonds in a New York department store". He was a "Four Minute Man" in the towns and cities of northern New Jersey, speaking about Liberty Bonds to all kinds of service club luncheons and other organizations. At the end of the war the "Four Minute Men" were disbanded. They were praised for their patriotism and aid by President Woodrow Wilson in an acknowledgement of their final report. A letter written by J. C. Auchincloss on the status of the "Four Minute Men" was published in the *New York Times* in September, 1917.

Lincoln's son Freeman wanted to serve in a more active way. He went to Boston and enlisted in the Army, with or without his father's permission, something, we surmise, which upset his father and strained relations for a while. Freeman was in service only a short time before the Armistice was signed and the war ended. He never saw any foreign service.

In 1918, Joe wrote and produced a one act play, *Grandpa,* for the benefit of the Cape Cod Chapter of the American Red Cross. He was anxious to do his bit and to serve his country. He did it in what he felt was the most effective way that a writer can contribute. Joe acted in the title role, and his friend, Hayden Richardson and his son

Freeman, and an unknown young woman played the other parts with him. Hayden Richardson was the proprietor of *The Sign of the Motor Car,* an inn in Dennis, and President of the Cape Cod Chapter of the American Red Cross. Joe and his company produced this play in several places on Cape Cod in the summer of 1918 for the benefit of the Red Cross.

One of the places where it was produced was the Town Hall of the Town of Bourne. Colonel Eugene Clark of Sandwich was the stage manager of this production . Miss Evelyn Perry, Music Teacher in the schools of Bourne and Wareham, played the piano, accompanying Mr. Percy H. Harling, an art student employed during the summer by F. K. Irwin in his General Store at Cataumet. Mr. Harling played the violin during the intermissions. They played to a packed house at $5.00 a seat. Mr. Harling, who retired as a commercial artist at the *Boston Herald Traveller.* remembers the event in these words, "We played to a packed house — it was a great thrill to meet Joseph C. Lincoln whose books I had read — Many of Mr. Irwin's summer customers to whom I had delivered groceries were surprised to hear me playing the violin".

Grandpa was also produced by Joe Lincoln at the Unitarian Congregational Church in Hackensack, May 2, 3, and 5, 1919. Joe played the title role; Freeman, the grandson; and Ben Wells, the artist and a Miss Marion Hodges played the other parts. To the best of our knowledge, the play was never published — it exists solely in a mimeographed form.

The friendships that the Lincolns made in the simple and unpretentious towns of Cape Cod meant a great deal to them. Joe particularly made friends easily and appreciated their worth.

On the 15th of January, 1921, Joe Lincoln wrote "An Appreciation" of Dr. Louis A. Crocker, who had died in Brewster, Mass. on the 8th of January. This piece, written in New York where the Lincolns were spending time during the winter, was published in the *Harwich Independent.* We quote as follows:

"Doctor Crocker was born in Brewster, he spent his boyhood there, he married a Brewster wife — Miss Hannah Knowles, daughter of the late W. W. Knowles — and it was to Brewster that he came, shortly after his marriage, to practice as a physician ....

"For approximately twenty years he lived and practices his profession in his native town. which is also mine. I had known him slightly as a boy, but he was older than I and in childhood a few years is a wide gulf. It was not until 1904 that, returning to Brewster for a summer stay, I again met him, was thrown much into his society, and our intimate and firm friendship began. It was a friendship the value of which is beyond estimate to me ....

"His would be called, I suppose, a simple life. It was never in the limelight, he never strove for public applause or publicity of any kind.......And for my own part, if I were asked to think of the ideal American citizen — one who was faithful always to the highest ideals for which our republic is supposed to stand — I should think of my friend, Louis A. Crocker."

We have been told that when the Lincolns came to Brewster for a summer vacation prior to the building of "Crosstrees", and expecting to stay at the old "Consodine House", they were often farmed out to the home of Dr. Louis A. Crocker. From Joe's remark in the above "appreciation" we can assume that the intimacy arose from the Lincolns being guests in the Crocker home. Royalties from the first novel, *Cap'n Eri,* were providing money for the vacation in Brewster.

In the year following the publication of Sinclair Lewis' *Main Street,* the people at D. Appleton & Co. in New York decided to re-publish all of Joe Lincoln's early books, namely *Cape Cod Ballads and Other Verse, Cap'n Eri, Partners of the Tide, Mr. Pratt, The Old Home House,* and *Our Village,* in two similar volumes in a neat box. In all of these they put their "first edition" number on the last page, making some confusion for present day dealers and collectors.

Thus when the madness of America in the twenties was becoming epidemic, the Appleton people offered an antidote to the smartness of *Main Street.*

Dr. Albert Perry Brigham, Professor of geology at Harvard University, in a book entitled *Cape Cod and the Old Colony,* (G. P. Putnam's Sons, New York 1921), wrote this about Joe Lincoln's people, "This is the fascination of Mr. Lincoln's homely heroes of Cape Cod. Rough they may look, plainly and profanely they may speak, but they are no longer common persons, they impersonate struggle, daring and achievement, they have gone down to the sea in ships, they have done business in great waters, they see far beyond the doors and dooryards of their low, shingled cottages, and you see with them".

In contrast the people in the clever novels that were mirrors of the day could not see the end of *Main Street,* while many of the people in Joe Lincoln's novels had walked the decks of ships that sailed in and out of the harbors around the oceans of the world. In their homes they had miniature museums of foreign cultures that were old before the savage Indians taught the Pilgrims at Plymouth how to plant corn so they could continue to eat.

The collection of Joe Lincoln's books published by the Appleton people did not save the United States from the economic depression which was the inevitable result of the decade's smartness, but who can tell how many of those that survived the depression were encouraged to begin again upon the example of the homely people in Joe's books?

During the years 1923 - 1924, Joe spent his writing time developing two novels on subjects in which he was deeply interested. *Dr. Nye of North Ostable* was about a doctor who returns from a period in jail to fight water pollution in his home town.

In a review of this book published in *World's Work,* the following comment is made: "As homely as it is, it is a relief to turn from this sort of thing (*The High Place,* by James Branch and *Horses and Men,* by Sherwood Anderson) to *Doctor Nye* by Joseph C. Lincoln. Mr. Lincoln is a conscientious worker in a purely American field and has succeeded in introducing an American atmosphere into real stories, which we are not ashamed to have in our homes. This alone entitles him to distinction."

Rugged Water, published in September, 1924, dealt with one of Joe's favorite subjects. It describes the life and work of the men who man the lifesaving stations on Cape Cod.

As a boy living in Brewster, and during vacations when he returned to Cape Cod, Joe Lincoln was acquainted with and visited the lifesaving stations situated "down Cape".

His admiration for the bravery and dedication of the men who manned these stations is expressed in his poem, "The Life-Saver", written in 1898. This poem was included in *Cape Cod in Poetry,* edited by J. F. and F. H. Crowell and published by The Four Seas Company in Boston in 1924. The Reverend Alfred R. Atwood quoted the entire text of "The Life-Saver" in his address on "Cape Cod and Its Life Saving Service", printed in the East Dennis Old Home Week Booklet of 1937.

Chatham lighthouse in 1980

The Life-Saver
(Dedicated to the men in the United States Life-Saving Service)

When the Lord breathes his wrath above the bosom of the waters,
    When the rollers are a-poundin' on the shore,
When the mariner's a-thinkin' of his wife and sons and daughters,
    And the little home he'll, maybe, see no more;
When the bars are white and yeasty and the shoals are all a-frothin',
    When the wild no'theaster's cuttin' like a knife;
Through the seethin' roar and screech he's patrollin' on the beach, —
    The Gov'ment's hired man fer savin' life.

He's strugglin' with the gusts that strike and bruise him like a hammer,
    He's fightin' sand that stings like swarmin' bees,
He's list'nin' through the whirlwind and the thunder and the clamor —
    A-list'nin' fer the signal from the seas;
He's breakin' ribs and muscles launchin' life-boats in the surges,
    He's drippin' wet and chilled in every bone,
He's bringin' men from death back ter flesh and blood and breath,
    And he never stops ter think about his own;

He's a-pullin' at an oar that is freezin' to his fingers,
  He's a-clingin' in the riggin' of a wreck,
He knows destruction's nearer every minute that he lingers,
  But it don't appear ter worry him a speck:
He's draggin' draggled corpses from the clutches of the combers —
  The kind of job a common chap would shirk —
But he takes 'em from the wave and he fits 'em fer the grave,
  And he thinks it's all included in his work.

He is rigger, rower, swimmer, sailor, doctor, undertaker,
  And he's good at every one of 'em the same:
And he risks his life fer others in the quicksand and the breaker,
  And a thousand wives and mothers bless his name.
He's an angel dressed in oilskins, he's a saint in a "sou'wester",
  He's as plucky as they make, or ever can;
He's a hero born and bred, but it hasn't swelled his head,
  And he's jest the U. S. Gov'ment's hired man.

About 1923, the year that Freeman graduated from Harvard College, the Lincolns gave up their house on Summit Avenue, which was becoming increasingly a business area, and moved into a fine old Colonial house on the river at 9 Knapp Place, which they rented from a Mr. Johnson.

Freeman became a reporter on the *Philadelphia Public Ledger,* a job which lasted only a year or two. He gave up newspaper work to become a freelance writer. In 1929 we find Joe and Freeman collaborating on a novel entitled *Blair's Attic.* When they were not together, they discussed plots and progress over the telephone. Joe wrote the parts which referred to Cape Cod; Freeman the off-Cape parts. This arrangement worked successfully, and they would write two more novels together — *The Ownley Inn,* published in July, 1939, and *The New Hope,* published in September, 1941.

In 1925, Joe Lincoln dedicated his play, "The Managers, A Comedy of Cape Cod", "To B. B. Wells, the first 'Timothy Tidditt', and my comrade in this and so many other dramatic adventures. From his friend of twenty years, Joseph C. Lincoln". Joe had acted the part of Hiram Salters, opposite to Wells when they produced the play at the church. This is the one and only play by Joe Lincoln that was ever published. D. Appleton & Co., published it as No. 13 in their pamphlet series of short plays in 1925. The play was subsequently included in a volume of plays edited by Kenyon Nicholson and entitled, *The*

Appleton Book of Short Plays, published in 1937. In 1972 a limited edition of 500 copies was printed by The Baggia Press of East Bridgewater, Mass. for the Elmwood Bookshop.

Following the publication of "The Managers", and after Joe had moved away from Hackensack, he seems to have given up dramatics. We make no critical analysis of Joe's plays, but let it be said that when produced, they played to "capacity audiences", even though the print publishers might not be interested. Notice had been taken in other quarters of Joe Lincoln's novels, however, and several motion pictures were adapted from them.

In a letter to his son, dated January 27, 1925, Joe wrote, "My first check on account of the movie sale of *Rugged Water* came this morning. The Appleton's take ten per cent commission on the sale, so I got $18,000 instead of twenty; But now that isn't so bad, is it."

The motion picture version of *Rugged Water* was copyrighted by Famous Players-Lasky Corp., on August 17, 1925. The screen play was written by James Shelley Hamilton: the Director was Irvin Willat: and the photographer, Alfred Gilks. This silent, black and white, 35 mm., 6 reel (6,015 ft.) film was presented by Adolph Zukor and Jesse L. Lasky, and was distributed by Paramount Moving Pictures. The cast consisted of Wallace Beery as Cap'n Bartlett, with Lois Wilson as Norma Bartlett. Warner Baxter played Calvin Homer, Phyllis Haver was Myra Fuller, and Thomas Delmar played Seleucus Gammon.

In 1915, the Eastern Film Corporation of Providence, Rhode Island, made an average-sized feature film of *Cap'n Eri.* The Eastern Film Corporation was incorporated by Frederick S. Peck of Providence in 1914, and made quite a few motion pictures in the Newport and Providence area in the following years. The film version of Joe Lincoln's first novel was directed by George Lessey. Frank Andrews portrayed Cap'n Eri Hedge, Martha Nelson (Mrs. Martha Knapp Burlingham Freeman) was Elsie Preston, and George Bunny was Ralph Hazeltine. The film was made in the old Park Brewery on Elmwood Avenue in Providence and on the shores of Narragansett Bay at Conimicut.

A feature film was made of *Partners of the Tide* by the Eastern Film Corporation of Providence, Rhode Island in 1916. It was filmed in the Newport, Rhode Island area and at the studios in Providence. Capt. Titcomb and Bradley Nickerson were portrayed by a Mr. O'Neil and a Mr. Swenson. A copy of this film is in the Film Archives of the Rhode Island Historical Society in Providence.

The novel, *Mary-'Gusta,* was made into a motion picture with the title, "Petticoat Pilot". The five-reel film was released by Paramount Pictures on February 20, 1918, and featured Vivian Martin and Theodore Roberts.

The information on the film "Petticoat Pilot" is from a period catalog card file system in the possession of the Library of Congress. The card file system was established by The Community Motion Picture Bureau during World War I in order to be able to pick, choose and censor films which were to be shipped overseas to entertain U.S. troops. The card for "Petticoat Pilot" is over-stamped "Rejected" because it was considered a children's picture.

Irvin V. Willat made a seven reel, black and white film of *Partners of the Tide,* which he copyrighted March 20, 1921. J. P. Lockney was cast as Capt. Titcomb, Jack Perrin as Bradley Nickerson, Daisy Robinson as Augusta Baker, Gordon Mullen as Sam Hammond, and Florence Midgley as Temperance Allen. This film is No. F2.4154 in the *American Film Institute Catalog of Feature Films, 1921-1930.*

Holtre Productions made a seven reel, black and white film with the title "No Trespassing", which they copyrighted June 11, 1922. This film was based on Joe Lincoln's *The Rise of Roscoe Paine.* The film starred Irene Castle as Mabel Colton with Howard Truesdale as her father. Ward Crane was Roscoe Paine and Eleanor Barry was his mother. Blanche Frederici was the housekeeper, Dorinda, and Charles Eldridge was her husband Lute. *The American Feature Film Catalog, 1921-1930,* lists this film as a "Rural melodrama": the scenario was written by Howard Irving Young, and the movie directed by Edwin L. Hollywood.

C. Gardner Sullivan adapted Joe Lincoln's *Dr. Nye of North Ostable* for a six reel, black and white film, with the title, "Idle Tongues" It was copyrighted November 11, 1924 by Thomas H. Ince Corp., and distributed by First National Pictures. Percy Marmount was cast as Dr. Ephraim Nye, with Doris Kenyon as Katherine Minot. Claude Gillingwater was Judge Daniel Webster Copeland, with Lucille Rickson as his daughter, Faith. Vivian Ogden was Althea Bemis, the gossip, and Dan Mason was Henry Ward Beecher Payson, Dr. Nye's housekeeper. *The American Film Institute Catalog, 1921-1930* lists this as a "Drama" involving "Physicians, Judges, Biologists, Public Funds, Embezzlement, Epidemics, Typhoid, Water Pollution, and Gossip" — certainly a full package.

The only one of these films from which Joe Lincoln had any known revenue was *Rugged Water.* Joe seems not to have mentioned any of these films to interviewers. We cannot imagine a modern author ignoring the possible income from the motion picture rights to his book, but with the exception of *Rugged Water,* Joe seems to have ignored all of the others.

In early 1925, rheumatism in Joe Lincoln's shoulder made him wish that he could quit work. His physical condition began to make him wonder whether he had anything more to say. But instead of quitting, he followed "a course of sprouts" set for him by a Dr. Brown in Hackensack. He reports on this to his son, Freeman:

Hackensack, N. J.

Joseph C. Lincoln
Tuesday, January 27 — '25 — 11.20 A. M.

My dear boy:

I have worked steadily at the sixth chapter of my novel and tomorrow, if my schedule of that novel is to be lived up to, I shall finish it. Whether or not I can quite do so this time is a question. If I don't, I shall almost do so, which is fairly good. Meanwhile, having done all that I feel capable of doing this forenoon, I am going to have my weekly chat with you, son. There isn't so very much in the way of news to write. Since you and Virginia left us on Sunday morning the time has gone as it usually does with mother and me. Sunday morning I did not go to church. Saturday night I began the "course of sprouts" which Brown prescribed for me and as "calomel" was the first "sprout" I felt that church attendance might be a risky proceeding. So I remained at home and did some of the writing I did not do on Saturday. When you are here, my boy, I can't drag myself to the desk — minutes with you are too precious to waste on mere work. In the afternoon, however, I did go down to MacKay's "Bible class". He is teaching, or lecturing, on the modern view of the Old Testament and is very interesting. It would be "old stuff" for you, of course, as you had it, with more detail, in your course at Harvard.

To bed early Sunday night and at the novel next morning. Nothing happened Monday except the second "sprout" which was a blood test. I went with Hallett to the Laboratory at the Hackensack Hospital and the fellow there dug a needle — or a broomstick; it felt more like the latter — into my arm and pumped out a gill or two of my blood which he is to analyze and report upon today. It was a peculiar performance, seeing one's life fluid pumped out into the glass-pump, and gave me an odd feeling. I called to my mind the fact that our granddads had that sort of thing done to them whensoever they happened to feel "off their feed". And those old butchers in those days took away a quart at a lick. It is a wonder that they did not kill the entire population — and they did kill many, I suppose. Last night we heard President Coolidge preach "Economy" to the National Budget Association over the radio, and then turned in.

This afternoon the third "sprout" — an X Ray by Haggerty of my teeth. What will come of that the Lord only knows! A double set of false ones, very likely. Well, I must get back into shape and I can't have another attack of rheumatism — so here goes! The pain in my shoulder is no worse; sometimes I think it a little better. Mother's foot seems just the same. The swelling has not yet gone down, but perhaps it won't until the bone has set. She reads a great deal and is just now hard at the surgical dressings. It is snowing hard outside. We are having more snow this winter than for the three winters past. I don't like the stuff and I know well that you don't. "P........." will not come out here for her visit until Thursday, or perhaps, Friday. Her doctor wishes to have her under his observation following the blood transfusion and it would be foolish for her to go back and forth to the city from here. So she will be here when you come over on Saturday and will, I know, be very glad to see you. She is in miserable shape and mother and I are much worried concerning her. My first check on account of the movie sale of "Rugged Water" came this morning. The Appleton's take ten per cent commission on the sale, so I got $18,000 instead of twenty. But now that isn't so bad, is it.

We hated to have you and Virginia leave us. The house seems doubly lonely after you young people have been here to brighten it up. And we shall look forward — as we always do— to your visit on Saturday. I am wondering whether or not you saw your " ...." yesterday — the person who wishes to be "publicized", I mean. It will do not the least harm to see and talk with him — and, very likely — and as you, yourself, said — not the least practical good. But, good or not, I am eagerly awaiting your report. Mother and I discuss plans for our future a great deal. If you do settle down there in Philadelphia, I feel quite certain that we shall come there, too, perhaps, as you suggest, taking an apartment in the city or better — in a pleasant suburb, and living there during the fall and spring, the summers at Chatham, and — it may be after you are married and have a home of your own, travelling a bit in the winter months. Considering my health and that I don't have to live here, it seems almost foolish to stay amid the ice and snow. But, in order to carry out such a program comfortably, I must put by a sufficient principle to give me a fair-sized income. This, as you know, I am trying hard to do. Well, that is all future — so we won't worry about it this particular winter . I hope you are having some interesting assignments this week. And I should certainly punch up ....regarding the salary increase. Of course the actual amount of your earnings is of secondary consideration now, but an increase — even if but a small one would, I know, be an encouragement to you. We are very glad Virginia thinks she could accompany us to Hot Springs, provided that, by and by, I am sent there to continue the "sprouting". She would be company for mother and I hope, too, that she might enjoy it, herself. As soon as the busted foot shows signs of being whole again we shall seriously consider the trip. I hope we may have a letter from you by tomorrow or Thursday, dear. Mother sends ever so much love and to

Virginia, when you write her. Write us, won't you. Keep well and in good spirits. With oceans of love and looking forward to your letter — and then, Saturday — I am, as always

Your own devoted

Dad

In a later letter he writes:

"The weather is fairly good today, but we are having a ghastly winter. The proverbial groundhog did not see his shadow — at least in this vicinity — but I take small stock in 'hog prophecies' ".

Four days before Joe Lincoln's fifty-fifth birthday, W. Dunning Haggerty, D.D.S., 244 State St., Hackensack, N.J. extracted all of his natural teeth — this is the fourth "sprout", what he called his "boiling experience". They stayed until March 19, having taken the baths and played some golf, and after returning to Hackensack, we hear no more about the troublesome rheumatism.

We asked Mr. Rider to make an analysis of a letter Joe wrote to his son in 1925 when Joe was fifty-five years of age. Here is our account of Mr. Rider's report.

Joe's mind has improved, he has picked up a sense of humor, and the speed of his writing has increased considerably. His enthusiasm is accented, and his goals are set far ahead. He takes advantage of his "cloud nine" ideas, and begins to show education and culture — he has a tremendous interest in cultural things. He has remarkable power of concentration, and because of his dignity and pride he has to do his best. He has a keen and inquisitive mind, and reads widely in all that interests him. His fluid way of thinking has improved since boyhood, and he is a dedicated person. But he is more of a loner than ever — he could hole up for a whole day. He is very content and not restless like his father, and is not too much interested in other people — they were incidental to him.

He has very deep emotions and shows a great deal of sensuousness. But his loyalty, pride and high ideals confine his sexual activities to their proper place.

He is very persistent, and good order comes natural to him. He realizes that he has faults, but he has himself under control. He has some irritability and on occasion could be hard to get along with. He would not like to be interrupted, and here is where he shows irritability. He is very down to earth and has very little vanity left — again in contrast to his father. He is secretive, a hard man to understand — no one ever really knows him (in this he is like his mother). He is not a

91

great talker except when he has something to say or is reminded of an anecdote.

He has no great desire to possess money, but he shows a great deal of possessiveness of the people and things close to him. He is very selective and direct in his approach. He is very particular in choosing his friends and limits the number to a very few. People could easily think him to be snobbish.

Freeman Lincoln and Virginia Cross, daughter of Albert L. and Anne Sargent Cross of Weston, Massachusetts, were married in Weston on September 12, 1925. When Joe and Flo were invited to the engagement announcement party, Joe wrote a rather formal letter to Virginia saying they were sorry that they would not be able to attend the party but were happy about the engagement. One suspects that the formality was due to Joe's possessiveness. From letters to his son before the marriage, Joe indicated that he is glad Freeman has a job as a reporter with the *Philadelphia Public Ledger* but that he anxiously awaits Freeman's letters and week-end visits. The fear that marriage might mean that Freeman would have an absorbing interest other than running home every week-end seems to come through the cool letter to Virginia.

This attitude did not last long, however. The Freeman Lincolns were most understanding of Joe's love of family and desire to have them close by. He became very fond of his daughter-in-law and adored his grandchildren, Anne and Josephine.

In a recent letter to us, Mrs. Freeman Lincoln pays this compliment to Joe: "Our oldest daughter, Anne, named him 'Daddy Joe', and from then on all his friends called him that. He had a marvelous calm disposition, — in all the years I knew him I never heard him say a cross word to anyone."

Chapter 11
The Move to Villa Nova, Pennsylvania, 1925-1944

After their marriage, Freeman and Virginia went to live in the Merion Apartments in Merion, Pennsylvania, on the "Main Line", west of Philadelphia. Late in 1925, the year of Freeman and Virginia's marriage, Joe and Flo left Hackensack, New Jersey, and moved into an apartment in the same building in which Freeman and Virginia lived.

Shortly thereafter, Freeman began to build a house but Joe persuaded him to give up that location and project. They subsequently bought adjoining lots on Ashwood Road in Villa Nova, Pennsylvania, and built houses side by side with Joe's sunporch placed so that from it all that went on at the other house could be seen.

They were living here when two grandchildren were born, Anne Sargent Lincoln, on March 10, 1928, and Josephine Crosby Lincoln, on March 15, 1932. Joe took great pride and joy in these granddaughters.

In an article for the magazine, *Country Life in America,* April 1924, entitled, "Ten Houses for Ten Authors" with paintings and sketches by Andrew Avinoff, Thomas L. Masson includes Joe with nine other contemporary authors. The other authors were Edith Wharton, Booth Tarkington, Kathleen Norris, Zane Grey, Scott Fitzgerald, Willa Cather, Joseph Hergesheimer, Christopher Morley and Gene Stratton-Porter. By an analysis of the author's work and life-style, the writer of the article tries to design a house for each which will express what each of them is. About Joe Lincoln he wrote, "And we don't

93

believe he would be happy in anything but the simplest of houses, for the simplicity and friendliness of his Cape Cod stories are largely responsible for this author's great popularity."

The house which he designs on this basis is a comfortable colonial type which, depending on the meaning of simplicity, a relative term, would seem to fit. Certainly Joe Lincoln could afford to build and maintain such a house, but whether he and Mrs. Lincoln alone needed a house of this size is another matter. In any case, it was a long path of persistent work that led from a second floor rear apartment in Chelsea, to the house on Ashwood Road in Villa Nova.

Villa Nova, Pennsylvania, is a residential and university town on the "Lincoln Highway", ten miles west of Philadelphia, Penna. It is one of the so-called "Main Line" towns because the main line of the Pennsylvania Railroad connected it with Philadelphia and the West.

Villa Nova College was founded by the Jesuit order of the Roman Catholic Church in 1842, and is one of the many institutions of higher learning in the area west of Philadelphia.

We know of no contacts that Joe Lincoln had with Villa Nova College. In his writings he shows no prejudice against any religious denomination, but there is almost no reference to the Roman Catholic Church. This is not strange when we learn that the first Roman Catholic Church on Cape Cod was St. Peter's Church at Sandwich, which was founded in 1825 at the time of the beginnings of the Boston and Sandwich Glass Company. Many of the employees of that company came from East Boston and were members of the Roman Catholic Church there. This first Roman Catholic Church building on Cape Cod was dedicated on September 19, 1930.

So if there are no Roman Catholic people in Joe Lincoln's writings, it is because in the period of the History of Cape Cod about which Joe writes, there were no Roman Catholic Churches and few if any people of this religious persuasion. The population explosion on Cape Cod after World War I has changed all that so that now there is a large Roman Catholic element in all of the towns of Cape Cod.

Corpus Christi Catholic Church in Sandwich, which sprang from the original St. Peter's Church mentioned in the text.

Large numbers of Catholics came to Sandwich in 1825 from Cambridge and Boston to work in Deming Jarves' new glass making plant. A wooden chapel was built by them in 1830 on Jarves Street. Outgrowing this, in 1851 they built a large brick church called St. Peter's at Church and Willow Streets. The original chapel was moved and incorporated into the Sandwich Hardware Store.

St. Peter's Church was a handsome structure costing $25,000. It had a high spire surmounted by a ruby glass ball. The light reflected from this could be seen great distances and was a boon to mariners. A northeast gale in 1852 brought down the steeple and in 1898 the famous "Portland" gale caused cracks in the structure so, regretfully, the church was pulled down. Earlier, in 1865, St. Peter's Cemetery, the oldest Roman Catholic one on the Cape, was established.

The modern Corpus Christi Church was built in 1901, with dedication on July 7th of that year. Incorporated in it were bricks, stained-glass windows, and wood carvings from the earlier structure. In 1921, the Drew homestead near the church was purchased for a Rectory and the old Rectory was converted into a Social Hall.

The interior was again redone with natural wood and carvings by Alois Schmid in 1946. An old USO building was acquired later for a Parish Recreation Center. Though the church mothered several parishes, its only mission now is St. Theresa's Church in Sagamore.

Courtesy Pierre and Marion Vuilleumier from *Churches on Cape Cod*

The Lincolns at Crosstrees in the 1930's. Left to right, Mrs. J. Freeman
Lincoln, her daughter Anne Sargent Lincoln. J. Freeman Lincoln, Mrs.
Florence Sargent Lincoln (Joe's wife) and Joseph C. Lincoln the author.

Courtesy Mrs. J. Freeman Lincoln

Chapter 12
Speeches, Clubs, Honors

Joe Lincoln the writer was also a speaker. He told Arnold Patrick how it began when he was with the American Institute of Bankers in New York in 1899.

"Never having made a speech," he went on, "I was sent to Cincinnati to talk on banking and the Association."

Patrick comments "This was his first speech, and he admits that he was filled with confusion. Would he be able to hold his audience, to convince them of what he had to say? He is glad now that such an opportunity came to him, for it gave him confidence and taught him something of how to interest people. Since then he has delivered hundreds of lectures. His anecdotal talk on 'Cape Cod Folks' has delighted men and women all over America. For the most part he now enjoys lecturing, although it is harder work than writing, in his opinion — "takes more out of you!"

On August 1, 1912, before he began to spend his summers at "Crosstrees" in Chatham, he was invited to read some of his poems at the celebration of the Two Hundredth Anniversary of the Incorporation of the Town of Chatham on Cape Cod. He read the poems "Matildy's Beau", "The Parlor", and "The Surf Along the Shores". He prefaced his reading with a few facetious remarks, which were also printed in the official report of the celebration. One wonders what people from Brewster thought when they heard a native of Brewster say, "I was, as I say, born in Brewster. That is not Brewster's fault, of course; so far as I know it is, in other respects, a perfectly respectable community. But until you have tried it you cannot realize the disappointment of being so near to the real thing and missing it by a matter of ten miles."

On February 5, 1917, Lincoln was chosen to make a speech at a dinner given in honor of the Reverend and Mrs. James A. Fairley by his Unitarian friends. It was held at the Warner Restaurant in Hackensack. Joe chose as the title for his talk, "So Long Jim — A Pluck From a Hackensack Harp."

Joe gave the address of welcome in his native village on July 27, 1930, at the Union Tercentenary Service (of Harwich and Brewster) on the school grounds in Brewster, his indiscretion at Chatham eighteen years before notwithstanding.

In his *Cape Cod Yesterdays*, Joe refers to one of his speaking tours as a time "when I was doing some story-telling and public reading throughout New England". He says that he was in at least nine towns, mentioning only Danbury, Connecticut by name.

Off Cape people roared their pleasure at Joe's tales, but Cape Codders made wry faces when they heard of the roar over tales about them.

"I plainly remember a night when he read from his own material to a jam-packed church in Harwichport", wrote Freeman Lincoln in his Introduction to the *Joseph C. Lincoln Reader,* which he edited. He continues, "After two hours, the audience gave him a standing ovation that lasted a full ten minutes." One suspects that that audience may have been made up largely of "summer people".

Twice during the years that his son Freeman was at Harvard, Joe gave lectures there. To the Freshman class in a series on vocations, Joe's subject was, naturally, "On Being an Author". On another occasion, Joe read poems and told Cape Cod tales to the Dramatic Club.

In the late nineteen-twenties Mr. Percival Hall Lombard, President of the Bourne Historical Society of Bourne, Massachusetts, got together a group of notable men from Boston, New York, Washington, D. C., and Cape Cod in a Building Fund Committee. Mr. Lombard and others had excavated the sight of the ancient trading post of the Plymouth Colony at Aptucxet near the village of Bourne, Mass. He proposed to build a replica of the building that had been destroyed by a hurricane and flood in 1635. This was one, and the first, of the three trading posts established by the Pilgrims of Plymouth to help them pay off their debt to the people in London, England, who had financed their adventure. It seemed appropriate that a suitable memorial should

Above, Joseph Freeman Lincoln upon graduation from Harvard.
Below, his two daughters and wife, from left, Anne Sargent Lincoln,
Josephine Crosby Lincoln, and Virginia (Mrs. J. Freeman) Lincoln.

Courtesy Mrs. J. Freeman Lincoln

be erected at Aptucxet, "the cradle of American commerce", for it was here that the Pilgrims, trading with the Indians and the Dutch from New Amsterdam, got the American free enterprise system underway.

When Dr. W. H. Faunce, President of Brown University in Providence, Rhode Island, and a member of the Aptucxet Building Fund Committee died, Mr. Lombard chose Joseph C. Lincoln of Chatham and Villa Nova to take Dr. Faunce's place on the committee. Just what Joe contributed in time or money is not recorded, but his inclusion with the illustrious names on the committee is an indication of his standing among men at this time.

At the Tercentenary Banquet in Barnstable, Massachusetts, in 1939, Joe Lincoln was an honored guest and speaker. The Toastmaster, Chester A. Crocker, in introducing Joe, said, "We call him a citizen of Cape Cod, and we share our pride in a native son who has given the world a clean, wholesome, entertaining picture of Cape Codders". Mr. Crocker also said, "He has written more novels about Cape Cod, and his novels have won greater popular acclaim, than any author the old peninsula has ever produced. Why, we Cape Codders have to read Joe's books to find out how to act, so we won't disappoint summer folks".

We quote some of what Joe said from the *Report of Proceedings of the Tercentenary Anniversary of the Town of Barnstable, Massachusetts,* edited by Donald G. Trayser, as follows:

> "You have heard this afternoon much learning, very great eloquence, scraps of biography and history and now you have got to fiction...... I was thinking, ... of my first visit to Barnstable...... it was when I was a boy and that would put it back a good many years. There are days when with a little help I think I could remember Noah .... I remember that I had my ticket to the Fair or the price of it and my return ticket from Barnstable and also so much budgeted for my dinner....... We all had oyster stew and the reason we had it was because it was only fifteen cents and that left us ten cents, for we had budgeted twenty-five cents for our dinner..........
> To all of you, to the town and its people, our friends and neighbors, my fellow Cape Codders, the old time honored birthday wish, many happy returns of the day, with a strong accent on the happy".

Joe Lincoln was not addicted to club membership. He was for a time a member of the Salmagundi Club in New York, but used it so little he gave it up. He did belong to and enjoy the Dutch Treat Club in New York, which was made up of authors and artists who met once a week for lunch and shop talk.

In Hackensack, he was a member of the Union League Club, but used his membership in the Hackensack Golf Club much more — the course was very near his house and he tried to play a little as often as possible.

In Chatham, he belonged to the Beach Club, mostly for the benefit of his family, and he was a member of the Eastward Ho Golf Club where he played quite frequently and for a time was chairman of the publicity committee.

He joined some clubs in Philadelphia while living in Villa Nova — The Contemporary Club, The Art Club, and The Franklin Inn Club. But again he dropped out because he did not use the clubs enough to make membership worth while.

He must have played golf somewhere in the Villa Nova area, and we know that he played golf in Winter Park, Florida, when he was there in the winter.

One of his golfing friends was Irving Bacheller, the journalist and novelist, and another was Barton W. Currie, editor of *The Ladies Home Journal,* which published many of Joe's writings.

But Joe did not spend all of his time in Winter Park golfing. He was well known and very popular on the Rollins College campus. Students who wrote for the student newspaper, *The Rollins Sandspur,* interviewed him and wrote interestingly of their conversations. They quoted him on his first trip to Winter Park as saying, "If I were to select a winter home for myself I should certainly feel that I were making no mistake in choosing Winter Park. I like it, and I can see no reason why anyone fond of quiet beauty and charming surroundings should not like it." Joe liked it enough to go there winters from 1930 to 1944, when he died there.

Under the leadership of Dr. Hamilton Holt, President of Rollins College from 1926 to 1949, a unique one-of-a-kind magazine was "published" annually. The first issue appeared in February, 1927, when a group of writers and others were asked to prepare articles for the new magazine which they would read live to the assembled "subscribers" at the college. At the suggestion of Dr. Edwin O. Grover, Professor of Books at Rollins, the project was named *The Rollins Animated Magazine.* Joe's first appearance in the list of "Notable Contributors" was in the issue of 1932. He read two of his poems, "The Cooky Jar," and "The

Cuckoo Clock". A reporter for *The Sandspur* made this comment:

Bright and breezy Joseph Lincoln,
   blowing clear the clouds of passion
Sang the joys of chewing cookies,
   mother's cookies, many cookies,
Chewing all the day from morning,
   noon and evening, even snoring.

Once I bought a Cuckoo clock
Every hour the bird would mock
The door would ope, and the bird come out
Flap its wings and begin to shout
   Cuckoo
   Cuckoo.

Now at last the damned thing's dead
I broke the poker on its head,
For all one day I sat in the rain,
To keep myself from going insane
   Cuckoo
   Cuckoo.

Joe's next appearance was in the issue of 1934 along with Dave Sholtz, Governor of Florida, Fannie Hurst, Homer S. Cummings, Attorney General of the United States, Marjorie Kinnan Rawlings, Arthur Guiterman, Daniel C. Roper, Secretary of Commerce of the United States, Roger Babson, and others. Joe's contribution to this issue was his poem "The Woodbox", about which *The Rollins Sandspur* said, "The beloved Joseph Lincoln was the last on the program. He typified his character in reading a lovely little poem entitled "The Woodbox". It was most humorously touching in its own environment and seemed to be thoroughly enjoyed as all of Lincoln's works." The large crowd of approximately 7,000 people was much appreciative of the efforts of the leading creative writers who gave them a living and animated piece of their work."

In the issue of 1935, the year Joe received his honorary degree from Rollins, Joe was on the program with H. V. Kaltenborn, Andre L. de Laboulaye, French Ambassador to the United States, Rex Beach, Cordell Hull, Secretary of State of the United States, Stephen S. Wise, and others. On this occasion Joe was introduced by Dr. Richard Lloyd Jones, Editor of the Tulsa, Oklahoma *Tribune*, with these words: "No periodical of literary prestige would presume to go to press without a poem by Joe Lincoln, and so we conclude this *Animated Magazine* with a Cape Cod Ballad, and Joseph C. Lincoln will deliver it." Joe read his poem "The Parlor".

Joe was scheduled for the issue of 1941, but trouble with his eyes prevented him from appearing — Irving Bacheller took his place along with Maurice and Countess Maeterlinck, Osa Johnson, Robert Osceola, Faith Baldwin and others.

At the Founder's Day Convocation held in Knowles Memorial Chapel at Rollins College, Winter Park, Florida, on February 25, 1935, Dr. Irving Bacheller, a trustee of Rollins College, made the following recommendation to the President of Rollins College, Dr. Hamilton Holt:

"I bring to you an author who has won the approval of many readers for his insight, his humor, his art, and his understanding. He has written of a people who dwell near the sea. Their fathers spent most of their lives in sailing ships, carrying treasure to and from the distant coasts of the world. They lived between two great deeps, the one above and the other beneath them. They had to deal with appalling hostilities — the lightning, the hurricane, the tumbling seas, the baffling of wind and wave and fog and tide. They acquired a patience, a courage, a wisdom, a dauntless un–yielding strength of purpose far above those of most other men. Of these mariners and their descendants this man has written worthily, with playful wit and an imagination equal to the task of seeing and vividly presenting character affected by heredity and changing environment. Moreover, in his work he has shown a respect for the honored traditions and restraints of old New England. I therefore present for the degree of Doctor of Literature, Mr. Joseph C. Lincoln — novelist, poet, philosopher, friend of the vital ideals of America, who has created by his manner of living a character in itself as admirable and delightful as any of which he has written. Mr. President, I have the honor of recommending to you Joseph C. Lincoln for the degree of Doctor of Literature."

The citation was then made by President Holt:

"Joseph C. Lincoln, romancer, humorist, master of the art which is nearest akin to tears, for the warmth you have kindled in the hearts of the American people, for the demonstration you have made in your life that nobility of character ever comes from high endeavor, for the lofty inspiration which you, like another Lincoln, have received from the lowly, Rollins College confers upon you the degree of Doctor of Literature and admits you to all its rights and privileges."

Thus the wise Hamilton Holt, perceiving the quality of the man before him, expressed in succinct phrases Rollins College's reasons for honoring a man who began his education in the Brewster, Cape Cod village school and finished school at the end of the ninth grade in Chelsea, Massachusetts, to become, in 1935, one of the most popular writers in America.

Strange as it may seem, only one newspaper noted this honor when all wrote obituaries of Joe Lincoln in 1944. That one was the *Harwich Independent,* and they didn't know what the degree was or who gave it to Joe Lincoln. Even the report of the *Boston Herald* Testimonial Luncheon given Joe on September 30, 1941, doesn't mention his degree. Today no one knows the why of the omission.

Joe Lincoln touched the lives of hundreds of thousands of people through his books, his lectures, and his personal contacts. This "local color author" seemed to his readers to be one of them, one of them who could spin a yarn and make sense while making them laugh. As Grant Overton said, "his writing is transparent", so that the reader sees the scene, the situation, and the people, people who are like folks one knows and lives with. Sometimes Joe holds up a mirror and one sees himself. Had Joe been a preacher, he would have evoked "Halleluiahs" and "Amens" and sometimes "No! No!" as well.

If you tell Joe's readers that none of his writings has any literary significance, they will likely say, "Is that so? I didn't know", and go right on chuckling with Joe over the way he expressed the wisdom of Solomon Pratt when he said of Miss "Agony" Page, "her one idea in life was to feed ice cream to children that hankered for fish balls and brown bread".

In most public libraries, the copies of Joe's books on the open shelves are battered and worn from long hard use — many libraries are putting their best copies of Joe's books on reserved shelves, some behind locked, glass doors. This is the situation thirty-plus years after Joe's last novel was published in 1943.

Books by Joe Lincoln were read aloud to individuals and family groups in homes across the nation. People who lived in the western part of the country were interested in stories about the lives of people who were like their ancestors.

Janet Gillespie, in *A Joyful Noise,* a biographical book about her father, Robert Russel Wicks, Dean of Princeton University Chapel, gives the following account of one family's reading: The family was at their summer place in Westport, Massachusetts after Labor Day and she comments, "A new season in a familiar place is as exciting as a journey into a foreign country". And continues, "Mum, who had learned to cook by then, made us little suppers that tasted wonderfully good, and then we'd build up the fire and draw our chairs up close around the kerosene lamp while she read Joseph C. Lincoln aloud. Every night was the same, and we eventually got through the complete works of this New England hero".

This family would have had some twenty-five of Joe's books to read in the 1930's. Apparently they didn't have radio or television in every room of the house so that the individual who was forced to be at home of an evening could be obsessed alone with his own choice of program and never know the downright human joy of a family evening together.

William Dana Orcutt, in *From My Library Walls,* tells one of Joe's own stories about the reading of his books as follows:

"A good many years later, Lincoln was asked to recite some of these Cape Cod Ballads at the centennial celebration of the town of Provincetown, Massachusetts. At the end of the program he was approached by two Cape Cod sisters. 'You don't know who we are', one of them said to him, 'but my sister and I thought you would like to hear about our poor, dear father. He was blind and helpless, and we read your books aloud to him until he died'.

" 'I asked her which of my books delivered the coup de grace,' Joe chuckled as he related this to me; 'but she just shuffled away.' "

Joe Lincoln loved to go fishing on the fresh-water ponds of Brewster, Harwich, and Chatham, and he often ate some of the fish he caught. Some of his fishing companions, when he did not go alone, were Harold Brett, the artist and illustrator, Dr. Gorham Bacon, a New York physician who had retired to his native Barnstable, Anthony Elmer Crowell, the bird carver of East Harwich, John Emery, the candlemaker of Chatham, and Charles Owen.

In *Cape Cod Yesterdays,* Joe tells the story of the Smallmouth Black Bass (Micropterus dolomieu) which Elmer Crowell carved for him. The back of the board on which the fish is mounted is inscribed, "My Dear Friend, Joseph C. Lincoln, maker Anthony E. Crowell, Cape Cod, Mass., 1917". Joe said that this was the first fish Elmer Crowell ever carved — it is still in the possession of the family.

Anthony Elmer Crowell was born in East Harwich, December 5, 1851. He raised cranberries, ran blinds for many gunning sportsmen, and then began making decoys for these sportsmen. His decoys were so perfect that the business occupied his full time. As gunning on the Cape declined, he turned to carving shore-birds and song-birds. These carved birds are in museums and many private collections.

Carving of the small mouth black bass done for Joe Lincoln by Anthony Elmer Crowell. *Courtesy Mrs. J. Freeman Lincoln*

Three of the small birds carved and decorated by Anthony Elmer Crowell, which among others were purchased by Joseph C. Lincoln.

Courtesy Mrs. J. Freeman Lincoln

Mr. Crowell wrote a chapter entitled *Cape Cod Memories* for the book, *Duck Shooting Along the Atlantic Tidewater,* edited by Eugene V. Connett. A biographical sketch of Mr. Crowell is contained in Elroy Sherman Thompson's *History of Plymouth, Norfolk, and Barnstable Counties,* published in 1928, and Jack Frost has a sketch of him, "The Man Who Makes Birds", in his *Cape Cod Sketch Book,* published in 1939. The most recent account of Anthony Crowell can be found in an article, "The Greatest Decoy Maker of Them All", by Margaret H. Koehler, published in *Yankee Magazine* of October, 1969.

Cleon Stanley Crowell, son of Anthony Crowell, carried on the work of carving birds with great skill and artistry until his death in 1961.

Dr. Gorham Bacon was an eye, nose and throat specialist in New York City until he retired to his ancestral home in Barnstable. Joe had consulted the specialist and that is where the friendship began.

Among other things, Dr. Bacon was the Senior Warden of St. Mary's Protestant Episcopal Church in Barnstable. During his term of office, which ended in 1940, the need for a new furnace in the church was matched only by the lack of money for that purpose. He discussed the matter with Joe, and the two of them dreamed up the idea of a program that might provide the necessary money for the furnace. The "idea" was this — if they could persuade Martha Attwood, the Metropolitan Opera star, who was the daughter of Captain and Mrs. Simeon Attwood of Wellfleet, to join them, they would put on "An Evening with Martha Attwood and Joe Lincoln". This "idea" was cooked up in the Bacon's dining room, as Mrs. Bacon remembers it. The two men took off for Wellfleet to invite Martha Attwood, who was home on vacation, to join in the scheme. She readily consented. The unusual affair was held in the Barnstable Town Hall, and tickets were $5.00 apiece. The two schemers also induced another summer vacationer, the Right Reverend Frank W. Sterrett, Bishop of the Protestant Episcopal Diocese of Bethlehem, Pennsylvania, to preside as "Master of Ceremonies". The packed house was treated to a program in which the opera star would sing a group of numbers, using her own accompanist, after which Joe would tell some of his endless string of Cape Cod yarns, then Madam Attwood would sing again, etc. Perhaps only on Cape Cod could such a program be put together so successfully, but Joe Lincoln had a facility to make such unusual programs possible. Madam Attwood had made her operatic debut in Siena as Mimi in "La Boheme", and Tullio Serafin had engaged her for the Metropolitan in New York. So here she was, with all of the dignity of the Mettropolitan, teamed with one of the nation's outstanding humorists — an unusual combination. But they raised the money for the furnace and some of "God's frozen people" were a little more comfortable.

In the September, 1937 issue of *The Cape Cod Beacon*, a magazine published in Yarmouthport by Charles W. Swift, is contained an article by Peter Ray, entitled "Meeting the Famous". The Editor, Harold Dunbar of Chatham, said of Peter Ray, "We have seen him, talked with him, received his contribution, yet we know absolutely nothing about his life. . . . . ."He didn't look like an author: one who writes seldom does. He was dressed in the style of a successful business man on a summer vacation: colored shirt with tie to match; light brown coat; white flannels; sport shoes; his socks I didn't notice. His face is round; eyes restless, behind silver-rimmed glasses; hair, light grey. His voice is low, pleasant to hear. He didn't talk much, just signed his name. I asked him if A. L. Burt, the publisher's name which was on the majority of the books, published all of his works. 'No'. he answered quietly, 'Appleton publishes my works. Burt publishes the cheaper editions'. I had had a conversation with Joseph C. Lincoln."

One of the ways which the members of a profession have of honoring their own is to produce a collection of writings in a book and inscribe it to the one to be honored. *Cordially Yours* is such a book. Published by the *Boston Herald* for their book fair in 1939, it is inscribed, "This book was printed especially for Joseph C. Lincoln". It contains, "A Collection of Original Short Stories and Essays by America's Leading Authors". Now since "a prophet is not without honor except in his own country", it is something when a group of leading authors take time to write a piece just to honor another of their kind.

Joe Lincoln was accompanied by his wife, his son and daughter-in-law, and his granddaughter, Anne, when he sat down at the head table in the Copley Plaza Hotel in Boston for a luncheon sponsored by the *Boston Herald* on September 30, 1941. This luncheon was a tribute to "the Literary Dean of Cape Cod" on the occasion of the publication of *The New Hope,* by Joseph and Freeman Lincoln. There were approximately 600 guests present, including the Governor of Massachusetts, Leverett Saltonstall, and the Mayor of Boston, the Hon. Maurice J. Tobin. The Toastmaster, Dr. Claude M. Fuess, Headmaster of Phillips Andover Academy, said of the honored guest, "[he has captured in words] the clean salt air and sand of Cape Cod". There were people present representing William Cardinal O'Connell, Old South Church, the Association of Jewish Philanthropies, the *Boston Herald,* the *Boston Post, Yankee Magazine,* Coward-McCann, Inc. of New York, publisher of *The New Hope,* and many others.

Messages were read from the governors of all the New England states, and Governor Saltonstall of Massachusetts made the main address. In part the Governor said, "As we grow older, we have realized that a Joe Lincoln story has other and perhaps more important qualities; an appreciation is in them of the best and most enduring elements of the New England way of life, and ability to find the good which is in all of us".

A special front-row table was reserved for Joe Lincoln's classmates from the class of 1885 of the Williams Grammar School of Chelsea, twenty out of thirty-three of whom were still living.

The newspaper reports said that Joe's address in reply sparkled with anecdotes of Cape Cod people, that is, his fictional "children". He told the assemblage that when a Cape Cod friend was informed of the Luncheon, he said, "You don't look as if you needed any extra luncheons", the kind of comment one could expect from a Cape Codder.

Alice Dixon Bond, Literary Editor of the *Boston Herald,* read the following prose composition, which includes the names of all of Joe Lincoln's books:

The Lincoln Story by Alice Dixon Bond

"He has gone back to *Cape Cod Yesterdays,* and found *The Ownley Inn* in *Our Village* which is situated near the *Rugged Water* of *Fair Harbor. All Alongshore* you will find *Partners of the Tide, Cap'n Eri, Mr. Pratt, Keziah Coffin, Galusha the Magnificent,* and even *Queer Judson.*

When *Storm Signals* flew, *The Depot Master,* and *The Post-master,* and sometimes *Doctor Nye* would gather at *Cy Whittaker's Place,* and *Mr. Pratt's Patients* would be left to the tender mercies of *Cap'n Warren's Wards.*

The Big Mogul of the town was *The Aristocratic Miss Brewster,* although *Great-Aunt Lavinia* owned *the Old Home House,* and considered everyone *Back Numbers.*

It was a town of political differences, of obstinacies and generosities, of strong loyalties and clannish insularity, *The Rise of Roscoe Paine* was attributed by some to *The Peel Trait* of perseverance, but others thought it due to *Thankful's Inheritance* which was so helpful in *Extricating Obadiah* from the clutches of *A. Hall & Co.,* and the machinations of *The Portygee.*

When *Christmas Days* drew near, and the great *Head Tide* could be seen full and deep *Out of the Fog — Silas Bradford's Boy,* who lived in *Blair's Attic* would walk with *Cap'n Dan's Daughter* along the curving shore, letting their fresh young voices soar above the pounding surf in old *Cape Cod Ballads* or *Rhymes of the Old Cape.* He called her his *Storm Girl,* but when the wind was *Blowing Clear* they would drop in at *The Managers* who were known as *The Woman Haters,* and there with *Shavings* on the floor, and *Kent Knowles: Quahaug* — he got his name because of his trade — and with *Mary-'Gusta* to join them, they would plan their future, full of *The New Hope* which the world needs so much."

(In order to bring the story up to date we have added this epilogue.) The grandchildren of *The Bradshaws of Harniss* will seek their ancestry in *Cape Cod Stories* about *Cape Cod Characters,* and rejoice in the heritage they will find in *The Joseph C. Lincoln Reader.* (This last by Percy F. Rex, your author, in *The Falmouth Enterprise,* February 13, 1970.)

B. O. Fowler, in his review of *Cape Cod Ballads,* aptly called Joe Lincoln "a singer of the common life". This was the first of many epithets used to describe one of the most prolific writers of the Twentieth Century.

Hamlin Garland called Joe Lincoln "Cape Cod's Genial Chronicler", and said of him, "He looks like......... an old skipper, hearty, unassuming and kindly. The task which he has set himself is one which calls for a keen sense of character, democracy of sentiment, and fancy which never — or very seldom — loses its hold on the solid ground of experience. His plots are sometimes negligible, but his characters, even when they seem a bit repetitious, are a joy. His prosperity is well earned.

The blurb on the dust jacket of *The Aristocratic Miss Brewster* calls the author a "humorist, philosopher, storyteller", and certainly Joe is all of these.

Someone dubbed Joe Lincoln a "Cape Cod American", and Ray M. Owens called him "Cape Cod's Champion". An extremist said, "The man who put Cape Cod on the map". His "friend and summer neighbor", William Dana Orcutt, called him the "Interpreter of Cape Cod", which is what Joe Lincoln really is. He was "the master of New England coast fiction" as the *Sea Story Anthology* says of him. One could go on and on citing these epithets, but perhaps the one Joe himself liked best of all was his name in the family, "Daddy Joe".

In 1942 nothing written by Joe Lincoln was published. He was working on a new book, not knowing that when finished, it would be the end of the Cape Cod Saga. William Dana Orcutt tells us that Joe was having trouble with his eyes and was fearful that he would not be able to finish this book. He had never dictated his thoughts to a stenographer, preferring to write everything out in long-hand, and he never used a typewriter.

While he is recovering and finally finishing *The Bradshaws of Harniss,* let us take another look at this man. He stands among that small company of writers who know one corner of the world well.

Gilbert White, the Vicar of Selborne, Hampshire, England, was one of these. His *Natural History of Selborne,* published in 1789, has

111

gone through over one hundred editions, and is a genuine English classic. Richard Kearton, in his edition of White's book says, "These things may be regarded as trivialities, but they inevitably link one to the spirit of the lovable old Hampshire parson and his times".

Henry David Thoreau wrote that he had "travelled a great deal in Concord". His American classic *Walden* deals only with the life about the pond where the naturalist-philosopher spent much of his time. Yet *Walden* has appeared in over one hundred fifty editions in America, England, Scandinavia, South America, India, and Japan.

Thornton Waldo Burgess wrote about the Briar Patch (a small area in Sandwich on Cape Cod), where the Green Meadow and the Laughing Brook were, and later along the Purple Hills. Over eight million of his books have been sold.

Joe Lincoln wrote about one island on this planet, simply, with sympathy, respect and humor. The so-called trivialities recorded in his verses and yarns link us to the "genial chronicler of Cape Cod", as Hamlin Garland called him. William Rose Benet wrote in the *Saturday Review* of March 18, 1944, a few days after Joe's death, "He immortalized human character in a particular 'neck of the woods', and made a vital part of our land his own". And the dust jacket of *The Bradshaws of Harniss* would say, "Seldom has one man contributed so much to the fame of a locale as Joseph C. Lincoln has done for Cape Cod. His Cape Cod novels are known from Maine to California. His fictional characters — such as *Cap'n Eri, Shavings, Great-Aunt Lavinia, Keziah Coffin, Galusha the Magnificent,* and many others — are famous the country over, and are part of the great American tradition. As clean and wholesome as a sea breeze, as interesting and romantic as Cape Cod itself, the books of Joe Lincoln will endure as long as good fiction is read".

Joe Lincoln's books are not treatises on human or de-humanized behavior, but rather they are made up of the stuff of life as people lived it. They tell it "the way it was" in the times in which they lived. Hildegarde Hawthorne, granddaughter of the great American novelist, Nathaniel Hawthorne, in her pamphlet "Joe Lincoln's America", says, "He is saving for us a previous part of America, writing down before it is too late, a past recent enough, but changing fast, a past closely woven into the very fibre of our character and meaning as a nation".

Chapter 13

Death and Memorials, 1944

Musing about "Our Oldest Inhabitant" in his memory sketch, published in *Collier's Weekly,* August 29, 1908, and subsequently included in *Our Village,* Joe wrote, "But the yarns are gone and the old skippers who spun them have gone, too, on the longest voyage of all — the voyage we shall all take, and for which our passages were booked the day we were born.''

Joseph Crosby Lincoln began his 'longest voyage of all' at 7:30 a.m. on March 10, 1944, while at the Virginia Inn, Winter Park, Florida. A rather sudden heart attack ended his life, and his prolific pencil was no more.

His body was cremated and the ashes were buried in the Lincoln lot in Union Cemetery in Chatham, Massachusetts. The ashes of Florence Sargent Lincoln, who died of a heart attack on February 15, 1954 at "Crosstrees" in Chatham, are also buried there. The lot also contains the ashes of Joseph Freeman Lincoln, who died on February 11, 1962. Nearby is the Brett lot, where the ashes of Harold M. Brett, Joe's warm friend and illustrator, who died January 7, 1956, are buried.

According to the *New York Times* of April 14, 1944: "Joseph C. Lincoln, author of Cape Cod stories, left an estate of $200,000., according to his will on file today in Probate Court in Barnstable, Massachusetts." But the real legacy of Joseph Crosby Lincoln are the novels, short stories, essays, poems and letters which immortalize the strengths and frailties of the human spirit.

Joe Lincoln wrote verses and poems, yarns and short stories, sketches and essays, collections of short stories and novels, and many letters. He wrote a different kind of letter, something he called "Poetry Letters", written to his teen-age grandchildren. The two girls have saved these letters and hope someday to publish them. These letters reveal a very affectionate grandfather who sought to keep in communication with his grandchildren. The question of literary quality is quite beside the point — he was not writing poetry for the critics to chew apart, but communicating with young girls whom he loved and whose love he sought and treasured. He loved to read to them, tell them stories, draw sketches and puzzles for them, take them on drives in his auto: being a possessive person, he always wanted them near him.

We quote a few lines from one letter merely to show the style and approach which Joe used:

"It's a beautiful day.

The sky is bright blue, though last evening 'twas gray
And all through the night it was raining — But, say!
this morning the clouds have been all blown away
And flowers and gardens are blooming and gay.
Though, out in the road, there are places quite muddy.
Now your 'Daddy Joe' is up here in his study
(He calls it a study, although it is small
And some might insist 'twas a garret, that's all)
But, anyhow, here he is writing this letter
And you'll say, I know: 'It's high time and he'd better'!"

On the 15th of March, 1944, the younger grandchild received a birthday letter from "Daddy Joe", who had died only five days before. We quote a few lines from this letter as follows:

"And now, my goodness! this girl has grown
To a Thirteenth Birthday all her own
She's 'most a lady, so big, you see,
that pretty soon she'll be holding me
And, maybe, calling me this or that
like 'Pig' or 'Elephant ' — something fat.
Well, I shan't care what I'm called — No sir!
I'll sit and love it, for I love her
And names don't matter, between us two;
At least, I'll never believe they do."

114

Obviously Joe wrote this letter in preparation for the birthday, not knowing that in a few days he would not be around any more.

Joe sent copies of each of his new books to special friends. In 1930 he sent a copy of his *Blowing Clear* to his "friend and summer neighbor" William Dana Orcutt, and inscribed the fly-leaf with the following verse:

> "It's years since first you voy'ged to Rome,
> Dear friend and summer neighbor,
> The questing of the perfect tome
> Your aim, your joy, your labor.
> The wide world's now your hunting range,
> Good books — you never miss one ....
> Ah well! it's time you had a change,
> And so I give you this one."

William Dana Orcutt was a world authority on typography. He was decorated by the Italian government in 1924 for his *The Book In Italy,* because they said he had "interpreted Italy to America in the sister arts of literature and typography" — hence the reference in the fly-leaf verse of *Blowing Clear.* There must have been quite a few of these fly-leaf verses, but this is the only one the author has seen.

Looking at a large portrait of Joe Lincoln after Joe's death, Orcutt wrote that he would personally miss Joe, because for many years they had discussed the books they were writing before publication. This piece, called "Joe Lincoln — Interpreter of Cape Cod", served as Orcutt's obituary on Joe published in the *New York Times,* and was included in his book, *From My Library Walls.* It is followed in that book by a piece entitled, "A Cape Cod Rhapsody Before the Hurricane", in which Orcutt, writing of his own summer place in Chatham, describes the Cape that he and Joe knew and loved before the hurricane — the hordes of people who sweep into Cape Cod like a hurricane and leave their destruction and litter to be swept up by the year round residents.

In head-lines and editorials, newspapers of Cape Cod, Boston, New York, and many other places announced the death of Joe Lincoln, and commented on his life and works. One said, " 'Joe' Lincoln, Author, Dead," another said, "J. C. Lincoln, Noted Author, Dies at 74"; another said, "Joseph C. Lincoln is Dead at 74; Wrote 36 Novels on Cape Cod"; another added, "Joseph Lincoln, Novelist, Dies, Wrote 40 Books with Cape Cod as Scene". The *Cape Cod Standard Times* announced, "Death Claims Joe Lincoln; His Cape Lore is Immortal", and the *Barnstable Patriot* editorialized, "Famous Pen of Joe Lincoln Laid Aside Forever".

William Rose Benet noted in the *Saturday Review of Literature* of March 18, 1944 that, "Four American writers of wide popularity have recently left us: Irvin S. Cobb, Joseph C. Lincoln, Hendrik Willem Van Loon, and Colonel John William Thomason of the Marines. All were read by many thousands if not millions, at least two were widely known abroad, all were writers in whom one prime ingredient was a humorous philosophy of life, different as these were. Cobb had his roots in the Blue Grass, Lincoln was a Cape Codder, Thomason was of the Lone Star State, Van Loon was our own Flying Dutchman direct from Holland."

Harold Brett, in a tribute to Joe Lincoln in the *Barnstable Patriot* of March 16, 1944, wrote, quoting from a recent letter from Joe in Florida, "I walk a little, and 'putt' a little, but mostly I sit in the sun and cuss the Nazis and the Japs. Not an exhilarating kind of exercise: who invented this 'old age business' anyhow — Roosevelt, probably".

If a "prophet is not without honor save in his own country", then what about this from the Selectmen of Chatham: "It was a rare privilege for all of us to know and live in the same community with Joseph C. Lincoln".

The *Barnstable Patriot* of March 16, 1944, published the one poem we know of written on the death of Joe Lincoln. The poem is by Margaret Morse Coffin and bears the title, "Joseph Crosby Lincoln, in Memoriam":

> You did not, so you said,
> Make choice deliberate
> When weaving romance round Cape Cod.
> But her son born and bred,
> Heir of her sea and sod,
> You knew each byway intricate.
>
> Her slender white church steeple,
> Her still pool where trout may leap
> Were yours. In heart and mind
> Held close. Her folk, plain people,
> With humor true yet kind
> You painted for our world to keep.
>
> Joe, while we scan each treasured page,
> We know you gave to us your heritage.

Three hours and forty-five minutes after the death of Joe Lincoln, Irvin Shrewsbury Cobb, American author and humorist, died at the age of sixty-eight, six years younger than Joe. Their deaths occurring so close together on the same day provoked several editorials about them. One editorial said, "Although neither Joseph C. Lincoln nor Irvin S. Cobb will probably be considered a major figure of American literature, the audience of each was larger and more devoted than the followers of the most adroit of our craftsmen".

Joe Lincoln is not a "major figure in American literature", but it is very unfortunate that the canons which determine what is literature and what is not exclude such a writer. Books which purport to be histories of American literature do not even mention his name. Is there no category for such truly American writing as that of Joe Lincoln? Histories of American literature carry the names of authors whose books gather dust in the back corners of used book stores. Should there not be a place in American literature for a writer whose books bring premium prices a hundred years after his birth? But then again, Henry David Thoreau had to buy several hundred copies of his *Walden* from the publisher, and now there are over one hundred fifty editions of that book. Perhaps those who determine the canons of literature are not as neglectful as they are slow to see that the reading public's reaction is just as important as the notions of the so-called purists.

Alice P. Kenny, Assistant Professor of History at Cedar Crest College, Allentown, Pennsylvania, puts it this way, "A long-needed restoration of balance may be initiated by studying a writer of the Progressive era who deliberately, resolutely and consistently presented the good rather than the evil side of his material, and by so doing won the faithful devotion of a large popular audience."

In his tribute to Joe Lincoln, Harold Brett wrote, "I hope that perhaps a beautiful public memorial of some kind may be erected in his honor on the Cape, every inch of which was 'home' to him".

In 1947 the Chatham Historical Society began a drive for funds to build a Joseph C. Lincoln memorial. Barton Currie wrote articles for the *Harwich Independent* and the *Barnstable Patriot* announcing the project. People gave time, money, boards, nails, paint, and all sorts of things to make the Lincoln Memorial Room in the Atwood House on Stage Harbor Road in Chatham possible. Barton W. Currie gave a complete set of first editions of Joe Lincoln books to the memorial. Harold M. Brett gave a portrait in oils done by him in November of 1943. The family gave a large collection of original manuscripts written by Joe Lincoln. Many other people gave interesting mementos of the famous author.

The New Bedford *Sunday Standard Times* of April 26, 1959, announcing "New Edition of Joe Lincoln, Cape's Homer, Published." This was a reference to Freeman Lincoln's memorial to his father, *The Joseph C. Lincoln Reader*, published by Appleton-Century-Crofts, New York. This is a large volume of 562 pages and contains two complete novels, *Partners of the Tide*, and *Galusha the Magnificent;* four short stories from *The Old Home House;* and eight poems from *Rhymes of the Old Cape:* in all a good sampling of the writings of Joe Lincoln, to which Freeman added in the introduction, a very fine tribute to his father.

Being a writer himself, it is interesting to note which of all the writings of Joe Lincoln his son chose to have included in this volume.

Partners of the Tide is representative of Joe's early novels, and *Galusha the Magnificent* shows the middle period of Joe's maturing. The short stories, with the exception of "The Meanness of Rosy", represent Joe Lincoln the short story writer. The selection of poems shows only some aspects of the many kinds of delightful verses Joe wrote — the sea poems chosen are among his best. In any case, this one volume "edition" is a worth-while addition to a Joe Lincoln library, even though it does not comprehend the work of the prolific pencil of the father of the editor. But it stands as a son's memorial to his father and that is valuable.

During the expansion of the facilities of the Cape Cod Hospital in Hyannis in 1950, Mrs. Joseph C. Lincoln gave the money for the building and furnishing of Room 214 in the new Maternity Wing as a memorial to Joseph C. Lincoln. This is a very appropriate choice, because Joe loved children as many older people testify in their remembrance of him.

When David, the first child of Joe Lincoln's granddaughter Josephine, was born in 1957, "Crosby", as she is known in the family, was surprised and pleased to find herself in the Joseph C. Lincoln Room of the Cape Cod Hospital.

The *New York Times* of June 20, 1944, announced under a United Press dateline, South Portland, Maine, June 19, "Two Liberty Ships, named in honor of a New England novelist, and the discoverer of an important navigation principle, were launched today at the yards of the New England Shipbuilding Corporation here.

"One ship was named for Joseph C. Lincoln, author of Cape Cod folk stories, and was sponsored by his widow, Mrs. Florence E. Lincoln of Chatham, Massachusetts. The other vessel, honoring Thomas N.

Summer, who discovered a new celestial navigation principle in 1837, was named by Miss Elinor L. Lewis of South Portland, a nurse at the ship yard".

The keel of M C E Hull No. 3035 was laid down on May 8, 1941 at the yards of the New England Shipbuilding Corporation at South Portland, Maine. Upon this keel the company built a United States Maritime Commission basic design, steel, dry cargo ship of the ECS-S-C1 Type with the following specifications: length 441 feet, 6 inches; beam 57 feet; depth 37 feet, 4 inches; draft 27 feet, 7/8 inches; with a grain capacity of 562,608 cu. ft., and a deadweight of 10,497 tons. There were two decks, with a third deck forward. The single screw propeller was driven by a reciprocating engine built by the General Machine Corporation of Hamilton, Ohio, with Water T — oil boilers, and a speed of ten and one half to eleven knots. In all respects this vessel was a typical Liberty Ship.

Mr. Walter Lloyd, Virginia Inn, Winter Park, Florida, suggested to Secretary of the Navy Frank Knox, that a Liberty Ship be named for the author Joseph C. Lincoln. The official records of the United States Maritime Commission state that the S.S. Joseph C. Lincoln was launched June 24, 1944.

The "christening bottle" with its red, white, and blue ribbons, used by Mrs. Lincoln when she named the M C E Hull No. 3035 the "Joseph C. Lincoln", is lovingly kept in a specially made glass-topped box with a silver plate inscription, by Mrs. J. Freeman Lincoln, daughter-in-law of the Lincolns, who was present at the christening ceremony in South Portland, Maine.

The S.S. Joseph C. Lincoln was delivered to her first owners, the Eastern Gas & Fuel Association (Mystic S.S. Div.), on July 8, 1944, at South Portland, Maine, and sailed under the American flag. The Stockard Steam Ship Corporation of Baltimore, Maryland, bought the ship September 26, 1946. On November 28, 1949, the Waterman Steam Ship Corporation of Mobile, Alabama, took possession of the ship. The Triton Shipping Company of Mobile, Alabama assumed ownership on January 19, 1951, and on February 2, 1951, the ship was delivered to the Traders Steam Ship Corporation at Jersey City, New Jersey.

The Alvarez Compania Maviera, South America, took possession of the S.S. Joseph C. Lincoln on August 27, 1954, re-naming it the "Purplestar", and it sailed under the flag of Liberia. On August 22, 1960, the name of the ship was changed to the "Epos", and sailed under the flag of Greece from Piraeus. The Synthia Shipping Company, South

America, acquired the ship September 11, 1962, and re-named it the "Rea". On June 22, 1965, the Golden Marine Transport, Inc. bought the ship, re-named it the "Pelikan", and sailed it from Morovia under the Liberian flag.

The Hua Eng Copper & Iron Industrial Co., Ltd., a corporation of the Republic of China, bought the Pelikan on November 30, 1966, and it was scrapped at Kaohsiung, Taiwan — the official record states that after all these changes of owners and flags, the old S.S. Joseph C. Lincoln was broken up in December of 1966.

Joe Lincoln, whose ancestors sailed the high seas of the world, was not able to be a mariner himself, but the ship named for him after his death did him honor on the high seas.

Continuum

Since the death of Joseph Crosby Lincoln, Litt. D.

America has dropped atomic bombs on two cities —
    an act of violence unbelievable

America has sent men to walk on the surface of the Moon —
    an accomplishment witnessed by millions

And the books of Joe Lincoln about people
    are still read with pleasure and profit
    by people seeking relief
    from the extremes of violence and greatness

. . . The Author

Death Claims Joe Lincoln; His Cape Lore Is Immortal

"Cross Trees," Mr. Lincoln's home on Pleasant Bay in Chatham

CHATHAM, March 11—Life for "Joe" Lincoln, who used to talk about the neighbors around the dinner table when he was a boy in Brewster and who gained fame by talking about them in his books, has "come to anchor."

The man who was said to have been "stuffed to the ears with Cape Cod" died yesterday at the age of 74 in his hotel suite in Winter Park, Fla., but like the salty characters he wrote about, "Joe" lives on.

An unpretentious writer. and a modest man, who insisted upon signing himself as "Joe Lincoln" rather than Joseph C. or Joseph

Novelist Joseph C. Lincoln in his study

them live, too. Just a ... Lincoln wrote ... intimate, confiding ...

... an enemy plane overseas. The typical Lincoln story bubbled with salty philosophy, homespun honor, sharply - drawn characterizations and youthful romance.

Found Life Interesting

Keep interested, Lincoln would say. To which he would add, "No matter how old you are, life is a grand game so long as you can keep interested." Joe Lincoln saw to it that no one lost interest in the Cape. He turned out 47 books in 42 years, never once using the trusty typewriter of most authors. A bunch of yellow paper and a batch of stubby-soft-lead pencils were good enough for him.

The story of Lincoln starts way back in a day when the town frowned on a young man who didn't go to sea. "Shouldn't wonder if he lacked ambition, they would say. All the same, he didn't go to sea.

was about the Cape, yes, for that was his life. After that there was a book for every year—with a few to spare. His 47 books included 39 novels, three volumes of collected short stories, three books of sketches and two of verse.

Among Joseph C. Lincln's best-known books are "Cap'n Eri," his first novel; "Silas Bradford's Boy," "Keziah Coffin," "Shavings," "Mr. Pratt," "Ownley Inn," "The New

One of many articles that appeared at the death of Joe Lincoln. Published in in a local Cape Cod newspaper. *Courtesy Ralph and Nancy Titcomb*

121

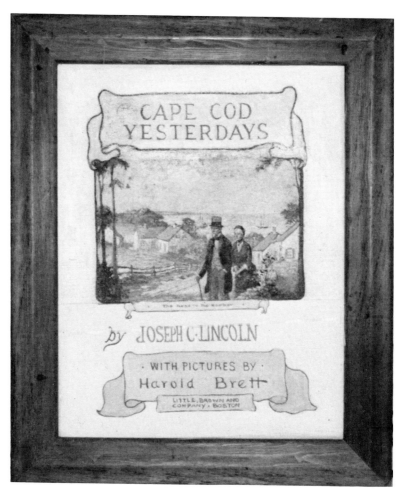

The painting by Harold Brett used for the title-page of *Cape Cod Yesterdays.* Note that the printing is not that used in the book. A letterer was hired to do the final inscriptions. *Courtesy Mrs. Ralph C. Chamberlin.*

Part III

Chapter 14
The Beginning of the Cape Cod Saga

Joe Lincoln's Cape Cod Saga extended over a period of about forty years (1904-1943) . Counting his volumes of poetry and his one published play, Lincoln's books numbered forty-seven, which was an average of a little better than one book a year. Three of these were in collaboration with his son, Freeman.

Alice Dixon Bond, Literary Editor of the *Boston Herald,* in an article in September, 1941, written after an interview with Joe Lincoln, stated "What he has done for New England is priceless, for he has made her traditions, her manners, and her people a part of America's memory, while his characters reach out into universal living."

In another place, she wrote that "the world owes Ripley Hitchcock a vast debt for it was he, back in the early days of Joe's career, who convinced young Lincoln that he could write a novel." James Ripley Wellman Hitchcock (1857-1918) was known as the "discoverer of *David Harum*".

After one of my lectures on Joe Lincoln, a lady came up to me and said, "I was born and raised in Pittsburg, Pennsylvania — we bought, read and kept in our library every one of Joe Lincoln's books as they came out each year". I often wonder how many families in many parts of the country did the same thing.

The Bookman, An Illustrated Magazine of Literature and Life, (published by Dodd, Mead & Co., N. Y., in their Sales of Books Department) listed the ratings of books sold every month. This list was made up from reports of dealers in many cities.

In checking through these lists one can see that book after book from the prolific pencil appeared on the best seller list in many cities from which *The Bookman* received reports. All of Joe Lincoln's books made the best seller lists, some making the No. 1 spot, even though they didn't hold that spot for long.

The first book in the Cape Cod Saga of Joseph Crosby Lincoln is *Cap'n Eri,* which earned him fame and fortune at home and abroad. Published by A. S. Barnes & Co. of New York in February, 1904, it went through six printings before the end of the year, and ten printings by the end of 1906. No doubt the printings were in the thousands as compared with today's hundreds of thousands, but *Cap'n Eri* was a great success for a first novel.

Even though this was his first novel, Lincoln's name was known across the country for his poems and short stories published before 1904. His verses and accompanying sketches in the *League of American Wheelmen Bulletin* went to many states outside New England. In 1897, well over 100,000 copies of the *Bulletin* went to subscribing members of the Bicycle Club each week. His short stories and poems published in *Ainslee's Magazine* and in the publications of the American Press Association were known in many areas of the nation.

Cap'n Eri was reviewed in *Ainslee's Magazine* in May, 1904:

"In his first attempt at novel writing Lincoln shows here the inventiveness and imagination, the restraint of plot development and the coherence on characterization of a seasoned writer of novels; and this is rather remarkable in the case of one whose reputation is chiefly that of a humorist. There is humor in the tale, plenty of it, and it is of the genuine kind which provokes a laugh from the solitary reader — which is perhaps the best test of humor — it is spontaneous and sane, and never diverts the interest from the main thread of the story.

"But the story is something more than mere vehicle for the expression of Mr. Lincoln's humorous sense. It has an ingeniously worked out plot in which all the necessary ingredients of action, drama and character are judiciously combined and molded together into one organic whole with a nice sense of proportion.

Cap'n Eri, of course, occupies the center of the stage throughout, and to anyone familiar with the New England coast he appears as a living, breathing man. A retired sea captain, he lives with two of his cronies, Captain Jerry Burgess and Captain Perez Ryder at Orham. Their decision to reduce their domestic chaos to order by the introduction of a woman's influence into the household gives the first impetus to the forward movement of the story. Martha Snow, Ralph Hazeltine and Elsie Preston are successively brought in, each contributing his or her share of interest, adding vitality and accelerating the movement. The characteristic life of a New England coast village with its quaint people is shown with such skill as to give a harmonious setting to these characters."

In *Cap'n Warren's Wards,* Published in October, 1911, Joe gives this account of the reception of Jim Pearson's first novel; "The reviewers praised it, the reading public — that final court of appeal which makes or unmakes novels — took kindly to it and discussed and recommended it; and , most important of all, perhaps, it sold and continued to sell. There was something in it, its humanity, its simplicity, its clearly marked characters, which made a hit. Pearson no longer needed to seek publishers; they sought him. His short stories were bid for by the magazines and his prices climbed and climbed. He found himself planted suddenly in the middle of the highway of prosperity with a clear road ahead of him, provided he continued to do his best."

This is a very revealing bit — Joe is saying here how it went when *Cap'n Eri* was published and became such a success.

The basis of *Cap'n Eri* appeared in a short story with the title, "The Woman From Nantucket", published in *Ainslee's Magazine* in November of 1900. Into the story of the novel he introduces another short story, "Through Fire and Water", also published in *Ainslee's Magazine,* in April, 1901. This was one of Joe Lincoln's methods of writing a novel, — among others, as we shall see later.

In "Moral 'Suasion and the Able Seaman", published in the *Woman's Home Companion,* March 31, 1904, and included in *Cap'n Eri,* Cap'n Eri Hedge undertakes to make a seaman out of a teen-age street urchin from the city. The boy, named Josiah Bartlett, is a nephew of Cap'n Perez Ryder, who is completely floored by the behavior of the lad. Cap'n Eri takes over, saying that the boy knows too much about some things and too little about others. He 'signs on' the boy as an apprentice seaman and, remembering what his old school teacher called 'moral 'suasion', proceeds to make an able seaman of him. It would appear from the story that Josiah came to respect Cap'n Eri. The older man physically "knocked the sass" out of the youth, taught him everything he knew about sailing, and then proceeded to send him on to the Naval Academy at Annapolis, Maryland.

Joe Lincoln does not let less than good human behavior dominate his writings, no more than he creates an idealistic world. He does, however, raise the question of allegiance to the 'law of God' as set forth in the Bible in opposition to obedience to the laws of man. Many have fallen into great trouble in these days by disobeying the laws of the state, believing that they are obeying a higher law. The story of Cap'n John Baxter in Lincoln's first novel deals with this problem. Cap'n Baxter was "as smart a skipper as ever trod a plank", but on a voyage to Manila he suffers a sunstroke and fever. When he gets home he becomes so involved with religion that he becomes the leading Come-Outer in Orham. He is fanatically opposed to the existence of the pool hall in the village. One day he says to his life-long friend, Cap'n Eri Hedge, "Eri, do you believe that man's laws ought to be allowed to interfere with God's law?" Cap'n Eri made a very perceptive answer: "Guess the fust thing would be to make sure 'twas the Almighty that was callin'." Cap'n Eri was worried about his friend, and the next day comments to Cap'n Ryder: "Perez, seems to me some kinds of religion is like whiskey, mighty bad for a weak head. I wish somebody'd invent a gold cure for Come-Outers." (Come-Outers were a religious group which did not find favor with Unitarians and Congregationalists).

Cap'n Baxter finds in the Bible what he mistakenly believes to be a command from God, providing him with the incentive to take action. What he finds is an historical passage about the Israelites burning the cities of the Midianites (Numbers 31:10): "And they burnt all their cities wherein they dwelt and all their goodly castles with fire", which is in no way any sort of command from God. However, Cap'n Baxter proceeds to set fire to the pool hall, and dies from injuries received while running away from his triumphant act. Here then is a story which shows that destructive violence produces nothing but destruction, as so many have found out by experience in the violent '60's in America, and as Joe was saying in 1904.

In this very first novel we see a pattern which appears again and again. In the midst of a humorous yarn, Joe sets forth shy comments on the social scene, even though the humor hides the message from the unwary.

People come to Cape Cod looking for the towns about which Joe Lincoln writes. They are not actual places, however, but composites, just like his characters.

"In writing of a Cape Cod town or village", Joe once told an interviewer, "although I purposely refrained from describing it as any one

town in particular, I have tried conscientiously to give it the characteristics of the Cape Cod towns I am acquainted with". Anyone who
knows the Cape will recognize familiar features carefully portrayed,
but when he tries to pin point the place he will find that Joe has added
other features, truly Cape Cod but not of that particular place. Someone suggested that a map of Cape Cod should be made locating the
names of the villages in Joe Lincoln's books and short stories. It would
be easy to see that "Ostable" county is the geographical and political
unit known as Barnstable County. The actual places Joe names, like
Cohasset Narrows, Pocasset, Sandwich, and Provincetown would go in
their actual places. But to sort out the rest would be a task impossible.

Some possible combinations that come to mind are:

OSterville + BarnsTABLE makes Ostable
DENnis + BORO makes Denboro
EAStham + BORO makes Eastboro
ORleans + EastHAM makes Orham
TRUro + PaMET makes Trumet
WELLfleet + YarMOUTH makes Wellmouth
EAStham + HarWICH makes Eastwich
Cape Cod BAY + YarmouthPORT makes Bayport

But where they are on the map we do not believe to be important;
in fact, if they could be actually located Joe would have failed his purpose.

The same situation pertains as to people and names. Joe once
said, "I have never knowingly drawn the exact, recognizable portrait
of an individual". Many have played the game of finding out who this
or that character really was, but with no success, because all of Joe's
fictional "children" are actually composites, and so the game is fruit-
less.

This is not to say that Joe's pictures are inaccurate. Listen to
what he says about language, "in attempting to transcribe the habit
of language I have made it a rule never to use an expression or idiom
I have not heard used by a native of the Old Colony".

It is inconceivable that Joe ever wrote anything that would offend
or hurt an actual Cape Codder.

To quote Joe Lincoln further:

"I use Cape Cod and its people not because I consider all the humor
and drama in the world is concentrated on a fifty-mile stretch of sandy
soil. I realize fully that these things may be found in almost any lo-
cality where human beings live....... And I know the people and the

country as I could never know any other people or country ....

"I shall try to make my characters normal people or at least what I consider normal people to be . A specialist in nervous diseases might find interest in a morbid lot of disagreeable individuals, married or unmarried, quarreling through the labyrinths of sex or divorce entanglements. I truly doubt whether the average healthy man or woman cares for such problems, and I write upon the supposition that he or she does not."

In an article in the September, 1941 *Better Homes and Gardens,* William Cary Tuncan quotes Joe as saying:

"You see, I want to write optimistic and healthy books, and to do that I must keep my optimistic and healthy outlook on life, if I can. With most of our poor, stricken earth torn by strife as it is now, and ruled by force and injustice and forgetfulness of all that is real and fine, I can't help feeling God's grand old sea and glorious blue sky offer a more inspiring outlook". And so Joe Lincoln regularly spent long summers at this place by the sea that he loved.

In his own way Joe sets about to deal with the fad of so-called "realism" by writing a story and having Cape Cod people act out his ideas. Miss Mabel Taylor, daughter of Cap'n Jonathan Taylor, comes home to Cape Cod from art school in New York in the short story "The Realist". Her secret fiance, Sergius Hartshorn, author of "The Life Veritable", the current rage, comes for a visit also. Cap'n Jonathan reads the book and sighs but is reluctant to make any further comment. Mabel prods him until he says, "A laugh is just as real as a tear, isn't it?"

When Mabel and Sergius are wrecked on Ogansett Island, the Howlands, who are the only people living on the island, take them in, feed and re-clothe them, and put them up for the night. Deborah Howland's philosophy of life is, "If you can't have cake, then take your hardtack and make the best of it. Growlin' and spite don't do no good."

When Sergius returns to the city he writes "The Grubbers", which the reviewers call "a photograph of real life". Mabel is upset and disillusioned because Sergius has used their benefactors on the island as the people in his book. Cap'n Jonathan's comment is, "I shouldn't call it more than a half way photograph of 'Bial and Debby. But as a real, revealing likeness of the fellow that wrote the yarn — humph! Well, as a photograph of him I don't see how it could be improved on."

And that is the trouble with what is called realism: it reveals too much about the writer or the artist and only one aspect of life. Some lives are lived in smog but not all, some lives are filled with sorrow but not all, some lives are lived in the glorious light of the sun but not all, some lives are lived in love but not all, the real is actually a mixture, birth and death are both part of the real.

Many years later, at the request of the Editor, Joe Lincoln wrote an essay, "The Average Man as I See Him", which was published in the *American Magazine* in January, 1926. "I like my fellow average man on the whole", he wrote, "and I like to have him like me. I am tolerant of his failings because they are my failings......... He is not a Socrates, nor a George Washington, nor a Galahad. Neither is he a Pecksniff, nor even a Babbitt. Such as he is, he is without doubt the backbone of this nation and every other......... He interests me and I like to write stories about him".

In this article, Joe continues his war on the so-called realists. "An author does not have to work harder, nor do better, truer work to make his hero and heroine end in a garbage heap than in a flower garden". "I insist that a reasonable cheerful attitude toward life is not optimism nor sentimental falderal. I maintain that it is the realest of realism, because it is the outlook of the average sane human being". Joe wrote these things in the midst of the "roaring twenties" when many people were de-bunking everything while swilling illegally gotten bootleg hooch and preparing for the smash, which would come in a short time.

Cap'n Foster Bailey Townsend of Harniss was no average man. He was the wealthiest and most powerful man in Ostable County, to whom his old girl friend said, "It must be a dreadful thing to be bowed down to and worshiped so long that you come to believe you are the Lord of Creation". This is the central figure in *The Big Mogul* — ("the big mogul" was what Cape Cod people called the self-declared important summer-people). Cap'n Townsend's wife is dead, and he lives in a big, empty house. This combination brings him to Miss Reliance Clark, milliner and Post Mistress in Harniss, who is raising his deceased brother's daughter. The Cap'n proposes to take Esther Townsend into his house and give her everything, to which Reliance replies, "Most of us have got a conscience somewheres on the premises, even if some of us have kept it packed away up attic so long we've pretty nigh forgot it". Reliance Clark has made her way in the world without the likes of Foster Bailey Townsend, and she lets him know it.

Before one has read very much of this novel, he is aware of the reality of the human problem of a man who could say, "Well, independence is a good thing if you can afford it". But the author makes us aware of something else when "Nabby" Gifford, the Townsend housekeeper, says, "Oh, well! We're here to-day and tomorrow the place thereof don't know us, as it says in the Bible. Ah, hum-a-day!"

METHODS OF MAKING BOOKS

Making books out of previously published short stories was one of the methods used by Joe Lincoln. Published in 1907 by A. S. Barnes & Co., New York, *The Old Home House,* a collection of such items became popular, and was reprinted in 1921 under the title *Cape Cod Stories,* by D. Appleton & Co., New York.

Our Village was published in 1909 by D. Appleton & Co. and consisted of seven short memory sketches which had appeared earlier in magazines

In 1931, *All Alongshore* was published and included eighteen short stories published in various magazines in the nineteen twenties.

Back Numbers, published in 1933, is similar in form, even to keeping the general look of the cover. It contains eighteen stories previously published in magazines.

Another method used to produce a book was to create a character and tell his story, and then introduce previously published short stories into the book — this is the method of *The Depot Master,* published in 1910, and of *The Postmaster,* published in 1912.

The *Saturday Review of Literature* noted, "The story is well put together. The joiner work hardly shows. It doesn't matter that the intellectual content could be reduced to a platitude, or that the moral involved is somewhat shopworn. Mr. Lincoln never leads his readers to expect too much — and he never disappoints them".

Still another method of making a book employed by Joe Lincoln was to expand a previously published short story into a full-blown novel. This was the procedure in *Mr. Pratt,* published in 1906 — Joe used the short story, "The Simplicity of It", published in *Everybody's Magazine* in August, 1905, changed the names of the people, and wrote the novel. Another illustration of this method is *The Woman Haters,* published in 1911 — a short story with the same title appeared in *Ainslee's Magazine* in May 1911, and the novel appeared in June, showing that the author was making hay while the sun was still shining.

Joe used parts of published short stories in some of his other novels — to find them one would need to have a complete knowledge of all of his stories. How many short stories did Joe Lincoln write, from his first in 1896 ("The Studio Puzzle", with Howard Reynolds) to his last in 1937 ("Mr. Expert", published in the *American Magazine*

130

in March)? Our list contains over one hundred and twenty-five, but we believe there are more. There are manuscripts of five unpublished short stories in the collection of the Lincoln Memorial in Chatham. The titles alone may indicate why they were not published.

"Dishonorable Mention", and "The Double Crossers" are not the kind of theme Joe enjoyed using. The other unpublished manuscripts bear the titles, "The Experts", "The Law and the Holloways", and "Luck is a Funny Thing".

Every time a tale is told, it lengthens, just as yarn lengthens when it is spun on a spinning wheel. Joe Lincoln liked to call his short stories "yarns" (the word comes from garno, meaning string). From the many land and sea yarns spun on decks and wharves, in stores and post offices, and in taverns and boarding houses, Joe collected a considerable store. With his knowledge of these "yarns" and his own great imagination, just a word or a phrase or a bit of a story could set him off spinning a new one.

It wasn't necessary for Joe to remember the names of the people in the original story, or the name of the village, or the road, or of the ship, because he always chose names for all of them from his great storehouse of Cape Cod names. Biblical names were given to the children by parents who knew their Bible well. Joe also had great fun naming people with names of the great, and he sometimes gives these names to domestic animals. Martha Phipps in *Galusha the Magnificent* has a cat named "Lucy Larcom" (a New England writer of the nineteenth century). Thankful Barnes' horse is named "George Washington" because his gait is "dignified deliberation".

It was no accident that Mr. Pratt's first name was Solomon: he was wise enough in his own way, and his observations bear notice. e.g., "The prices charged for things [at the church summer lawn fete] would have been highway robbery if it hadn't been a church that was chargin' 'em".

Joe shows his respect for the judiciary in naming judges — Judge Daniel Webster Copeland of Ostable in *Dr. Nye* is the "great man" of the place, and Judge Marcus Aurelius Knowles of *Fair Harbor* is a very much respected person. Then there is Issachar Ulysses Grant McKay in "Issy and The Other", a short story. The printer's devil in *Head Tide* is named Benjamin Harrison "Tippecanoe" Cahoon, with wonderful old Elisha Napoleon Bonaparte Dodson as the editor.

We have come to wonder how many poems Joe Lincoln wrote in the course of his life: we can count the ones in his two books of poems and we can add the ones published in magazines that are not in his books that we have found, but we suspect that there are more that have not been located. Our guess is that there are well over two hundred

Rhymes of the Old Cape, which appeared in 1939, is not a re-issue of the first anthology, *Cape Cod Ballads and Other Verse.* For *Rhymes,* Joe used seventy-one of the seventy-eight poems in the *Ballads* — he did not use what he had called *Other Verse* in the first book. He then added thirty-eight poems, written since the first volume was published. Apparently he did not write any new poems just for the *Rhymes.* Next he arranged the whole lot under subjects, which again he had not done in the first volume. Instead of Edward W. Kemble, Joe's friend Harold M. Brett did the illustrations and painted the picture for the dust jacket of the *Rhymes.* Joe used the original dedication to his wife with an explanation of the why involved. This adds up to a new book rather than a new edition of an old book.

HUMOR

Joe Lincoln was known primarily for his humor, and he used many of the literary devices available to the humorist. Many of them were used naturally, perhaps unconsciously, and most likely without knowing the technical names of the devices.

There are quite a few literary allusions scattered through his writings. Some of these came from his own reading and were drawn out of his remarkable memory, and others he copied out of *Bartlett's Familiar Quotations.* We know that he read most of the works of Charles Dickens. In *Great-Aunt Lavinia,* he says of the widow, Mrs. Octavia Devitt Pail, "There is a person named Bucket in one of Dickens' novels......... This one is a large Pail, more like a tub".

Joe Lincoln had a wide knowledge of the Bible and put many biblical quotations into his writings. He also used scriptural allusions on occasion. For example, in *Cap'n Warren's Wards,* when the good captain gets home from a service in a fancy New York church, he says, "He's a smart preacher, ain't he! And he knew his congregation. You might not guess they was meek perhaps, but they certainly did look as if they'd inherited the earth" — alluding to the Beatitude in Matthew.

As an example of a use of ambiguity — in the chapter on "Our House" in *Our Village,* it is said of Uncle Henry who was drowned at sea, "he made a barrel armchair out of his own head". This reminds us of Jed Winslow's comment in *Shavings,* "There seems to be a sort of family feelin' between my head and a chunk of wood".

An amusing surprise is a much desired device of the humorist. The sign on the store of Solon Snaith in "The Middleman" reads, "I Buy and Sell Everything Old, Except Eggs".

Joe went about Cape Cod collecting anecdotes and biographical incidents which he could use in writing or speaking. He gave his anecdotal talk "Cape Cod Folks" over and over again all over New England and elsewhere. In introducing the yarn of "The Meanness of Rosy", Cap'n Jonadab Wixon says of Julius Ceasar Sparrow, the original spinners of the yarn, "he put in his time swappin' lies for heat from the post office stove".

When Cap'n Sears Kendrick tells his former ship's cook that he is to be the manager of Fair Harbor for Mariners Women in *Fair Harbor*, Judah says, "sounds kind of Brigham Youngy", as he banters with his old friend. There is good-humored candor in Cornelius Rowe's comment about Cap'n Solomon Berry in *The Depot Master* when he says, "He always was stubborn as an ox and cranky as a windlass". And Cap'n Berry says, "I wonder sometimes the Almighty ain't jealous of Cornelius, he knows so much and is so responsible for the runnin' of all creation".

Joe Lincoln is not much given to caricaturing the form and features of his people, but in *Dr. Nye of North Ostable,* he describes Mrs. Vasco Rose as "a huge featherbed of a woman". Throughout his writings Joe Lincoln coins terse descriptions which need no elaboration. Roderick Howard Hilliard in "As He Thinketh" is "a hurricane on legs". Miller Jenkins, the antique dealer in *Blair's Attic,* is "a master of indirection". Galusha Cabot Bangs, archaeologist, in the novel bearing his name, is a "mummy-duster", and the Spiritualists in the same novel are "ghost-seiners".

There are very few comical figures in Joe Lincoln's yarns, with the exception of the gossips mentioned elsewhere. In "A Tarnished Star", Zebina Mayo is a comical figure with his tin badge, but the ending of the yarn does not leave him so. Issachar Ulysses Grant McKay in "Issy and The Other" becomes a comical figure in his vain attempt to stop a marriage.

Another device of the humorist is incongruous contrast. Caleb Ginn, the hermit in "By the Airline", describes Miss Mabel Knight as "looking as fresh, and summery, and sweet as a mudhole full of pond lilies".

Nautical jargon appears frequently in Joe Lincoln's writings, an excellent example of which is the comment by Uncle Gaius Beebe when he hears about James Carey Judson, Jr.'s financial failure in Boston. He is so taken aback that "he just lay to with his canvas slattin', knowing that he ought to pray for strength, but too weak to even cuss".

Jumbled proverbs are not the most effective kind of humor, so Joe Lincoln uses very, very few of this kind. Cap'n Samuel Doane in *Fair Harbor* says, "You can't make a silk ear out of a sow's purse".

There are a few malapropisms in Joe Lincoln's writings besides those of Hannah Parker in *Thankful's Inheritance,* a genuine example of the breed. Amaziah Holt, the light keeper in *Great-Aunt Lavinia,* takes a young man on a tour of the light and reports to his great-aunt, "When we was goin' aloft to the lantern-room, I explained to him that them windin' steps was called a spinal staircase. He said it looked to him like a bad case of curvature". Caleb Ginn, the hermit in "By the Airline", describes Mabel Knight's voice thus: " 'Twas the kind of voice they call a contractor, I believe". And in *Cape Cod Yesterdays,* a person back from Boston says of a new department store, "You don't have to climb stairs in that great place, you ride up and down on the cultivators".

Joe Lincoln has the old Captain use an example of meiosis in *Cap'n Warren's Wards,* "to give the minister a dollar and walk off with two hundred eighty pounds of wife is showin' some business sagacity, hey?" There is a good example of a contradictory epithet in *Blair's Attic,* when it is said of Miss Iantha Beasley Hallett, the Blair housekeeper, that after her days work is done she reads Edgar Allen Poe, "uttering periodic moans of delighted horror". I dare say that while Joe Lincoln never knew these examples of literary devices by their technical names, he certainly knew how to use them effectively.

We wonder whether Joe took a dim view of puns. He does not seem to be a punster, and about as near as he comes is in *Mary-'Gusta,* when Cap'n Shadrack Gould says, "The average sewin' circle meetin' is one part sew, and three parts what so-and-so said".

There is a fine example of sarcastic humor in the short story, "His Native Heath", when Cap'n Benijah Poundberry, Chairman of the Wellmouth Selectmen, says, "Sometimes the way this world's run gives me moral indigestion". Joe Lincoln does not resort to sarcasm very much. Nor does he use much satire. In the case of *Cap'n Dan's Daughter,* the whole novel is a gentle and humorous satire in which he holds up to ridicule "The Guild of the Ladies of Honor" in the same way that *Mr. Pratt* is a satire on "The Natural Life".

A lack of a sense of humor is described in *Cap'n Warren's Wards* in a comment on a member of the firm of Sylvester, Kuhn & Graves in New York: "Graves suffers from the absolute lack of a sense of humor. His path through life is about three feet wide and bordered with rock-ribbed conventionality. If a man has a joke in his system, Graves doesn't understand it and is suspicious". Or as Solomon Pratt said of Mrs. Sophrony Gott, a tea-leaf reader, in *Mr. Pratt's Patients,* "Fur's jokes was concerned she was an ironclad old frigate".

Joe Lincoln likes to use similes. In the short story "Jonesy", Barzilla Wingate says that Peter Theodosius Brown was "as high-toned as a ten-story organ factory". And in his "By The Airline", Caleb Ginn says of something that it was "as convenient as a cow's tail in flytime".

There are many examples of proverbial wisdom, such as this one from Cap'n Ben Hopkins in reference to a summer sailor. in *Blowing Clear.* "Them that knows everythin' can't be told nawthin' ", and of course the Cap'n has to rescue the summer sailor. Solomon Cobb comments on an old proverb in *Thankful's Inheritance* as follows: "Honesty's a good policy, maybe, but it takes hard money to pay bills". In speaking of the relationship between two people in *Dr. Nye of North Ostable,* it is said that, "a drop of ink on a lump of charcoal leaves no noticeable smear".

The illustrations given above will serve to show the breadth of Joe Lincoln's use of humor. There are many other kinds used in his various writings, and to make a collection of his humorous sayings under their literary devices could pleasantly occupy a good deal of time.

In the novel, *Thankful's Inheritance,* Joe Lincoln creates what Thankful Barnes' second cousin, Emily Howes, calls "a genuine Mrs. Malaprop". Her real name is Miss Hannah Parker, who keeps house for her bachelor brother, Kenelm Issachar Parker, next door to Thankful's house. As Cap'n Bangs says, "she keeps watch over him same as the sewin' circle does over the minister's wife".

Mrs. Malaprop, a character in Richard Brinsley Sheridan's (1751-1816) first comedy, *The Rivals* (1775), was said to "deck her dull chat with hard words which she don't understand". Fowler's *Dictionary of Modern English Usage* (1965) comments, "She (Mrs. Malaprop) is now the matron saint of all those who go wordfowling with a blunderbus".

Joe Lincoln's Mrs. Malaprop, speaking of the status of a man who falls down stairs and breaks his collar bone, says, "the doctors are real worried because the fraction ain't ignited yet". When she tells a yarn about a young woman who swallows toothache lotion by mistake,

Hannah says, "it ate right through to her diagram". She brags that her brother has money enough, "to subside on comfo'tably, if he wanted to do it". She mothers her brother but says, "I bear up under my own burdens, but I get compressed in spirit sometimes". When something unusual happens it is "a dissipation of providence". Hannah says that she, her brother, and Cap'n Obed Bangs have all been "what the minister calls 'unattackted' all their lives".

Cap'n Bangs, who probably never heard of Mrs. Malaprop, explains Hannah's speech in this way, "Hannah Parker can get more wrong words in the right places than anybody I ever run across. She must have swallowed a dictionary sometime or 'nother, but it ain't digested well, I'm afraid". Hannah describes her situation by saying, "I'm a second fiddle nowadays and I cal'late that's what I'm foreordinated to be from now on".

Quite a few malapropisms are scattered through Joe Lincoln's writings, but Hannah Parker is the one and only genuine Mrs. Malaprop.

Then, of course, there are "Primmieisms".

A family by the name of "Cash" lives in the "Portygee Nest" on the edge of North Ostable in Joe Lincoln's novel *Doctor Nye of North Ostable*. Miss Martha Phipps' housemaid in *Galusha the Magnificent* is named Primrose Annabel Cash, and comes from Mashpaug Woods. We are not told whether "Primmie", as she is called, is Indian, "Portygee", or something else. All we know is that she is the creator of "Primmieisms", such as "my savin' soul" and "my Lord of Isrul", which sometimes is heard as, "Lord everlastin' of Isrul! My savin' soul!"

A collection of these ejaculations from some of the "characters" in Joe Lincoln's books would provide us with spice for much of our hum drum speech. "Well I want to know" is a common and rather mild one, but what about Judah Cahoon's "Limpin' Moses" or Cap'n Titcomb's "Great scissors to grind", said when you hear something new. Keziah Coffin's "Cat's foot" clearly tells us of her skepticism.

When Cap'n Zebedee Mayo, a retired whaler, hears that the new minister of the Regular Church, the Rev. John Ellery, is engaged to marry Miss Grace Van Horne, an orphan and ward of the leading light of the Come-Outer sect in Trumet, he says, "Well, by the flukes of Jonah's whale!"

The contents of the Holy Bible were very familiar to Joe Lincoln. Like the people of the times about which he writes, he used biblical names for his created "children". He rarely if ever cites chapter and verse when he uses a quotation from the Judeo-Christian scriptures.

When one of his characters misquotes the Bible, one of Joe's most delightful forms of humor is created. Here are some examples:

When Bradley Nickerson, who had been raised by old maids, comes home after his first trip to sea, they tell him of the cash windfall they are now receiving—

"You see", explained Miss Tempy, "it come so sudden that it was almost like Providence had heard us talkin' that night and provided for us same as it did for Jonah in the Bible, when the robins fed him".

" 'Twan't Jonah", breaks in Miss Prissy, " 'twas Elijah, and they wan't robins but ravens".

"Never mind, 'twas birds and they fed somebody. I'm sure poor Jonah needed it, after the time he had, bein' eat up by whales and things". (The reference to ravens is to I Kings 17:6, the story of Elijah by the brook Cherith where the ravens fed him).

Mrs. Azure Crisp, housekeeper for Miss Mary Brewster in *The Aristocratic Miss Brewster,* does a real job of setting forth a new biblical saying. The "Sermon on the Mount" contains the well known saying about not laying up treasures upon earth, as well as the saying, "Love your enemies, bless them that curse you, do good to them that hate you, and pray for them which despitefully use you and persecute you; that you may be children of your father which is in heaven".

On one occasion Azure says to the minister of the New Church, "I did say I'd never demean myself by comin' to this church again, but I'm a Christian, I hope, and we're commanded not to lay up treasures or whatever it is, against them who despitefully use us".

The creator of Azure Crisp had something to say about the saying in the Sermon on the Mount that could turn this world completely around, but is generally considered so impractical that it is forgotten.

In a more serious light, in *The Bradshaws of Harniss,* Joe Lincoln makes use of clams in a perceptive comment by Zenas Bradshaw, "jealousy and spite are considerable like clams. At high water you'd never know there was any around, but when the ebb is under way they commence to spout". Joe knew how clams behaved, and he hated jealousy and spite.

While the Lincolns were in England, they had also visited France and Switzerland — all in the year before the out-break of World War I in Europe. Joe was at work on a new book, and this book is *Kent Knowles: "Quahaug".*

In the light of the above we can see that Joe wrote into his new book much of what he saw and felt when he was abroad. With great ingenuity Joe uses the quahaug as a symbol of what he is talking about. "the trouble with all the folks of all the nations; they stay in their shells and they don't try to know and understand their neighbors." And "That's who makes wars like this dreadful one — quahaugs. We've found out that, down underneath, there's precious little difference. Humans are humans." "I guess that's it: American or German or French or anything — nice folks are nice folks anywhere."

Remember that Joe wrote this when it was just great to hate the savage Germans!

JOE'S CHARACTERS

In *Cape Cod Yesterdays,* Joe Lincoln raises the question, "What is a character?", and answers his own question by writing, "Why, he or she is, apparently, an individual who speaks and acts and, perhaps, thinks in a manner different from that in which you, yourself, speak, and act and think."

In his essay on "The Average Man as I See Him", Joe makes the observation, "when we look for a 'character' we never think of looking in a mirror". He uses this again in *The Ownley Inn* when Seth Ownley says, "The average summer boarder is forever hunting 'characters' and forgetting to look in the looking glass for a specimen".

Joe Lincoln created many "characters" in his prolific writing. Old Higgins in *Our Village,* "died proudly boasting that no person in the county owed more money than he did"; Emma Kelly in *The Old Home House* was "pretty nigh old enough to be a coal-barge, but all rigged up with bunting and frills like a yacht"; Hettie Bradford in *Silas Bradford's Boy,* "I'd rather be a first-class cat than most any man I've run across in my life"; Peter T. Brown in *The Old Home House* "could talk a Come Outer into believing that a Unitarian wasn't booked for Tophet"; Luther Millard Filmore Rodgers in *The Rise of Roscoe Paine* believed that "work is all right....... but to work when you don't have to is wrong"; Mrs. Phoebe Light in *The New Hope,* "Her tongue always has a full breeze astern of it", and her husband Ezra, the peddlar, "he could make a living peddling brimstone in Tophet"; and Mrs Elizabeth "Betsy" Lemon in *The Bradshaws of Harniss,* whose one mistake was to marry Jacob Lemon who is "misjudged merit and injured innocence".

The sayings of these characters are indicative of Joe's understanding of human nature.

Some of Joe Lincoln's favorite characters are ministers, doctors, sea captains, housekeepers (both male and female), hermits and women.

Galusha the Magnificent is dedicated "To James A. Fairley" — the Reverend James A. Fairley who was the minister of the Unitarian Congregational Church in Hackensack, from 1904 to 1913. At that time the church was located on Park Street near Central Avenue, but since then the congregation has moved to another location. This is the same church in which Joe and Flo were active all the twenty-five years they lived in Hackensack.

Joe was one of the speakers at a dinner given to honor the Rev. Mr. and Mrs. Fairley by their Unitarian friends on Monday evening, February 5, 1917, at the Warner Restaurant in Hackensack, on the occasion of the Rev. Mr. Fairley's becoming a Chaplain in the United States Army during World War I.

With the one notable exception of the Rev. John Ellery in the novel *Keziah Coffin,* the ministers in Joe Lincoln's writings are not memorable characters. One suspects that Joe found much to admire in the Rev. Mr. Fairley, and used this when he created the Rev. Mr. Ellery. Most of the ministers in Joe's books appear on the scene to conduct weddings and funerals, but are otherwise completely uninvolved in the everyday life of the communities in which they live.

No doubt many ministers felt that it was wise to be out of their homes on Monday mornings. This notion causes Cap'n Josiah Dimick's comment in the short story "An Inherited Eden": "I'm to home and wish you was, as the woman said, when the minister called on wash-day morning", thereby asking what on earth a minister was doing calling at such an hour on such a day.

Joe named the minister of "the regular church" in *Fair Harbor* the Rev. David Dishup. He must have done this with malice of forethought, for this was the fellow who "preached a sermon on the sin of theatre-going" on the Sunday before the Universalist young people put on a play. Joe did not intend the man's name to be complimentary, since he denounces one of the joys of Joe Lincoln's life.

Joe does show considerable perception about ministers' roles in relation to their communities and congregations. John Ellery in *Keziah Coffin* is very much a case in point. Here, a young man just out of seminary tries to live with people who "know" exactly what a minister should say, do and think; where he should go and not go; where and how he should live; with whom he should or should not associate; what clothes he should wear on all occasions as well as in the pulpit; and most of all, whom he should not marry. In the so-called "Free Churches", there is no freedom for the minister. Every aspect of his life is determined by the freely-expressed notions of the congregation. For the good of his soul he is kept in poverty, and any deviation on his part in word or deed jeopardizes not only his salary but his position.

In the case of John Ellery, his attempt to heal the ungodly and unbelievable attitudes of the 'Regulars' and the 'Come-Outers' is condemned by both sides. His personal sacrifice for a sick, unknown sailor is counted as foolishness. It would seem as though anything Christ-like in a minister's behavior is contrary to what the congregation determines he should be. It seems to me that this is as true at the present time as it was in 1879.

The literary critics, having stereotyped Lincoln as a writer of unimportant funny stories about a small place, and of knowing about the life of a minister, completely missed the point of *Keziah Coffin*. Here are typical reviews: From the *New York Times*, November 29, 1909; "It is a simple tale of simple people in whom, nevertheless, runs the red blood that makes plain every-day life a strong story in the hands of a strong writer." And from the *Outlook*, October 16, 1909; "It is rich in Cape Cod characters and Keziah Coffin's shrewd remarks on human nature are keenly amusing."

"When the Minister Comes to Tea" is a very funny poem — a boy's remembrance of a laughable situation caused by the absurd behavior of a household when the minister is present. Joe might well have called this poem "God's Policeman".

In the days before policemen were prime targets for rock-throwing and bottle-throwing, and we had not heard of "police brutality", the approach of a man in the uniform of "law and order" or of a man in the uniform of ecclesiastical piety quickly changed people into law-abiding citizens or pilgrims on their way to heaven.

Joe's readers were no doubt amused by the minister who came to tea and the behavior of the members of the family, but "God's policeman is not amused when at his approach the cussing and the gossiping stop and the speakers suddenly become solicitous of the minister's health and of the affairs at the church: it is a lonesome role being a policeman for God or the village.

There are many physicians in the writings of Joe Lincoln. As characters, they seem to be about as useful as the ministers and lawyers. Joe's Cape Codders seem to use these professionals only when it is absolutely necessary.

In a letter to his son, Freeman, Joe tells about having a blood test, and goes on to say, "I called to my mind the fact that our granddads had that sort of thing done to them whensoever they happened to feel 'off their feed'. And those old butchers in those days took away a quart at a lick. It is a wonder that they did not kill the entire population – and they did kill many, I suppose."

The short story "Dusenberry's Birthday" appeared first in *Ainslee's Magazine* in December, 1901, and was included in *The Depot Master,* and in *Back Numbers.* The story of the sick little boy is an appealing one, but the tribute to the eminent Boston physician, Dr. John Spencer Morgan, redeems the profession in Joe's writings. The professional skill and devotion of Dr. Ephraim Nye in the novel which bears his name is colored by the physician's successful effort to re-instate himself as a man of honor in the community. The "older physician" who becomes a worshipper of the "great man of the community" does not enhance the profession.

When Elias Thanks, who is the janitor for the office of Cap'n Mark Hanson in the Wellmouth Savings Bank, hears that Mrs. Crockett has another attack of "nerves", he says, "Sylvia Crockett's nerves are Dr. Bingman's old-age pension". It's hard to fool even the foolish on Cape Cod. This bit is in the novel *Out of the Fog.*

In *Partners of the Tide,* Cap'n Ezra Titcomb wants the job of salvaging a wrecked lumber boat, but the representative of the insurance company laughs at the idea that the partners' schooner, the "Lizzie", can do the job. Cap'n Ezra replies, "Yup, with this tub. If you've got a loose tooth a string and a door'll snake it out as quick as the dentist will, and you don't have to pay for silver-plated pinchers and a gilt name-plate".

When Dr. Ephraim Basset Nye comes back to North Ostable after five years in jail to again take up the practice of medicine and try to re-establish himself as a man of honor, he chooses for his housekeeper a man who bears the name of Henry Ward Beecher Payson. Joe does not tell us why the parents give their child the name of the greatest preacher of the mid-nineteenth century, Henry Ward Beecher (1813-1887). Beecher was the brother of Harriet Beecher Stowe, author of *Uncle Tom's Cabin.* He made the pulpit of Plymouth Church (Congregational) in Brooklyn, New York, the greatest pulpit of the day. But Henry Ward Beecher Payson was something else again. Henry had one leg of flesh and one leg of cork. He was a regular in the post-office gang, "the news-distributing center of North Ostable". and on occasion could be enticed to imbibe too much 'good-natured' alcohol.

In telling Dr. Nye about a friend being arrested by Thop Pound-berry, the town constable, he says, "Some folks are so everlastin' like 'em". To which Dr. Nye replies, "Who can tell the mischief that the very virtuous do?" This saying can be found in *The Newcombes,* by William Makepeace Thackery. Did Joe know it from Thackery's book or did he take it from *Familiar Quotations,* by John Bartlett? There are quite a few quotations in this novel, something unusual for Joe, and most of them can be found in Bartlett.

Joe was a rapid and omnivorous reader, and with his excellent memory he could pull things that he had read out of his head as well as quote them from his resource books.

Having been a very well-respected physician and citizen when he lived in North Ostable, the reception Dr. Nye receives upon his return prompts two remarks made to his friend and housekeeper, "Henry, if you wish to live a carefree existence, don't ever become a universally respected citizen" (a saying we do not find in Bartlett), and "A certain-er-thief fell among friends and the friends sprang up and choked him". Here Joe combines words from the parable of the Good Samaritan (Luke 10:30), with words from the parable of The Soils (Matt: 13:7) to make the kind of original saying he knows so well.

Joe showed unusual ability in characterizing Cape Cod House-keepers, both male and female. Keziah Coffin takes a prominent po-sition among these with her pithy sayings and her deep understanding of people.

Typical quotes: "If you can't get cream, you might as well learn to love your saucer of milk." "Sulphur's alright for a spring medicine, maybe, but when June comes I like to remember that God made roses." "Six days shalt thou labor and wear comfortable clothes; on the seventh you must be lazy and dress up." "A minister hasn't got any private affairs; he's a public character."

One of Joe's most entertaining male housekeepers is Lorenzo Weeks, who keeps house for John Huyler "Hi" Heath, a cod-fisherman in Nanticook. In *Blowing Clear,* Heath, whom nobody knows any-thing about, has bought the late Joshua Burgess' shack on the shore. This place comes to be known as "Seven Up", because it is occupied by "Hi" Heath, "Lo" Weeks, and "Jack", the dog: Joe must have known about the card game called Seven Up.

Lorenzo Weeks coined memorable sayings that tell us what manner of man he was. On dish-washing he says, "that's the kind of job that's just mean enough to be righteous". He is a great reader of religious tracts. One evening he is heard to say, "Well, my salvation's sins!" while smoking his pipe and reading a tract against "tobacker". He becomes involved in The Society of the Pure in Heart, which Heath calls "the heart laundry". But you cannot fully appreciate "Lo" Weeks unless you read about him in the context of the whole yarn".

Mr. Isaiah Chase is the male housekeeper and steward for Cap'n Shadrack Gould and Mr. Zoeth Hamilton of South Harniss. While the two partners are managing "Hamilton & Company, Dry Goods, Groceries, Boots, Shoes, and Notions", Isaiah keeps house, cooks, and looks after his employers and their inheritance in the person of Mary Augusta Lathrop, known as "Mary-'Gusta", an orphan. Isaiah, he with the greatest of the Old Testament prophets' names, is no servant , but rather a partner in the total operation. Cap'n Shad, named for one of the Three Children in the Fiery Furnace in the book of Daniel, says to his partner, "You couldn't be wicked if you was apprenticed to the Old Harry for ten years, Zoeth." "You don't know how to be and the devil himself couldn't teach you. Now, don't waste time tellin' me I'm speaking lightly of sacred things," he added. "For one thing, the Old Scratch ain't sacred, as I know of, and for another I want to hear that secret."

"The Old Harry" is a widely used name for the Devil or Satan, and "The Old Scratch" was in common use on Cape Cod for the unmentionable ruler of the lower world. "Scratch" is a variant of a similar-sounding Middle-English word meaning monster. People had some superstitious fear that if they said his name the evil one might just appear.

Zoeth Hamilton was deserted by his wife years ago, and the unusual name he bears appears in the genealogy ot the twelve tribes of Israel (I Chron. 4:20). It is the name which Joe Lincoln used for six of his fictional "children".

When numbers of affluent "summer people" came to Cape Cod and bought or built large establishments called "summer cottages", they brought their servants from the city with them to do the work so that they could enjoy their vacations. These "servants" were just that, and were treated as servants. They were in no way like the housekeepers of the Cape Cod people. These servants worked for wages, not to have a home and be a member of a family. Many of them resented the deprivations of this rural area, and stayed on only because they would soon return to the "real" life of the city. Their influence destroyed the respected status of the housekeeper on Cape Cod so that the likes of Keziah Coffin, Azuba Ginn, Rachel Ellis, "Nabby" Gifford, Azure Crisp, Iantha Beasley Hallett, Phoebe Light, and "Betsy" Lemon were no more. The women of Cape Cod who for one reason or another had to work, found jobs in stores and offices or left the Cape and became time-clock punchers in jobs in the cities.

Joe has a delightful story about a Cape Cod woman who goes to the city and hires out as a housekeeper. He calls it "Deborah and the Wizard". Deborah is Miss Deborah Hannah Larkin of Ostable, who gets "a place" in "the multicolored, Babel-tongued poverty of the East Side" as housekeeper for Prof. Montgomery, Inventor and Proprietor of the "Wizard Appliances and Remedies - Wizard Magnetized Stockings, Gloves, Flannels, and Liniment". This yarn ends when the Professor gets sick and Deborah makes a sign which she hangs in the Professor's office waiting-room: "Prof. Montgomery is laid up in bed with rheumatic fever. The doctor he's called in to cure him says he won't be up for a month". Deborah returns to Ostable with a yarn to repeat the rest of her life but no fortune. The yarn was published in *Munsey's Magazine*, issue of July, 1910, but not included in any of Joe's collections of short stories.

Many of the characters in Joe Lincoln's books are retired sea captains. Joe loved to tell stories about skippers, and although few of them are actively sailing at the time in which Joe writes, he makes them a living and breathing part of part of his yarns. They tend lighthouses, take part in town politics, live alone or together by two's. They are interested in other people and distribute wisdom and advice as a matter of principle. Captains, by virtue of their experiences on the sea, are able to face and conquer any situation. Take the case of two retired captains in the short story "Two Pairs of Shoes" (later incorporated into *The Old Home House*).

Cap'n Jonadab Wixon and Barzilla Wingate attend the wedding of their business partner, Peter Theodosius Brown, in a mansion on the banks of the Hudson River in the winter. The two men from Cape Cod manage, after a fashion, to survive the unfamiliar doings of a New York society wedding. Another guest, who is a practical joker, gets the two Cape Codders on an ice-boat on the river. They are at home on a boat, and much to the chagrin of the joker, the Cape Codders say "When it comes to boats that's a different pair of shoes", the unstated point being made that every man is at home in his own skill.

The men actively engaged with the sea and its perils are those who work at lifesaving stations. Joe had the utmost respect and admiration for them and wrote a novel about them entitled *Rugged Water*. In it, Calvin Homer and Seleuous Gammon live and work at the Setuckit Life Saving Station.

This work was dangerous and hard; to quote Cap'n Myricks: "This life-saving is man's work and boy's pay."

Joe Lincoln had begun his poetical tribute to the "Life Savers" with the line:

"When the Lord breathes his wrath above the bosom of the waters".

In the great poem of creation at the beginning of the Bible it is written "And the earth was without form, and void; and darkness was upon the face of the deep. And the Spirit of God moved upon the face of the waters." (Genesis 1:2)

When David sings his song of deliverance he sings "And the channels of the sea appeared; the foundations of the world were laid bare at the rebuking of the Lord, at the blast of the breath of His nostrils." (II Samuel 22: 16)

The words, concept, and atmosphere of the first line of the "Life Savers" are in the Old Testament notion of the relationship of God to the sea.

The primitive mind reacts to sea as it reacts to a God — with love, respect, fear and dread. People, like those in Joe Lincoln's books who live near the coast, learn to love the natural beauty of the sea and to respect the power seen from the shore. But the people who go down to the sea for their livelihood, as many of Lincoln's people did, learn to fear the suddenness of the anger of the sea and to dread it in a storm. A thousand and more seamen have lost their lives on the shoals around Cape Cod shores.

Other characters which show Joe's interest in people include business men and football players.

The story of Balaam's talking ass in the book of Numbers is one of the most interesting animal stories in the Bible. But Joe Lincoln's Mr. Balaam Griggs has no friendly ass to warn him of the danger of his ways. Balaam Griggs is a moral and pious man who, like many church members, "seldom permitted piety and morality to interfere with his business". Balaam was into Real Estate, Insurance, Money Loaned on Mortgage, and Genuine Antiques Bought and Sold, in all of which there was opportunity to turn a dollar one way or the other. Balaam's step-daughter keeps house for him as a penniless orphan who has never been told by Balaam that she will inherit $25,000 when she is twenty-one years of age — Balaam holds the money in trust.

Cap'n Noah Newcomb comes along and rescues his erstwhile ship's cook from Balaam's machinations, saying to Obadiah, "Balaam's meaner than a vinegar pie, and he'd cheat his deef aunt out of her ear trumpet".

Mr. Horatio Pulcifer, in the short story, "An Honest Man's Business" and in *Galusha the Magnificent,* is another of Joe's business men whose morality has nothing to do with making a dollar. "Raish" is an agent for the Rising-Sun Ready-Tailored Outfitting Company, and the Diamond City Watch & Jewelry Distributors, and handles Real Estate, Insurance, and Money Loaned. When his deceptions in the restoration of Miss Ethel Hedge's inherited property are discovered, he makes the ironical comment, "It's got so nowadays that an honest man can't hardly make a decent livin' ".

A third example of this type in Joe's writings is Mr. Nathan Scudder, about whom Solomon Pratt comments, "It takes a strong man and a cold chisel to separate "Nate" Scudder from a cent". In the novel, *Mr. Pratt,* when the two young men from New York hire "Nate" Scudder to do things for them, Solomon Pratt warns, "Lambs foolin' with Nate Scudder was likely to lose not only wool, but hoofs, hide, and tallow".

These three are well-drawn characters, and represent what happens when "Yankee shrewdness" gets into the hands of men driven to make dollars, regardless of the consequences. It is to be noted that this kind of man is generally humorless, in spite of the humorous things Joe writes about them.

In a short story entitled "The Moral Tone", the Hon. Atkinson Holway returns to his native village, "bald-headed and bay-windowed, sufferin' from pomp and prosperity". He sets about improving the village by first improving the church. Of this improvement someone comments that he has given "stained-glass windows and velvet cushions to the meetin' house, so's the congregation could sleep comfortable in a subdued light".

The billiard room in the village, run by Jotham W. Gale, is thought of as not being a good influence on youth and as lowering the moral tone of the community. The Hon. Mr. Holway sets about getting rid of this blight. In the end, Jotham W. Gale, who still operates the pool room, says, " 'The trouble with you reformers', he adds solemn, 'is that, when it comes to political doin's, you ain't practical' ". Joe here briefly joins the great muck-raker of the early twentieth century, Lincoln Steffins, in an observation of great truth no matter how painful.

Joe Lincoln never played football in his life. How many football games he attended when his son was at Harvard College we do not know, but in a short story and in two novels, Harvard football heroes play a prominent part.

The short story was entitled "Willie", and first appeared in *Ainslee's,* in April, 1909, and subsequently in *The Depot Master.* Willie, a waiter at the Old Home House, is actually Bung Bearse, a native of Cape Cod, and a Harvard football hero. About the only thing Joe tells us about football here is Willie's amazing forward pass, which plays a part in solving the mystery of a robbery.

The football heroes in both *Mary-'Gusta* and *Blowing Clear* are young men with very complex backgrounds who, by becoming football heroes at Harvard, are offered jobs in New York City to which they are not fitted in any way. Joe's descriptions of the games in which these boys starred would lead us to believe that the author was reporting from a detailed newspaper account, in the case of Edgar Smith in *Mary-'Gusta,* and from his own observations at an actual game in the case of Ralph Raymond Condon in *Blowing Clear.* In any case, the inclusion of these three among his characters illustrates the broad scope of Joe's interest in people.

WOMEN

The women in the writings of Joe Lincoln lived at a time when great changes were taking place in the status of women in the nation. There were wives, mothers, sisters, and sisters-in-law who spent their time caring for their houses and their families, and in activities connected with their churches. There were spinsters, old maids, and widows, and occasionally some of these married somewhat late in life, but there were practically no divorcees. Joe writes about several orphan girls who find homes with relatives or friends, and also about some of the spoiled girl-children of the rich: some of these girls stay at home and a few go off-Cape to school.

Among the women in Joe's novels there are managers of boarding houses, and one manages a poor farm. There are store-keepers, postmistresses, and one is a telegrapher. There are newspaper columnists and poets, an editor, an artist, and a singer, along with seamstresses, milliners, clerks, and secretaries, but no factory or sweat-shop slaves. There are school teachers, nurses, and even one minister of a church. The women of the summer people are usually rich and important in appearance and manner.

Some of Joe's women are soft and gullible, pushed around by their men, but others are independent, able, and strong-willed, pushing around weak husbands or brothers. A few are local "gossip columns", a few are nosy "people-watchers", and some are "a whole sewing circle in themselves". Some are gregarious club-women, others are naturally retiring, and some are humorists, while others have no sense of humor at all.

Throughout his writings Joe Lincoln shows more respect for women than male chauvinism. He did not write especially for women, in spite of the charge that he wrote mostly for women's magazines. He wrote for the prominent magazines of the day and was of course read widely by men as well as women.

In general, Joe's women characters show strength, wisdom, and understanding. The novel *Great Aunt Lavinia* ran serially in *Good Housekeeping* from July through December, 1936, and was published in book form in October of the same year. The announcement of this novel was made in June and described it as being "about a gallant old lady who keeps a weather eye on the state of her young niece's eager heart".

Lavinia Hall Badger of Wapatomac shows her business acumen by investing money from inherited mining stock, which she feels is questionable, into Government Bonds, Class A securities, and savings banks.

As in the case of many of his women characters, Joe Lincoln not only endows Lavinia with good business sense, but blends it with a dash of "woman's intuition". Lavinia explains, "From the minute I got those Accidental certificates I was suspicious of 'em. Anything that Judah Badger had anything to do with I couldn't believe in. I would have liked to, but I just couldn't. I hung on for a spell, even against my better judgment, but then, when the stock got to sellin' at those ridiculous big prices, I began to peddle it out — or have Philander's [her lawyer] brokers peddle it for me — four or five hundred shares at a time. Poor Philander fought with me about every sale. He was certain sure I was makin' an awful mistake, wreckin' my chance of bein' worth a million and all that. But the way I looked at it, a hundred-odd thousand on earth was a whole lot more dependable than any amount of millions up in the sky."

And to Ethel's admission of misjudging a person merely by his looks, her aunt replies "Needn't blame yourself for that. You aren't very old yet. It takes years and hard knocks to make most of us realize that it isn't the shell of the nut that counts, it's the meat".

There is not much worth in writing about people who conform, who think and "act like folks", but when a Mary Brewster of the Brewsters of Wapatomac takes a job in the local National Bank, a story of an individual is born, one of Joe Lincoln's stories about the new women who do everything.

The story of the packing of the missionary barrel in *The Aristocratic Miss Brewster* would be one of the most humorous of all of Joe Lincoln's yarns except for the tragedy of its implications. Some Cape Codders didn't like Joe Lincoln's books because they thought he made money out of making fun of Cape Codders. In this yarn he is holding up to ridicule one of the church's most precious sins. Lured by the yarns of returned missionaries who bragged about their self-sacrifice in giving up steaks, cigars, and comfort, to bring the message of how wonderful it was in Christian America to the poor unfortunates in foreign lands, women formed missionary societies to help. One of the ways of helping was to "pack missionary barrels" — moth-eaten, woolen clothing that was supposed to help the naked heathen of the tropics to want to live like an American Christian.

An example will illustrate the point: The President of an insurance company in a New England city brings in a box "for the missionary barrel". When the church social worker opens the box, there are three white vests for men's formal evening wear. "What shall I do with these?" she inquired of the rector. With a dead-pan face, the rector solemnly answered, "The witch doctors in Africa will love them".

Cap'n Cummings knows from experience, in his days of sailing there, that many people in the south sea islands are actually naked children who doted on bright-colored "throw-aways" brought them from America, and he also knows that these things do not change their primitive religious beliefs or practices. It is almost impossible now to imagine the feelings of a really dedicated Christian missionary who needed books, medicines, and hand tools when he opened the newly arrived "missionary barrel". The contents of the "barrel" covered the bodies of the naked Hawaiians, whose descendents now watch the grandchildren of their benefactors walk about naked on Hawaiian beaches. Has religion changed, or did clothes have nothing to do with religion in the first place?

Another way in which Joe portrays women's strength is when a daughter takes over family responsibilities.

When the mother of a large family of children dies, the father may be so overwhelmed by his situation that he retreats into ill health because he is unable to cope with it. It is then that one of the daughters, with a know-how beyond her years, takes over and keeps the house and raises the children, all with the burden of a semi-invalid father who is more of a handicap than a help. This situation is neither rare nor common, but serves as the background of the short story by Joe Lincoln called "Idella and the White Plague". Idella realizes that her father can't work because he is unwell, and that he is unwell because he doesn't work. He is suffering, he says, from one disease after another, and if someone would just understand he would be comforted.

This story appears in *Mr. Pratt,* and Idella's name has been changed to "Eureka". She brings her father to the house on "Ozone Island", where she is the housekeeper. She convinces him that he has consumption, applies the "out-door, fresh-air" treatment, and her father makes a miraculous recovery.

The father, Washington Sparrow, names his oldest child Eureka Florina, and later ones Lycurgus, Editha, Ulysses, Napoleon, Dewey, and Marguerite. Eureka explains by saying, "Pa says there's nothing like hitching a grand name to a young one; gives 'em something to live up to. His own name's Washington, but he ain't broke his back livin' up to it, far's I can see."

Eureka Florina Sparrow appears again in *Mr. Pratt's Patients,* and achieves goals that were only dreams for most girls with her background. Eureka is the type of fictional person common in Dickens, Horatio Alger, and others whose successes are compounded from hard work, native ability, and a touch of luck or destiny that conspires to smile upon some but never shows up for others. This type does not dominate Joe's writings, nor does he hold any of them up as examples for all youth.

Fair Harbor for Mariners' Women is a home for widows of sea-going men. Judah Cahoon, the handyman, often entertains these lonely women by singing sea chanteys for them. Where might Joe Lincoln have learned the sea chanteys he has Judah Cahoon singing in *Fair Harbor*? We searched a source book of sea chanteys and found several of Judah's. We were not surprised to find different words — every sailor sings his chanteys as he remembers them and uses his own words as he pleases. Can't you just see the individual residents of Fair Harbor for Mariners' Women listening to Judah sing the old familiar songs and then complaining about "that uncouth noise from next door" when they were in a group?

Judah Cahoon thinks of Fair Harbor as "a genteel hen-house", and when he hears that his old captain, Sears Kendrick, will become its manager he says, "sounds kinda Brigham Youngy". Judah describes his present employer as a fellow who speaks "as if the last half of every word was comin' on the next boat". His horse is named, "Foam Flake", and is a "barrel of oats" who provokes Judah into "Limpin', creepin' prophets" on many occasions. Such a man's chantey singing would be hearty and full of fun, even if shocking to Miss Tryphosa Taylor's Shakespeare Reading Society, which met at Fair Harbor to help up-hold the cultural level of the inmates, and was treated to Judah's dis-tracting rendering of "Whisky is the Life of Man".

Mrs. Aurora Chase, widow of Ichabod Chase who had been second mate on a guano bark, is dubbed "Northern Lights" by Judah Cahoon. She continuously follows Miss Elvira Snowden about with, "What's he sayin' Elvira?" and would have been tickled into being able to hear if Elvira had been able to make her do so.

There follows a list of Judah Cahoon's repertoire of sea chanteys.

> Dreadnaught Chanty
> Yankee Ship on the Congo River
> The Blue Juniata
> Dinah
> Sally Brown
> Whisky is the Life of Man
> Oh, my Name is Captain Kidd
> Fire Down Below
> Reuben Ranzo
> The Coast of Barbaree
> Old Storm Along
> Light in the Darkness Sailor (actually a hymn)

LOVE, ROMANCE, AND HERMITS

There are courting couples in all of Joe Lincoln's novels. Some are young people, others are older. Some are bachelors and some are old maids, and still others are widows or widowers. There are instances of older men and younger girls marrying, with gossips running wild with joy over the fact. Some couples are separated for years, even marrying someone else, but in time they find each other again and marry.

The couples in Joe's novels do not practice bundling, which was a cozy way of courting in a house that had no central heating system. Henry Reed Stiles, in his study of the practice, defined it as, "a man and a woman lying on the same bed with their clothes on". If the couple were courting, they were usually tucked in by the girl's mother. Stiles, in his book, *Bundling, Its Origin, Progress and Decline in America,* published in 1934, says, "In New England, we believe that Cape Cod has the dubious honor of holding out the longest against the advance of civilization, bundling, as we have it on good authority, having been practiced there as late as 1827." According to the Records of the Brewster Congregational Church, the incidence of fornication before marriage confessed in the church was so high that the pastor felt moved to speak out against the "wicked practice among young people in their courtships" in 1730. Coal stoves in all of the rooms of the house on the first floor ruined bundling by making it unnecessary, so Joe Lincoln had no occasion to include it in his yarns.

Young couples who announced that they would marry expected the good-natured banter of their friends. One instance of this is in *Extricating Obadiah.* When Cap'n Noah Newcomb meets Irving Clifford and Mary Barton Barstow, he says to "Irve", "Are you prepared to sign away your rights as a free man and a bachelor for the privilege of buyin' this young lady's bunnits and shawls for the rest of your life?"

Couples who plan to marry in Joe Lincoln's novels show no rose-pink sentimentalism. They incline to be more straight-forward and down-to-earth than romantic. There are no blood tests, no licenses, and no books on how to plan and execute a proper marriage, nor wedding secretaries who make the fertility festival bearable for the mother of the bride. Joe's couples go to the minister of a church and get married, and that's it.

Some weddings and would-be weddings have surprise elements, as in "Independence for Two".

Zephaniah Bloomer, bachelor, and Miss Clara Everdean, drive to the Universalist Church in Denboro to get married and find that the minister is a woman, which provokes "Zeph" into saying, "Women do most anything nowadays, don't they? Pretty nigh as independent as men".

In *Thankful's Inheritance,* we find a delightful yarn about Caleb Hammond and Miss Hannah Parker leaving secretly at midnight to drive to Bayport to get married. They get lost in the fog and barely get home to their beds in separate houses before daylight, having given up the idea of marriage.

Sometimes it is difficult for bachelors to remain bachelors, as in the attempt of "Seth Atkins" Bascom and "John Brown" Russell Agnew Brooks to be "woman haters" in the book of the same name. The attempt turns into a complete fiasco when Emiline Bascom appears at a near-by cottage with Miss Ruth Graham.

Other times only one of a pair of bachelors succumbs to a woman's wiles, as in "The Petticoat Cruise".

Cap'n Abishai Thanks and Cap'n Heman Tinkham are both bachelors, both are "oracles" in South Trumet, and both are retired fishing captains who had been rivals in their working days. Now they live together in South Trumet and are each in his own way deeply devoted to each other. When Cap'n Tinkham takes a second look at the school teacher, Miss Georgiana Collins, Cap'n Thanks says, "Goin' crusin' after a petticoat and leave me stranded after all these years".

In all of his stories, marriage is the normal way of life for men and women, but the marriages do not depend on the fickleness of romance for their permanence. In Joe's very last novel, *The Bradshaws of Harniss,* the widower, Zenas Bradshaw II, thinks his housekeeper, "Betsy" Lemon's marriage to "Jake" Lemon was the "one mistake of her life", but she does not divorce because of her "misjudged merit and injured innocence". But in *Blowing Clear,* "Lo" Weeks is really quite relieved when his new wife, Mrs. Hulda Bascom, runs away with the fake minister of "The Society of the Pure in Heart". Joe shows that there are marriages that are "for better or for worse until death do us part". There are others, but he is not unaware of the others: he intends to emphasize the good marriages in which men and women find in life most of what they are seeking. He seems to say, let others plumb the depths of human misbehavior and misery if they must, but as for me, I must show that there is another side to married life.

Just as most people know what milk tastes like even though they cannot define it, so Joe assumes that most people know what love is

153

and he sees no need to spend pages in defining that most abused of all words in our language.

Young people born and raised on Cape Cod may have a summer romance with a summer resident, but they rarely marry one. Joe has stories of courtships among summer residents, and in *Cap'n Warren's Wards,* he has something to say about love among city folks. He has Mrs. Michael Corcoran Dunn, widow of an Irish contractor and Tammany Hall politician, who in spite of all the bills locked in her desk drawer, considers herself and her friends "society", say, "Love! Love is well enough, but it does not, of itself, pay for proper clothes, or a proper establishment, or seats at the opera, or any of the practical, necessary things of modern life. You can't keep up a presentable appearance on love!" It is from this that wise old Cap'n Warren in his own way rescues his niece.

Peleg Myric calls Miss Emily Blanchard, an orphan girl of East Trumet, "the storm girl", and so Joe named his novel about her *Storm Girl.* She was born during a storm, her mother died during a storm, and her father was killed by lightning during a storm, Emily left Trumet to seek work in Boston during a storm, and she returned to Trumet during a storm. She becomes engaged to Captain Chester Brewster of the Trumet Lifesaving Station during a storm, and their wedding is postponed because Chester has to be at the station during the storm that occurs at the time set for the wedding.

After Emily Blanchard returns to East Trumet to live with her aunt, Mrs. Desire Hulda Knowles Coleman, a widow who runs a boarding house in the village, she spends quite a bit of time for a while with a young boarder, Bradford Dykes, who is from Illinois. Bradford and Emily have long discussions centering around his study of the proletariat, and a book with the title, "Frozen Souls". Bradford says of the proletariat, "the hordes of people we see around us every day......... They are sheep led by political shepherds. And they seem actually contented to be just that". Bradford has concluded that, "After all, life is pretty hopeless, isn't it?" Emily, who has more common sense than she has knowledge of the current whims of the sociologists, says, "everyday, common people..... we don't go about whining and complaining and hating, like the people in that 'Frozen Souls' book", and finds Bradford's company neither enjoyable nor desireable. Betty Schwartz, an earthy kind of maid in the boarding house, says of Bradford Dykes, "there is a dike not worth a dam".

Uncle Sim, brother of Desire Coleman's deceased husband, and handy man about the boarding house, sums up his feelings about Bradford Dykes by saying that he is "Goin' around pitying folks that don't want to be pitied and would punch his nose for him if they knew he was doin' it".

There are no divorces in Joe Lincoln's novels. In *Mary-'Gusta*, it is revealed that Zoeth Hamilton's wife had absconded with a former partner in the general store. Lavinia Holt Badger's husband has gone out West never to return before the story of *Great-Aunt Lavinia* begins. John Huyler Heath's first wife runs off with a traveling salesman before "Hi" comes to Cape Cod in *Blowing Clear,* where he is rescued from his pessimism by a widow, Mrs. Susan B. Harwell. Keziah Hall Coffin's husband Ansel Coffin is never home until he dies of smallpox in Trumet in *Keziah Coffin.* The marriage of Azuba Ginn and her husband Laban Ginn is satisfactory to them, even though it seems strange to others in *Cap'n Dan's Daughter* — Laban visits Azuba when he can. If and when an absent spouse dies, then the one remaining may marry, sometimes a former "intended".

Joe Lincoln often used the theme of the lover's quarrel in his yarns. Cape Cod folks, men and women, are "right independent". Even in matters of the heart their independence sometimes shows. Does the beach plum, a native Cape Cod fruit, get its independence from the land, and the folks get their independence from the same land? The beach plum is independent: it bears fruit when it pleases and not otherwise. Some bushes will be full of fruit and the ones around it will be bare. The fruit may be red or orange or red-purple, or just purple when ripe. If twenty-five seeds are planted, four or five may sprout after a long time and the rest just go on sleeping.

In the short story "A Question of Birthdays", Bertha Simpson Paine is an orphan adopted by Nehemiah Paine. The original Nehemiah of the Bible was a man of piety, of prayer, and of great faith in God, who led his people to re-build the walls of Jerusalem, but Nehemiah Paine is a man who fights with his wife until she runs away with a sewing-machine salesman: she must be quite desperate.

Bertha Simpson Paine takes up with Edward Bailey. When the affair breaks up, Bailey takes off. Years later he returns to Denboro, and one of his contemporaries asks him what he is going to do: "Goin' to set around and lame your wrist cuttin' coupons, like a trust magnet?". But Bailey is manager of the local cold-storage fish plant, and eventually makes up with Bertha.

155

Good Housekeeping, in which the story of Bertha and Edward was published in May, 1912, said of it, "Like a whiff of the sea is this Cape Cod story — refreshing and wholesome. And it is a Leap-Year story in more ways than one". Along with his poems and stories about the holidays, Joe also took note of Leap-Year, and more than one of his women folk propose to their chosen mates.

Cap'n Solomon Berry, depot master in East Harniss, finds himself in the Mountain and Mahomet situation with the woman of his choice, Miss Olive Seabury. *Bartlett's Familiar Quotations* quotes this from the essay "Of Boldness", by Francis Bacon (1561-1626), "Mahomet made the people believe that he would call a hill to him and from the top of it offer up his prayers for the observers of the law. The people assembled. Mahomet called the hill to come to him, again and again; and when the hill stood still he was never a whit abashed, but said, 'If the hill will not come to Mahomet, Mahomet will go to the hill'." The spelling of the name of the prophet almost makes certain the source from which Joe took the title of the short story, published in *Everybody's Magazine* in March, 1910, and used as a kind of structure upon which he built *The Depot Master.*

More than one of the couples in Joe's stories break up, but not for long. The reasons that keep them apart are never very important. In some cases one or the other marries someone else, and when that partner dies, the original couple finds ways to get together in marriage. Joe seems to be saying over and over again that "they were meant for each other".

In the case of Dr. Ephraim Basset Nye and Mrs. Katherine Minot Powell in *Dr. Nye of North Ostable,* both have married and their spouses have died before they come back together. Neither Albert Speranza nor Helen Kendall in *The Portygee* marry until they marry each other. In the cases of Silas Banks Bradford and Elizabeth Cartwright in *Silas Bradford's Boy,* and Esther Townsend and Bob Griffin in *The Big Mogul,* several forces work to keep these couples apart, but in the end their love wins out. Joe finds all of the ingredients for these stories of the troubles of lovers in the everyday affairs of ordinary human beings, and nowhere seeks to show any strange and sub-human forces at work in them or in their lives: — a simplistic attitude, perhaps, but his readers know that what he says about lovers is true, no matter what pseudo-psychiatry may put upon the reasons for their quarrels.

Hermits seem to fascinate Joe. He uses these solitary characters in several stories and books. They live in 'single-blessedness', which adds spice and variety when confronted with situations in which 'normal' people are involved. They seem to combine the qualities of wisdom and love as a background to lovers and others.

In "By the Airline", published in the *Ladies Home Journal* of December, 1923, Caleb Ginn is a "simple, artless, contented hermit" who lives on Spar Point near Wapatomac. His whole life style is upset by two eager young people who fix up his shanty and buy him new furniture and a battery-operated radio for his long winter evenings. When they come back the next summer, he decides to get a job in a remote lighthouse, crying, "What am I a hermit for?"

The hermit, unlike the restless hobo, was a loner, a solitary type who found out-of-the-way shelter and settled down to do only what he wanted to do. He is a recluse only in that he desires solitude, and may or may not have an aversion to society. Joe Lincoln's hermits are in no sense ascetic, practicing some austere form of self-mortification. They were more like the dictionary definition of the word "hermit" as it is found in cooking, "a spiced molasses cooky, often containing chopped raisins and nuts".

Joe's hermits live in shacks on the shore. In spinning yarns about them, he does not dig up their past, expound their psychological machinery, or invade their privacy. He accepts the fact that they are hermits and portrays them as colorful persons who have pushed individualsm to the limit. And although the villagers consider them "queer"; "they did not live like folks", Joe's hermits are always getting involved with villagers or summer-people.

ın *Mr. Pratt's Patients,* the summer folks think that Philander Doane is a hermit, "meaning somebody that's not loony, but is next door to it, being odd and queer and independent as a hog on ice". Philander has a concertina, which he teaches himself to play, the sounds he makes seeming to give him a strange kind of satisfaction.

Peleg Myrick first appears in "Peleg Myrick's Piano". He is a hermit who lives near Setuckit Point, outside of Orham. "He owned a concertina (which he called his piano) that squeaked and wailed, and a Mexican dog (called Skeezicks) that shivered all the time, and howled when the concertina was played". Peleg has a reputation as a weather prophet. When Peleg appears in *Partners of the Tide,* Cap'n Ezra Titcomb says of him, "I'll give in that it sounds foolish to think a bow-legged sandpeep with a sprained brain like Peleg's can know about the Lord Almighty's gales and such", but he is helpful to the partners, and when he appears again in *Rugged Water,* he is again a real part of the story.

Jehiel Bailey is a hermit who lives at Shell Point on Setuckit Beach in "The Boojoo Man". "Love had never come to him, possibly because it could not run as fast as he could". A sailor rescued from a British bark wrecked on Sand Hill Shoal gives Jehiel "the Boojoo man" for a bottle of wild cherry bounce. When Mrs. Caroline Tudor Boggs comes to Shell Point to gather material for her new book, Jehiel feels pursued and gives Mrs. Boggs the doll, saying, " 'E's a love charm, you'll see", and continues to be a hermit.

Bethuel Foster is a hermit living on Minister's Point near Denboro in "The Deep Sea and the Dog". He is a Democrat, and when his vote is needed in the Town Election for the Denboro School Committee, two young people are frustrated in their efforts to get Bethuel into town to vote by a dog they think to be Bethuel's savage bulldog, which he calls "Pet".

In another story, a well-meaning widowed sister plagues Asaph Black, so that he takes a house on the West Trumet beach — "he preferred his own company to that of others", and so the summer people called him "The Hermit". When his sister rents his house to "duck hunters" while Asaph is away, and the "hunters" turn out to be bootleggers, he cries, "There's limits!". So "Limits" becomes the name of the yarn as Joe finally writes it.

All of these men have a few things in common: they live alone, they work only when they want to, and they are mighty independent in most things, which makes them different from each other. In spite of their desire to be let alone, all of Joe's yarns about them put them into unwanted situations caused by people who seem not able to let these men have the solitude they desire. If Joe were writing today, he could use the stories of these men as parables of what is happening to his beloved Cape Cod — when the summer "hurricane" comes there is no longer any solitude for anyone, and no more hermits.

NEWS AND HISTORY

Before the days when everybody had a telephone in his house, news spread through a village by word of mouth, and then some of it appeared in the weekly newspaper. Most villages had a news-gatherer like Myra Simpson Crusit, who wrote the "Wellmouth Gleanings" column for *The Item*. In several of Joe Lincoln's novels, people not only make a business of spreading "news", but go about telling "what so-and-so said", and reporting everybody's evaluation of what was said. Miss Melissa Busteed, "Orham's human gossip column", about whom Cap'n Eri Hedge said, "She was cruisin' 'round the way she always does with a cargo of gabble, and she put in here to unload", was one of Joe's first creations of this type.

Cap'n Cy Whittaker describes the situation in this manner. "You know that three words hove overboard in Bayport will dredge up gab enough to sink a dictionary". Miss Olinda "Aunt Lindy" Pepper is described in *Dr. Nye of North Ostable* as a woman who is "as hungry for gossip as a gull is for sand eels".

It was said of Miss Althea Bemis, who was Dr. Nye's watchful neighbor when he returned to North Ostable after having been in prison for five years, "She's havin' more excitement than she's had since Eliza Perry's false front came off in prayer meetin'. (For those who don't know, "a false front" was a carefully made hairpiece, which when worn gave the woman the effect of having bangs).

In *Queer Judson*, Cap'n Tobias Higgins says of Miss Hannah Beasley, "That woman would make a fust-rate for'ard lookout on a vessel", but of Miss Letitia Cahoon, he says, "That's one good thing about that clam-shell mouth of hers. It can keep shut when she wants it to".

Most folks were really controlled by "what will people say?", and "Why can't he act like folks?", but Cap'n Mark Bearse shows the true independent Cape Cod spirit when his friendship with Dr. Nye is challenged by saying that "he did not give a sulphrous trifle what folks said".

It is a curious word, "gossip", which describes the cause of so much pain and trouble in this world. The word began by meaning, "a sponsor at baptism", god + sibb, or a relation akin to God. Then it came to mean, "a familiar and customary acquaintance", and ended up by meaning, "one who runs from house to house or goes about tattling and telling news" or "groundless rumor".

We are familiar with Joe Lincoln's use of the words and phrases common among people who live near or on the sea, but in *Shavings,* a novel with World War I as a background, he uses words that came into our speech from the military. Gabriel "Gab" Bearse has "his vocal machine gun" with him and goes about "to obtain an additional clip of cartridges before opening fire on the crowd at the post office", which was always "the gossip-sharpshooter's first line trench".

People came to the post office in town every day for more than the mail (most of them were not expecting any mail). There was a holder for a postcard beside the delivery window in the post office. Into this holder the postmaster placed the card, which came in the afternoon mail every day from the United States Weather Bureau. It was the "official weather" for the area for the immediate day, and its predictions were always thoroughly discussed.

The post office, "the news-distributing center for North Ostable", is made up entirely of men in *Dr. Nye of North Ostable,* and the Orham post office gossips in *Rugged Water* are all men. These post office assemblies in Joe Lincoln's novels are a kind of people's court, where cases are tried on hearsay and usually without kindness, as in the case of the post office crowd in Bayport in *Storm Signals* in their discussion of hearsay of the plight of Capt. Benjamin A. Snow.

These people's courts met at other places, notably the weekly Sewing Circle meetings. The after-church exchange of news, "have you heard?" or "Did you know that", replaced the more ancient in-church public confession. It seems that the community assumed the right to evaluate everybody's behavior with or without accurate information.

In a poem, "Waiting for the Mail", published in the *League of American Wheelmen Bulletin,* Joe describes the scene repeated every evening in small post offices all over Cape Cod, and in many other parts of the country. One suspects that Joe did not get all of his knowledge of post offices from his experience in his Aunt Martha's post office, as a boy, but that he got the idea there and then, and with his wonderful imagination spelled out the scenes as they appear in his various novels.

After Joe Lincoln gave up other employment and devoted himself to writing as his way of life, he read *The New York Times* every day. As far as we can find out, he was never employed in a newspaper office. However, he wrote several things in which he shows an uncanny knowledge of newspaper business and people.

His first newspaper piece was the poem "The Weekly Clarion", which was published in *The League Bulletin,* August 13, 1897. Here the subscriber sets forth what he expects of the newspaper.

The second was his long poem, "Carrier's Address 1901", published by the American Press Association in December, 1900.

In "Esteemed Contemporaries", a short story that appeared in *Everybody's Magazine* in June, 1907, and in 1933 became a part of *Back Numbers,* Benjamin Phinney, editor and proprietor of *"The Trumet Weekly Breeze",* is no little distressed by the success of his rival, *"The Trumet Weekly Gazette".* This last newspaper is revived by no less a person than the very attractive Miss Edith Foster, niece

160

of the former owner, representing another instance of Joe's increasing interest in "Women's Lib", 1907 style. Benjamin and Edith eventually marry, and then there is but one paper in the village, *"The Trumet Weekly Breeze-Gazette"*: could there be any other ending? Does the size of Trumet really need two papers? Joe seems to say that both Benjamin and Edith win, to the benefit of the village they both serve.

Head Tide appeared in book form in July of 1932. This is the story of Franklin Cobb and the people of Wellmouth. Young Cobb, sole heir of Beriah Higham's newspaper, *"The Eagle"*, and his job printing shop, comes to Wellmouth and decides to stay. Throughout the story Joe has a good deal to say about the place of a newspaper in local politics, and about the ways of local politicians. The power-center at Wellmouth Four-Corners is challenged by the rising self-consciousness of the South Side, and the newspaper is right in the middle of the fray. Joe brings in all of the human interest that is involved in the variety of a growing community. The political boss, the political hack, the fishing skipper, whose "barrels and cart smelled enthusiastically of fish" and who seeks office outside of the support of the party's leader's wishes, are all there, Cap'n Gideon Bates, Wellmouth's richest man, known as "King Gideon the First", stands in considerable contrast to Elisha Napoleon Bonaparte Dodson, whom Franklin Cobb makes Editor of his inherited paper. This story is so well presented that one feels as though he were reading local history.

Joe liked to incorporate actual historical events and places in his stories.

Degna Marconi, in her biography *My Father, Marconi*, wrote, "In January 1901, my father took a map of America and on it marked the area where the receiving station for 'the big thing' would be built. It was to rise on Cape Cod, the 'bare and extended arm of Massachusetts', where 'a man may stand and put all America behind him'. Chatham is its elbow, Truro the wrist, and up the forearm one long, high cliff of sand and clay rises 130 feet from the sea. No land intervenes between that cliff and Poldhu." At South Wellfleet, on the edge of the Great Beach, Marconi built his radio station, and on January 19, 1903, his wireless made possible an exchange of messages between President Theodore Roosevelt and Edward VII in London, England. "Three years after Marconi won the Nobel Prize in 1909, the H.M.S. Titanic sent its historic SOS, dramatizing unforgettably the full and vital significance of the wireless."

In December, 1923, the *Ladies Home Journal* published Joe

Lincoln's short story, "By the Airline", which was later included in *All Alongshore.* "Samuel Russell", last name assumed, comes to Wapatomac and boards with the hermit, Caleb Ginn, in his shack at Spar Point, trying to recover from shell-shock received in World War I. Miss "Mabel Day", another assumed last name, comes to Wapatomac to study music with Professor Dantzigg from Chicago. When Mabel seems lost to Sam after the summer is over, Sam hears her voice on Caleb Ginn's radio and the lovers are reunited, "by the airline".

In a letter to his son, Freeman, written February 4, 1925, Joe describes his new radio with its horn and draws a sketch of it. He writes of its improvement over the old one and that he thinks it would be fun to take it to Cape Cod in the summer, but that his wife thinks it would take up too much room in the car. Like many people when the radio was new to the homes of America, Joe and Mrs. Lincoln spent a lot of time, especially at night, "listening to concerts" and other programs, and bragged about the far-away places they had heard.

The Civil War and President Abraham Lincoln are the background for a Joe Lincoln sea story.

The loss of a ship was a very serious matter to a Cape Cod ship captain. When a ship was lost, it was expected that the captain would go down with his ship unless all hands were saved. Young Captain Benjamin A. Snow, son of a leading citizen of Bayport, comes home as the only known survivor when his ship is wrecked off Cape Hatteras, North Carolina. This is the basis of *Storm Signals* by Joe Lincoln. Since the wreck took place in 1860, the whole story has as its background the beginnings of the Civil War in the United States of America. Joe does not attempt to write an historical novel, but rather presents the human dramas upon which the facts of the war have considerable influence.

One of the concerns of the people of Bayport, as elsewhere, was the appearance of Abraham Lincoln upon the national scene. Abraham Lincoln was a descendent of one of the four Thomas Lincolns who lived early in Hingham. John Farmer, in his *A Genealogical Register of the First Settlers of New England,* published in 1829, says "Of the four persons of the name of Thomas Lincoln, above, two were admitted freemen in 1637 and 1642, but it is not easy to designate them. Twenty-two persons of the name had graduated in New England in 1826, among whom may be found divines, lawyers, physicians, and statesmen, who may trace to the above as their common ancestors."

The descendents of one of these Thomas Lincolns moved gradually south and were the ancestors of Abraham. Joe Lincoln was a descendent of Thomas Lincoln, the cooper, who was the ancestor as well of the famous revolutionary general, Benjamin Lincoln, and his famous brother, Dr. Bela Lincoln.

"The comparatively unknown Illinois lawyer" generated strong feelings on Cape Cod, as elsewhere. In the discussions in the Bayport Post Office one could hear him described as "that long-legged scarecrow from 'way out yonder", or as "an ignorant western boor". He was thought to be a "Black Republican" by many people of the two political parties.

In a diary kept by Fred B. Holway of Sandwich, Cape Cod, under the date of November 8, 1864, it is recorded that Sandwich polled 559 votes in the national election: 440 votes going to Abraham Lincoln and Andrew Johnson and 119 votes going to Gen. George B. McClelland and George H. Pendleton. This is cited to indicate something of the political make-up of Cape Cod at the time in which *Storm Signals* is laid.

One of the characters in Joe's story is named Laban Hallett. We find this little man from Wapatomac a shoemaker in Bayport. Not being an important retired ship captain, and his trade giving him no status in the community, no matter how useful and necessary he is, he is further a "crank" and a follower of William Lloyd Garrison, one of the most controversial figures of the day. Captain Benjamin Snow and his fiance, Miss Alice Evans, daughter of "the oracle" of Bayport, Cap'n Heman Evans, meet secretly in the shoemaker shop of Laban Hallett for long serious discussions of slavery, the possible war, etc. On one occasion Joe quotes Laban as saying, "This is a fool war — but so was every other war that ever was fought — foolish in itself". This from a man who served with distinction in the war when he felt it necessary to answer the call of the Great Emancipator.

Joe Lincoln was neither a "hawk" nor a "dove": he had great respect for soldiers, but nowhere does he have anything good to say about war, and he seems to find no glory in it.

ANTIQUES AND HANDCRAFTS

One of the "things to do" during a summer vacation on Cape Cod is to visit antique dealers, attend auctions, and collect one or more of the products of the craftsmen of colonial America. Joe and Mrs. Lincoln collected Sandwich Glass and early American furniture. They accumulated a good collection of furniture, which is still in the family.

Their specialties in Sandwich Glass were paper weights and overlay lamps.

Joe shows his knowledge of overlay lamps in the short story, "Sandwich Overlay", which was published in *The Country Gentleman* in 1928. Did he get his knowledge from the many dealers he visited? We also have no idea which of the few books on the subject he studied. In any case, the story of the people in the yarn overshadows the incidental lamp. The antique dealer Jehiel Bean, who is involved in the story, makes a profound observation: "this bein' honest in my line of business is a darned complicated job".

There are antique dealers in several other short stories and books. One of the most interesting is Ebenezer Tadgett of Denboro, who appears in *Silas Bradford's Boy*, published in 1928. Ebenezer's front was a second-hand shop, but in the rear room he had some good antique furniture, and he really knew the difference. Through Ebenezer, Joe shows his own knowledge of the points of good antique furniture. Silas Banks Bradford rents a room over Ebenezer's store for his law office. He is overwhelmed by Ebenezer's gift of an antique desk for his office, which gives the office a special kind of atmosphere. The young lawyer watches his friend and two associates in their "cut-throat euchre" sessions. Silas is amazed by the care and attention Ebenezer lavishes upon his wife, who sees visions. Ebenezer reminds us of an industrialist who, when told that he should put his mentally ill wife away said, "I married her for better or for worse, now that its worse I will not go back on the bargain". The principles and life-style of Ebenezer Tadgett makes him one of Joe Lincoln's finest creations.

In a short story, "The Antiquers", published in the *American Magazine* in January, 1906, Joe has his fun with people who buy antiques. This story was included in the collection called *The Old Home House,* and contains the devastating comment by queer old Adoniram Rogers, "Well, if you want another set, I cal'late, I can git it".

In one poem Joe wrote, entitled, "The Antique Business", which appears in *Rhymes of the Old Cape,* Joe has fun with antique dealers. We quote the last stanza:

"A plain ten-dollar bureau is nigh worth its weight in gold,
If you just bang it up a bit to get it lookin' old;
Them cheap blue sets of dishes bring a 'hundred' ev'ry lick
If you'll be a little careful and give every piece a nick.
So let them that swears by farmin' farm themselves clean off
  their legs,

And let them that's raisin' poultry keep prayin' for more eggs,
And let them that's takin' boarders put in 'ads' for weeks and
    weeks;
I'll stay a simple rustic and keep peddlin' out 'antiques'."

"The Antiquers" was illustrated by Frederick Rodrigo Gruger.
Gruger was an artist and illustrator born in Philadelphia, Pennsylvania.
The editors of the 14th edition of the *Encyclopedia Brittanica* chose
Mr. Gruger to write their article on "Illustration" in Vol. 12, pp. 102-
06. Since there are so many artists and illustrators who illustrated the
many writings of Joe Lincoln, it might not be amiss to look at what
one of them saw as his job in relation to the writing. Mr. Gruger writes,
"The illustrator's first obligation to himself and to his public is a complete understanding of the story for which he is to make illustrations".
What kind of a person is an illustrator— Mr. Gruger writes, "The illustrator must be a person of wide knowledge, that he may have understanding ; of wide sympathy, that he may know the people whom he
is to picture; of creative imagination, that the story may be real in his
vision". What about the people who look at the illustrations? Mr.
Gruger writes, "Many persons have had no opportunity for parallel experiences with the author. Many have not the power of original observation. But the majority can associate the two when someone shows
them how. That is the work of the illustrator".

Gruger did the illustrations for Joe's poem, "Christmas at the Windward Light", published in the *Saturday Evening Post,* December 7, 1901,
and for the short story "Seer and Serpent", published in *Everybody's
Magazine,* January 1909.

Searching for antiques has become a popular pasttime on Cape
Cod. Handcrafts are also eagerly sought. Joe Lincoln wrote about
two of these in *Shavings* and *Queer Judson.*

"Shavings" is the nickname of a man who lives a life of "give-ups"
and whittles toy windmills.

Toy windmills were all the rage among summer-people on Cape
Cod when Joe Lincoln wrote *Shavings* in 1918. The novel features
Jedidah Edgar Wilfred Winslow, known as "Shavings" or "Jed Winslow",
the windmill maker, a man of Solomon-like wisdom who always does
more for others than he is able to do for himself.

Along with the humor and wisdom of Jed Winslow, this novel
deals with some human problems. Young Leander Babbitt is the son
of Phineas Babbitt, political boss of the town, who operates a hardware

and lumber store in Orham. Phineas is the citizen who "discovered that the war was a profiteering enterprise engineered by capital and greed for the exploiting of labor and the common people", and he is loud in his denunciations. Leander faces the problem of being drafted against his father's wishes or of enlisting when his father isn't looking. After a long discussion with Jed Winslow, Leander goes to Boston and enlists. Phineas continues to be a conscientious objector, but tones down his voice considerably. Joe Lincoln treats this whole problem with sympathy and insight — in September of 1918 his own son, Freeman, went to Boston and enlisted, with or without his father's permission — we suspect without it.

The second human problem in the novel is the fate of the ex-convict, in this case the brother of Ruth Armstrong, who is spending time in the house next door to Jed Winslow's shop. The brother, Charles Phillips, just out of the Connecticut State Prison after five years for embezzlement, comes to live with his sister. Can he get a job in the local bank with or without revealing his immediate past? Can he marry the bank president's only daughter? Joe presents all of the human aspects of this problem and resolves it in a way contrary to the widespread public opinion on the matter in 1918, which was to make the ex-convict an out-cast in society.

We do not wish to indicate that *Shavings* is a novel about problems, for it is not, but rather to show that Joe Lincoln was not afraid of unpopular subjects, and in dealing with people he does not ignore their problems just as he does not spend the whole book dissecting their sub-conscious drives and rages.

The novel was dramatized by Pauline Phelps and Marion Short, and opened on the stage of the Tremont Theatre in Boston. Then, on February 16, 1920, it opened at the Knickerbocker Theatre on Broadway in New York City. Incidentally, the play was published by Samuel French in New York in 1930.

A review of the novel *Shavings* in the *Bookman*, December, 1919, stated: "This delightful, winsome maker of toys is the central figure of an excellent and entertaining story of American life, with the war as dramatic background; a story full of human nature and radiant with humour."

The popularity of the book and the stage play brought many people to Cape Cod to buy toy windmills, hopefully at "Shavings'" shop, and all of the "knowing" were sure that they knew who Jed Winslow actually was, but Joe kept his own counsel, knowing that he had never used an actual person in any of his novels. They were all composites, his own fictional "children".

It is interesting that Joe Lincoln should use the name "Babbitt" in this novel four years before Sinclair Lewis made it famous in his tortured sociology of middle-class America. Joe's Babbitt is an unpleasant person, but he is strong enough to be a complete contrast to and in no way the "helpless and distracted" character portrayed by Sinclair Lewis. America can do without a Lewis-type Babbitt, but when there are no more Phineas Babbitts, America will be the poorer.

One of the significant things in Joe Lincoln's *Queer Judson* is the accurate and detailed knowledge of bird-carving shown by the author. This knowledge came from Joe's great friendship with Anthony Elmer Crowell of East Harwich on Cape Cod. Carey Judson's life-like "beetle-head", which provoked Cap'n Tobias Higgins into wanting a rock to throw at the bird, was a realistic Black-bellied Plover. The details of the shop set up in one of Cap'n Tobias' buildings after the incident of the "beetle-head" did not come out of Joe Lincoln's imagination, but rather from his knowledge of Anthony Elmer Crowell's shop. How often did Joe watch his friend, the famous bird-carver, at work? Certainly enough so that when he wrote the story of Carey Judson he had enough knowledge of bird-carving to make the setting true to life. Although Carey Judson is in no way like Anthony Elmer Crowell in personal terms, Joe's knowledge of Crowell's bird-carving makes Carey Judson's development much more than a yarn.

CAPE COD YESTERDAYS

Along with *Cap'n Eri,* the book *Cape Cod Yesterdays* seems to be one of Joe Lincoln's most memorable books and certainly one of his own favorites.

The publisher's blurb about *Our Village* stated, "In a series of unforgettable little sketches, Mr. Lincoln describes the life and the people of Cape Cod thirty years ago. This book may now be had, together with *Cape Cod Ballads,* in a special, illustrated gift edition".

Our Village contained memory sketches first published in *Colliers Weekly, Good Housekeeping, Success Magazine,* and *Country Life in America.* These are erroneously often listed as "short stories", which they are not. Joe wrote these sketches between 1906 and 1908, when he was thirty-six and more years old.

When Joe was sixty-five years old, his second book of essays about Cape Cod appeared with the title, *Cape Cod Yesterdays.* If these two are read one after the other one can see what had happened to Joe Lincoln's writing in thirty years.

Cape Cod Yesterdays is in no way a history of Cape Cod. It is, rather, in the category of Henry David Thoreau's *Cape Cod,* published in 1864, years before Joe was born.

In 1868 Charles Nordhoff published *Cape Cod and All Along the Shore Stories* — did Joe Lincoln know of this book or at least its title when he sent forth his collection of short stories entitled *All Along Shore?*

Henry Crocker Kittredge's *Cape Cod, Its People and Their History* had been published by Houghton Mifflin Co., Boston, Massachusetts in 1930. Joe said his book would not be a history: "the Kittredge book covers that field", indicating that he knew of the book.

We know that Joe was aware of Joseph Henry Sears' *Brewster Shipmasters,* published by C. W. Swift of Yarmouthport in 1906 — Joe wrote the foreword for this book. Did Joe read John Wilfred Dalton's *The Life Savers of Cape Cod,* published by The Barta Press, Boston, Massachusetts, 1902, before he wrote *Rugged Water,* published in 1924? And did the Lincolns read Walter Muir Whitehill's *New England Blockaded in 1814: The Journal of Lt. Henry Edward Napier of H. M. S. Nymphe,* published by the Peabody Museum, Salem, Massachusetts, 1939, before they wrote *The New Hope* in 1941?

There were three men involved in the production of *Cape Cod Yesterdays,* "the author, the artist, and the publisher's representative": Joe Lincoln, Harold Brett and Roger L. Scaife of Little, Brown & Co.

Roger L. Scaife was a summer resident of Cape Cod for many years. He and his wife, Ethel Bryant Scaife, wrote the delightful little volume entitled, *Cape Coddities,* using the pseudonyms of Dennis and Marion Chatham, published by Houghton Mifflin Co. in 1920. There are a number of letters extant which Scaife wrote to the people of Little, Brown & Co., concerning the projected *Cape Cod Yesterdays.* The following quotations from these letters throw some interesting light on Joe Lincoln:

"Lincoln is a nervous, apprehensive and somewhat timid individual, and it is always difficult to get him started on an enterprise of this sort. When once started, I have no fear but he will come through successfully".

"Lincoln is a high priced man .... He is, however, a very warm, intimate friend of Brett, and he is anxious that Brett should get as much if not more out of it than he himself".

The title *Cape Cod Yesterdays* was suggested to the publishers by Joe Lincoln in a letter to Roger L. Scaife dated Villa Nova, December 14, 1934. In this letter Roger L. Scaife is addressed as the Vice-President of Little, Brown, & Co. The extant manuscript of the book bears the title "Our Yesterdays", which the publishers wished to change, hence Joe's suggestion.

Another title change concerned the name of the Preface. In the manuscript the title is typically Joe, "All Aboard" — someone has listed this as one more short story by Joe. The title of the Preface in the printed book is "A Warning and An Invitation".

In a letter to Roger L. Scaife, dated Villa Nova, Pa., January 9, 1935, there is a revealing paragraph about Joe Lincoln from Joe himself:

"Now about the duck shooting chapter. To be perfectly frank I am not keen about it, and would rather not do it. Shooting does not appeal to me at all, and I never killed a duck in my life; therefore I have, of course, no personal recollection of gunning on the Cape in the old days, and know very little about it in the present day".

More than seventy-five people made illustrations for the writings of Joe Lincoln. One of the best known of these artists was Harold M. Brett, (1880-1956), who was a summer neighbor and fishing companion of Joe's.

Harold Brett studied with Philip Hale and Frank Benson at the Museum of Fine Arts in Boston. At the Art Students League in New York, Brett studied with H. Siddons Mowbray, Kenyon Cox, and Walter Appleton Clark. He spent several years in Wilmington, Delaware, first at the Howard Pyle School in Chadds Ford, Pennsylvania, just outside Wilmington. He had his own studio in Wilmington for some time after.

His illustrations appeared in the leading magazines of the day, such as *Harper's Weekly, Colliers, Ladies Home Journal, Saturday Evening Post,* and *The Country Gentleman.* He made posters for Liberty Bond drives in World War I, and did work for the publicity department of the Pennsylvania Railroad. He turned almost entirely to portrait painting in a studio in New York City — he specialized in blue-water ship captains. He spent about eight months of the year at his home, "Old Squaretop", in North Chatham on Cape Cod. This house was built by Capt. Joshua Atkins in 1812 and is still a fine example of a blue-water ship captain's house.

There are eighteen of Brett's paintings in the Chatham edition of *Cape Cod Yesterdays,* and there are twenty-six of Brett's line drawings in that edition. The originals of the paintings are prized possessions of people who were fortunate enough to acquire them.

There is a fine photograph of Harold Brett and a brief account of him in the third volume of Thompson's *History of Plymouth, Norfolk, and Barnstable Counties.* Brett's last picture in connection with Joe Lincoln was his portrait of Joe, done in 1943.

Joe sent complimentary copies of *Cape Cod Yesterdays* to an interesting group of people, who were also his friends. One copy went to Newell Convers Wyeth, the artist in Chadds Ford. N.C. Wyeth (1882-1945), father of the equally famous artist, Andrew Wyeth, illustrated many writings of many authors, among them the classics *Robin Hood* and *Treasure Island,* published by Scribners. He did the end-papers and the dust jacket for the novel *Blair's Attic* by the two Lincolns.

Another copy of *Cape Cod Yesterdays* went to the famous author Kenneth Roberts of Kennebunk Beach, Maine. Mrs. Sara Ware Basset, author of over forty Cape Cod summer romances, got a copy. Complimentary copies went to Mark A. DeWolf Howe, Boston Athenaeum, Henry C. Kittredge, Cape Cod historian and retired master of St. Paul's School in Concord, New Hampshire, and Miss Elizabeth Reynard, professor of English at Barnard College, New York, author of *The Narrow Land,* a book of Cape Cod legends. In her will Miss Reynard left the copyright of *The Narrow Land* to the Chatham Historical Society. The income from the sale of the new edition of this book made it possible for the Society to repair and enlarge the Atwood House in Chatham, which contains the Lincoln Memorial Room.

Joe Lincoln's friends were not great in number, but they were people of quality in their professions, and all were ardent Cape Codders.

The misgivings of the publishers of *Cape Cod Yesterdays* about the sales of the book were soon dissipated after its publication. At least six printings were to be made, with slight variations in the content of the illustrations by Harold Brett, in the ensuing years.

When the book was first issued, *The New York Times* Book Review said, "Mellow, humorous, and delightful. One more authentic record of an American way of life which has changed greatly in a brief time, and to which many Americans look back with regret". And that's right, for the publication of the book was followed by the dehumanizing effects of technology and the Atomic Age. Perhaps that is why Joe Lincoln's *Cape Cod Yesterdays* has become such a sought after collector's item one hundred and more years after his birth.

COLLABORATION WITH FREEMAN

With the publication of *Blair's Attic* in September of 1929, something new happened in the career of Joe Lincoln. His son and only child was his collaborator. Joe had collaborated with Howard Reynolds on his first short story in 1896. He had collaborated with William Danforth in the dramatization of *Cy Whittaker's Place* in 1910, but the drama was never published. He had collaborated with Sewall Ford in writing plays for the Unitarian Dramatic Club in Hackensack, New Jersey, and he had written a large number of short stories and novels completely on his own. Now his son had given up his newspaper work and become a free-lance writer, and they joined forces in this new novel. The novel was published by a new publisher for Joe, Coward-McCann, Inc., of New York: Appleton had been his regular publisher. The novel first appeared as a serial in *The Country Gentleman,* beginning in July of 1929.

The structure of the novel was different from those Joe had been writing. Major characters tell sections of the story, with Freeman writing the off-Cape parts and Joe continuing his Cape Cod style. Joe and his son had many "conferences", either face to face or over the telephone, before the final manuscript was complete. They developed a method of collaboration which they were to use on two other novels. A study of Freeman's own short stories and novels for style might enable one to determine the sections he wrote and what were his father's work. But what would be the purpose of finding out? This kind of vivisection would not add to the enjoyment of the reading and certainly would not make the people of the novel more interesting.

"Anthy" Beasley Hallet, the *Blair* housekeeper, who reads *Dracula* and the works of Edgar Allen Poe, "uttering periodic moans of delighted horror", helps create the atmosphere for the search for "the thing". The figure of Jonas Cahoon Jones, an antique dealer, shows signs that the authors were familiar with the Sherlock Holmes type. Anyone who has been awake in his bed when a gale off the ocean was sweeping inland will recognize the description of the gale which wrecked "The Pride of the Fleet" by "the way those gusts of wind yelled when they went by the corners of the roof" and will understand what the authors meant by, "the Old Scratch's own fandango was being danced on the roof".

It will be noticed that the element of mystery plays a larger part in Joe's own novels after his work with Freeman in this first collaboration.

Samuel Gregg comes to board at the home of the Blairs. He loves to play chess, and his favorite expression is, "Bless my soul!". He also becomes very interested in antiques and says that, "Antiques were a mirror of the past". He spends a lot of his time working puzzles — the mystery in the Blair household becomes very intriguing to him and of course he gets caught up in it.

Joe Lincoln had very smooth, agile hands. He could not use tools of any kind but he did card tricks with great facility and was always drawing sketches and puzzles on small pads of paper. He often entertained his grandchildren with his tricks and his sketches. Joe and Freeman loved puzzles, and Cross-Word puzzles, Double-Crostics, and Jigsaw puzzles were always being worked on. They not only worked out word puzzles, but made Double-Crostics for others to do.

Because of this, it is not surprising that they introduced a "puzzleman" into *Blair's Attic,* and made the story a puzzle, the solution of which involved quite a few people.

The Ownley Inn, published in 1939, was the second novel written in collaboration with Freeman. He and Joe used the "big blow" of 1938 as a "curtain raiser", which caused *Time* magazine in their review of the book, August 14, 1939, to say: "If a hurricane blew everybody off Cape Cod, it could be repopulated overnight by the fictional offspring of Joseph Crosby Lincoln".

The book is written as a mystery, in which Seth Hammond Ownley, owner of the Ownley Inn, tries to find the thief who has stolen a copy of the rare *New England Primer.* Of course, summer boarders are involved. Here is a characteristic quote: "The average summer boarder is forever hunting characters and forgetting to look in the looking glass for a specimen.

In the novel *The New Hope,* Joe and Freeman tell the story of the community of Trumet in action. The community buys the two-hundred ton bark, "The Flyer", re-names it "The New Hope", and is engaged in re-fitting the ship to run the blockade of the British around Cape Cod during the War of 1812. This is not a fictional history of the war, but a story of Cape Cod people crushed economically by a war which they did not want, attempting to work their way out of their troubles. It is a story of all kinds of people, helping and hindering, loving and hating, trusting and mistrusting each other, being loyal and disloyal and sacrificing and profiteering: in short, all the ways people react to a community project.

There is a traitor in the midst of the community and several people are suspected, until finally the real traitor is uncovered. He is Eben Fowler, who operates a salt-works and is a member of the community council in charge of the project. Eben Fowler is a man of hate, who holds grudges, who seeks revenge to the extent that he is willing to see his community's project fail. He is a perfect illustration of how hatred burns up the hater.

Cap'n Isaiah Hamilton Dole is the chosen captain of "The New Hope". It seems that he almost never gets any sleep, but he has organized the people of the community according to their skills and he gets the job done. After a very discouraging town meeting he comments, "Human nature is a good deal of a disgrace when you get a lot of it together in a bundle" (Joe made this comment before the horrors of the mobs of the sixties blighted our national scene).

The day comes when the tide and the wind is right and "The New Hope" sails. The historical fact behind the story of "The New Hope" is that ships were built on Cape Cod to run the British blockade in the War of 1812. Capt. William Handy, a soldier of the Revolution, set up a boat-yard on Red Brook Harbor at Cataumet and built quite a few ships for the purpose. He hid his boat-yard behind Handy Point so that British ships in Buzzards Bay could not see what was going on. Sailed by wily old Cape Cod skippers, these ships brought some relief to the economic depression of the people in what was known on Cape Cod and along the coast as "Jefferson's War".

ON THE PRESERVATION OF CAPE COD

People have always been coming to Cape Cod, the American Indians sometime just after the glaciers left. The Vikings, wandering in the North Atlantic, may have visited the Cape. Portugese fishermen came, loaded their boats with codfish, and followed the Gulf Stream home long before Columbus was born. Champlain was here while exploring the eastern shore of the new continent. Gosnold tried his hand at colonizing but went home with a boat-load of sassafras. Queen Wetamoe came with her Wampanoag people for shell-fishing. The "saints and strangers", sometimes called "The Pilgrims", came and stayed and settled the Cape.

Timothy Dwight, a President of Yale College, travelled the length of the Cape by stage coach. Henry David Thoreau, the Concord naturalist-philosopher, came by rail and stage-coach, walked the Great Beach, and wrote an American classic about his trip, in which he predicted what we now see all about us. Joe Jefferson, the actor; Eugene O'Neill, the playwright; Daniel Webster, the orator; Agassiz, the naturalist; Marconi, the inventor; Grover Cleveland, the President of the U. S. A.; and many other V.I.P.'s have come to Cape Cod.

Things began to change when people "from away" began to buy up the land of Cape Cod. The Bible tells the story of Esau, a man of the open country, who sold his birthright for a bowl of soup (Gen. 25: 29f). The American Indians of Cape Cod were people without fences, but they sold their patrimony and their future for trinkets. Fifth and sixth generation Cape Codders, who were people of the open sea and the land, sold their patrimony for small amounts of hard cash.

And then came the "hurricane", as William Dana Orcutt called it. People came in trains and automobiles, which had replaced the stage coaches. They came on highways that had once been sand roads and ways. Mushrooming motels replaced the enjoyable old "boarding houses". Sprawling shopping plazas began replacing the community centers known as General Stores. Noisy, water-polluting motor boats replaced the silent-winged sail boats. Oil spills drove out the bluefish and stripers and killed the clams, quahaugs, scallops, and lobsters. Cans and junk replaced the driftwood on the beaches. Ear-splitting, air-polluting jet aeroplanes shattered the lives of wildlife and people.

People came to Cape Cod because it was "the edge of the sea", where the wildness of the ocean and the forested land provided a shore

174

where a person could "let his soul catch up with him". Insanely, the very things that made Cape Cod attractive are the things that are being destroyed.

Lincoln was very concerned with the concept of an overcrowded Cape Cod. As early as 1905, Joe reflected on the changes made up to that time and Thoreau's reaction to them. In the Foreword which he wrote to *Brewster Ship Masters* by J. Henry Sears, dated November 30, 1905, Lincoln wrote the following:

"Before noon of a day in October 1849, Henry David Thoreau, author and nature-lover, quitted the Cape Cod train at what was at that time the railroad terminus at Sandwich and took 'that almost obsolete conveyance, the stage, for as far as it went that day, as we are told by the driver'. 'As far as it went that day', was, as a matter of fact, as far as the down-the-Cape stage from Sandwich went on any other day, and that was as far as the Higgins Tavern in Orleans. It is probable that the driver was Mr. Higgins himself and if so, that he wore his carefully brushed silk hat and passed it about among his passengers as a depository for their fares.

"At any rate, Mr. Thoreau, as a passenger in the stage, was driven that day through Barnstable, Yarmouth, and Dennis, until late in the afternoon we rode through Brewster, so named after Elder Brewster, for fear he would be forgotten else . . .
This appeared to be the modern-built town of the Cape, the favorite residence of retired sea captains. . . . . . .

"Thoreau did not like Brewster; principally, it appears, because of the prevalence of 'modern American houses' and the evidences of thrift and prosperity. He did not alight there, but went on to spend the night at the Higgins Tavern in the next town. Therefore, Brewster missed the opportunity of figuring prominently in the Thoreau book, 'Cape Cod', and that book, so we of Brewster heritage believe, lacks just so much of deep sea flavor and local color. There was more of Cape Cod than odd characters, the poverty-grass and the sand dunes, that the hermit of Lake Walden found in '49, and more than the magnificent beaches and inspiring ocean views, which attract the summer resident today."

City people are always getting notions about "going to the country" to escape whatever is bugging them: crowds, noises, polluted air, bad-tasting water, tensions from syncopated successes and failures in money-making and love affairs, or from just being bored with it all. Encumbered with all of the comforting gadgets of city living, people seek the primitive things, such as fire-places, candle-light, walking on grass, digging in the good earth. With these things they try to become human once again.

In 1906 Joe tried to discourage would-be seekers of "the natural life" in a novel entitled *Mr. Pratt.*

What Joe describes in *Mr. Pratt* is not to be confused with Thoreau's facing life deliberately at Walden Pond, or feeling the sea on the Great Beach on Cape Cod, or his seeking the impact of the primeval forest of the American Indians in the Maine woods. Nor is Joe writing about the valiant efforts of modern young people to live and work in communes in the country.

What Joe Lincoln writes about is one example of people who want to live a "natural life" by having enough money to pay somebody to do all the work required to maintain them in their dreams. In *Mr. Pratt,* the two young men from New York come to Cape Cod with plenty of money, a man-servant, and a book. They hire Solomon Pratt, Nate Scudder, and Eureka Sparrow to do all the work at the house they rent on "Ozone Island". But when they are forced to work physically in order to keep warm and to eat, they quickly burn the book on the natural life and return to the city.

This satire on a fad of the time in which it was written is good reading for city folks who think of becoming country dwellers — they will all return to the soil, but even then someone else will have to dig their graves.

The great Louis Agassiz wrote that as the glaciers had created Cape Cod by depositing its sand and gravel at their retreating edges, so in time the ocean would wear away this sand and gravel and leave nothing of this most interesting bit of the New England coast. When one sees the amount of annual erosion along the Great Outer Beach at Nauset and at Truro, one fears that Agassiz was right. Unless the residents of "the bended right arm of Massachusetts" are sufficiently alarmed, not by the work of the ocean so much as by the works of men, the very qual--ities that make the Cape desireable will be eroded away, and there will be nothing for the ocean to wash away but the horrors of another noisy, smoky, unbearable city.

Joe Lincoln wrote a letter to the Editor of the *Cape Cod Beacon Magazine,* published in the issue of February, 1938, from which we quote:

"You may be quite sure that I am entirely in sympathy with you in any effort to keep Cape Cod from being further commercialized. I have repeated the opinion that the Cape Cod Advancement Plan has reached the point where it is beginning to advance backwards. If these people would only realize that what the worthwhile visitor to the Cape comes there for, is its individuality, its fine old simplicity, and its natural beauty! There are dozens of Coney Islands and Revere Beaches and the like. So far there is only one Cape Cod and it should be kept as the one."

The inside of the rear cover of the issue of March 1938 of the *Cape Cod Beacon Magazine* contained the picture and quote from Joe.

In an editorial entitled "Saving Cape Cod; The Descent of the Rabble: Its Cause and Cure", the Editor of the *Beacon* wrote, "We all agree that the chief charm and attraction of Cape Cod has been its simplicity and tranquility, first described by Thoreau, and later made immortal in fiction by Joseph Lincoln. This we would like to retain, but how is it to be done? Do we need to advertise Cape Cod at all? Does one need to advertise Heaven?" Many preachers and evangelists have done so — we are reminded of the street-car conductor who said to a clergyman, "Many people talk about Heaven, but nobody wants to go there, today!" Perhaps if it was advertised as Heaven fewer people who want to make something else out of it would come.

Lincoln's interest in preserving the status quo of Cape Cod is expressed in a letter he wrote to the editor of the *Boston Traveler* on December 26, 1935.

"The preservation of Cape Cod as Cape Cod is, in my opinion, a vitally important subject for consideration by Cape people. We are adding to our summer population each year. The great majority of the visitors to our county have been attracted to it because of its simplicity, the charm which is its own. There are thousands of summer resorts but only one Cape Cod.

"It seems to me that every Cape Codder and lover of the Cape should realize how important it is to save our towns and villages from becoming mere copies of towns and villages elsewhere. —

"In my opinion for Cape Cod to lose its individuality would be very disastrous from a business standpoint. Cape Cod all-the-year residents, its shop-keepers and business men and hotel keepers should, I am convinced, do everything in their power to save the old buildings and landmarks, to preserve the genuine Cape Cod flavor where it is possible. They will profit by doing so, I am sure. I am a Cape Codder, born and bred, and even now I spend almost half of each year on the Cape.

"I want to keep on doing so. My summer neighbors are, many of them, importations — they came to the Cape almost casually, were attracted by the charm and individuality I have mentioned, came again and again, and at last built homes here. And they are now as staunch lovers of Barnstable County as the rest of us. They are the sort of people we want here as summer residents; they bring their families here, they spend their money here. If Cape Cod becomes something other than the Cape Cod they know and love, they will continue to do none of those things. So, when any movement is on foot to save and preserve the real Cape Cod it should have the support of us all. Let's get together and work for that end. That the work will be worth working for I am certain. This letter is longer than I meant it to be. I apologize for the length but — well, you see, Cape Cod, its people, its welfare and its future are pet subjects of mine."

The story of Cape Cod could be written with the changing modes of travel as the framework for showing how Cape Cod has progressed from a quiet rural place to an area fought over by "the developers", such as those in *A. Hall & Co.*

Timothy Dwight, President of Yale College in New Haven, Connecticut, traveled from Wareham to Provincetown on Cape Cod by stage coach and was so "shook up" from the experience that his *Travels in New England and New York,* published in 1820 tells very little about Cape Cod.

In 1849 Henry David Thoreau rode the stage from Sandwich to Orleans, and then walked the beach to Provincetown, and he tells us about what he saw in his *Cape Cod*, a classic.

In Joe Lincoln's *Partners of the Tide,* Bradley Nickerson, an orphan, comes to live in Orham among people he doesn't know, on the stage coach, and is frightened almost speechless.

Franklin Cobb comes from Cleveland, Ohio to Wellmouth on Cape Cod by railroad in Joe Lincoln's *Head Tide,* published in 1932.

And when Estelle Hall returns from college at the beginning of Joe Lincoln's *A. Hall & Co.,* published in 1938, she arrives on Cape Cod by airplane, and rides to her home in West Orham in an automobile.

The contest between Andrew Hall, Estelle's strong-minded, pigheaded, but indulgent widowed father, and a wealthy, powerful citizen of Chicago, who has a grandiose scheme for the development of West Orham, is complicated by Estelle's interest in the son of the developer. The world-travelled Carver Hall, the would-be peacemaker,

178

asks Oscar Oaks, an old employee of Andrew Hall's, if he remembers the ending of the Beatitude about the peacemakers, and Oscar says, "Blessed are the peacemakers? Hum! Somethin' about the rains descending and the floods comin', ain't it? Sure that's it. They're blessed 'cause they're founded on a rock. Thought it would come back to me". This is another instance of Joe Lincoln's clever combination of passages from the Bible — in this case he combines Matt. 5:9 with Matt. 7:25 to say something very interesting about Carver Hall's efforts and eventual success.

Cape Codders of modern time would do well to read *A. Hall & Co.* very carefully and understand what Joe Lincoln was saying about "developers" before it is too late.

The Bradshaws of Harniss concludes the Cape Cod Saga by Joseph Crosby Lincoln. The grandson of an old family is more interested in airplanes than in keeping the independent family store going. He goes off to fly war planes — World War II is getting under way. But before he goes he secretly marries a young woman, one of Joe Lincoln's finest creations. Her name is Emily Thacher. Joe's mother was Emily, and his beloved grandmother was "Mother Thacher". Emily turns out to be a business woman of no small ability when she takes over for the ailing grandfather Bradshaw. At least for a short time, she is able to keep the store going in spite of the challenge from the new "chain stores", which were to put most independents out of business.

This last novel really describes the end of the era that Joe knew so well. The sailing ships are gone, and so are most of the blue-water captains and their staunch women. The grandchildren of the old families have either left the Cape, or run wildly about on the hard paved roads in sports cars, where the stage coaches used to groan and rattle along the sand tracks. The whole tempo and sound of life on the Cape has changed. *The Bradshaws of Harniss* is not really a transition piece— it is one of his best books, and in its own way concludes the story of what Joe knew, loved, and wrote about for so long.

Part IV

A Descriptive Bibliography of
Joseph C. Lincoln First Editions
Preface

I have attempted to place in the hands of the reader a full
description of the acknowledged first printing of each of Joseph
C. Lincoln's books. The intent has been to arrive at statements
about the books that are verifiable from a hands-on point of
view.

I have primarily come to rely on private collections and the
knowledge of dealers in Lincoln material to arrive at recognition of
the first printings.

I had begun to inquire of publishers regarding editions of Lincoln published by them only to receive general statements to the
effect that "no records from that period now exist."

As I began to compare available published material on Lincoln
with records of the Library of Congress and the mass of data left by
the Reverend Rex, more questions presented themselves than I had
originally intended to answer. In many instances, the publishing
history of a given title seemed to differ somewhat from one source
to another, and the job of verifying and assessing the importance
of each printing grew more convoluted, as well as the task of actually placing my hands on each and every printing of a title in order
to fully describe it. In fact, it became increasingly obvious that
where major sources were incomplete, or the data they held was
in another form from that which I had managed to collect, the task
before me would extend a great deal further then the time limit
placed on it for publication.

What seemed to offer itself as a positive statement was a listing to the best of my knowledge of the major valuable items within the forty-plus titles, together with a series of photographs to illustrate each item.

Many people were helpful in allowing me to view their Lincoln material, in particular the author's widow, Mrs. Percy Rex of Pocasset, Mrs. Ralph Titcomb of Titcomb's Book Store in Sandwich, and Mrs. Mildred C. Chamberlin of East Orleans, a prominent dealer in Lincoln first editions and later books as well as Cape Cod material. Mrs. Titcomb was especially helpful in supplying valuable information concerning dust jackets for the first printings, notably *Cape Cod Ballads.*

I must also thank Jeremy Morritt, a collector of Lincoln material, for his help in lending two needed dustwrappers.

A few words about the book entries are appropriate. The titles, be they novels, poetry, or collections of short stories, are presented in the order of their being published, chronologically by first printing.

The description of each book begins with a printed, line-for-line description of the title-page, each line separated by a slash, for example, CAPE COD BALLADS / AND OTHER VERSE / [etc.] . The only distinction made is between capital and lower case letters in a line. Italic, the size of the type, or small capitals are not differentiated, and space between lines is not noted. If space between words in a line occurs, an appropriate space is indicated in the description, although the space shown does not illustrate exact space.

The second group indicates important information to be found on the verso or reverse of the title-page. Mention is omitted of the book having been printed in the United States, or a notice of reservation of rights, unless that particular line or lines is located within important data. The reader may take it for granted that most of the books were printed in the United States and that rights to them were reserved originally by the company publishing the particular edition.

The next section describes the printed sequence of pages, each page or set of pages being separated by a semicolon, with blank pages noted. Where pagination fails to display a number on the page at the beginning or end of a sequence, the page number is given in parenthesis, as (1)-397, or 1-(361).

Tipped-in plates, usually printed on a better paper, are noted in the next section. Their locations are stated, as "facing page 293", etc. This occurs when the plate is "tipped-in", or glued in to the book. The reverse of the illustration side of the tipped-in plate is blank.

The height and width of each book are the measurements of the page within the covers, given as height and width, respectively, in even or half-centimeters to the nearest two millimeters.

The binding is given as a color of cloth on boards, with the color of the lettering and/or stamping, cover illustrations, etc., fully described. Texturing or embossing of the cloth is usually not specified, unless it is part of the design of the stamping, for instance as a ground for a title, or in the case of decorative blind-stamping. Endpapers are specified as being unprinted, or where printed are fully described.

The preface, foreword, and/or introduction are then mentioned, if they exist, together with a synopsis of each of their contents.

The dedication, if any, is fully given with, if necessary, appropriate slashes to indicate copy from line to line.

The next item gives the number of sections or chapters with the subjects or subject and the basic plot or story-line of the book. These short descriptions are, with one or two minor exceptions, the verbatim descriptions of Reverend Rex from his larger chronological bibliography.

The last item is a brief bibliographical statement about the book, including the number, if any, printed on the last page of the book, together with notice of the publishing history, if any, of the material in the book.

While editing the bibliography for publication, I was constantly surprised at the bulk of material collected and organized in various ways by the Reverend Rex. I was able to use several parts of the material to verify my basic edited material. The short stories and poetry are virtually unchanged as to specific information.

With all the difficulties that I have encountered, I remain in awe of the wealth of time and dedication to Joe Lincoln represented by the body of information the Reverend Percy Rex amassed before his passing.

S. W. Sullwold

Courtesy Ralph and Nancy Titcomb and Mrs. Chamberlin

Poetry

A Query, with sketch; first known published poem by Joseph C. Lincoln; *League of American Wheelmen Bulletin and Good Roads* (hereafter noted as *LAW*); July 17, 1896; Vol. XXIV, No. 3, p. 91.

The Song of the Scorcher; *LAW*; July 24, 1896; Vol. XXIV, No. 4, p. 130.

Deacon Jones — Reformer; *LAW*; August 28, 1896; Vol. XXIV, No. 9, p. 314.

And There Are Others; with sketch signed "Reynolds & Lincoln"; *LAW*; September 11, 1896; Vol. XXIV, No. 11, p. 387.

16 to 1; about "free silver coinage" issue; *LAW*; September 18, 1896; Vol. XXIV, No. 12, p. 411.

Old Sis's Politics; *LAW*; September 25, 1896; Vol. XXIV, No.13, p. 451.

A Stick-in-the-Mud; with sketch "The Leading Six States", by Reynolds and Lincoln, p. 478; *LAW*; October 2, 1896; Vol. XXIV, No. 14, p. 470.

The Ballade of Polly's Hat; *LAW*; October 9, 1896; Vol. XXIV, No. 15, p. 484.

Not that Kind; *LAW*; October 16, 1896; Vol. XXIV, No. 16, p. 512.

A Happy Man; *LAW*; October 16, 1896; Vol. XXIV, No. 16, p. 535.

Free Gratis; *LAW*; November 13, 1896; Vol. XXIV, No. 20, p. 636.

Extreme Measures; *LAW*; November 13, 1896; Vol. XXIV, No. 20, p. 647.

"Ole Ez Perkins"; *LAW*; December 11, 1896; Vol. XXIV, No. 24, p. 752.

Santa Claus "Up to Date"; *LAW*; December 18, 1896; Vol. XXIV, No. 25, p. 773.

An Archaic Idyll; *LAW*; December 18, 1896; Vol. XXIV, No. 25, p. 778.

"Sister Simmons"; *LAW*; December 25, 1896; Vol. XXIV, No. 26, p. 801.

Loafing; with sketch; *LAW*; December 25, 1896; Vol. XXIV, No. 26, p. 815.

The Pessimist; with sketch; *LAW*; January 1, 1897; Vol. XXV, No. 1, p. 12.

A Seasonable Lyric; with sketch; *LAW*; January 8, 1897; Vol. XXV, No. 2, p. 41.

The Cornettist; with sketch; *LAW*; January 29, 1897; Vol. XXV, No. 5, p. 116.

The Sociable Down to the Church; *LAW*; January 29, 1897; Vol. XXV, No. 5, p. 127.
(Humorous sketches on p. 159 of this issue signed "J.L." include "A Fellow Feeling", "Bicycle Terms: 'A Home Trainer' ", "Time is Money", and "A Dilution & A Snare".)

John Anderson, My Jo; with sketch; *LAW*; February 5, 1897; Vol. XXV, No. 6, p

"Yap"; *LAW*; February 8, 1897; Vol. XXV, No. 6, p

Cut It Short; with sketch; *LAW*; February 12, 1897; Vol. XXV, No. 7, p. 164.
(Humorous sketches appear in this issue on p. 183, entitled "Another example wherein 'The Clothes Make the Man' ".)

A Retrospective Ramble; *LAW*; February 19, 1897, Vol. XXV, No. 8, p. 201.

Don't Crowd; *LAW*; February 26, 1897; Vol. XXV, No. 9, p. 213.

Sugared Pills; with sketch; *LAW*; March 12, 1897; Vol. XXV, No. 11, p. 262.

The Bullfrog Choir; with sketch; *LAW*; March 19, 1897; Vol. XXV, No. 12, p. 295.

Circle Day; with sketch; *LAW*; April 2, 1897; Vol. XXV, No. 14, p. 346.
(Humorous sketches appear in this issue on pp. 349 and

358, entitled "Fashion Item" and "A Full Hand", respectively.)

A Springtime Ode; with sketch; *LAW*; April 9, 1897; Vol. XXV, No. 15, p. 371.

The Sailor's Bier; *LAW*; April 16, 1897; Vol. XXV, No. 16, p. 396.

Someday; with sketch; *LAW*; April 23, 1897; Vol. XXV, No. 17, p. 440.

The Spare Bedroom; with sketch; *LAW*; April 30, 1897; Vol. XXV, No. 18, p. 479.

Sermon Time; with sketch; *LAW*; May 7, 1897; Vol. XXV, No. 19, p. 508.

Waiting for the Mail; with sketch; *LAW*; May 14, 1897; Vol. XXV, No. 20, p. 540.

"Home Agin' "; with sketch; *LAW*; May 28, 1897; Vol. XXV, No. 22, p. 612.

Bird's Nesting Time; with sketch; *LAW*; June 4, 1897; Vol. XXV, No. 23, p. 653.

Hookin' Melons; with sketch; *LAW*; June 11, 1897; Vol. XXV, No. 24, p. 688.

"Goin' in Swimmin' "; with sketch; *LAW*; June 18, 1897; Vol. XXV, No. 25, p. 730.

Friday Evening Meeting; with sketch; *LAW*; June 25, 1897; Vol. XXV, No. 26, p. 762.

The Little Old House by The Shore; with sketch; *LAW*; July 2, 1897; Vol. XXVI, No. 1, p. 18.

Sam Oatcake's Philosophy; *LAW*; July 9, 1897; Vol. XXVI, No. 2, p. 40.

The Girl in the Calico Gown; with sketch; *LAW*; July 9, 1897; Vol. XXVI, No.2, p. 56.

Ninety-Eight in the Shade; with sketch; *LAW*; July 16, 1897; Vol. XXVI. No. 3, p. 76.

"Camp Meetin' "; *LAW*; July 16, 1897; Vol. XXVI, No. 3, p. 87.

Retribution; *LAW*; July 23, 1897; Vol. XXVI, No. 4, p. 112.

The Hen, A Dyspeptic Lay; with sketch; *LAW*; July 23, 1897; Vol. XXVI, No. 4, p. 127.

The Country Kitten; with sketch; *LAW*; July 30, 1897; Vol. XXVI, No. 5, p. 148.

Love's Greeting; *LAW*; July 30, 1897; Vol. XXVI, No. 5, p. 161.

The Lady and the Camera; with sketch; *LAW*; August 6, 1897; Vol. XXVI, No. 6, p. 204.

Hard to Suit; with sketch; *LAW;* August 6, 1897; Vol. XXVI, No. 6, p. 207.

A Love Spell; with sketch; *LAW*; August 13, 1897; Vol. XXVI, No. 7, p. 235.

"The Weekly Clarion"; with sketch; *LAW*; August 13, 1897, Vol. XXVI, No. 7, p. 238.

The Ambitious Rock; *LAW*; August 20, 1897; Vol. XXVI, No. 8, p. 260.

The Gospel Tunes; with sketch; *LAW*; August 20, 1897; Vol. XXVI, No. 8, p. 262.

The Unkindest Cut; *LAW*; August 27, 1897; Vol. XXVI, No. 9, p. 297.

When the Tide Goes Out; with sketch; *LAW*; August 27, 1897; Vol. XXVI, No. 9, p. 300.

A Celebrity; (signed "J.L."); *LAW*; August 27, 1897; Vol. XXVI, No. 9, p. 293.

Grandfather's "Summer Sweets"; with sketch; *LAW*; September 3, 1897; Vol. XXVI, No. 10, p. 327.

Uncle Peleg on Kickers; with sketch; *LAW*; September 3, 1897; Vol. XXVI, No. 10, p. 333.

The Popular Song; with sketch; *LAW*; September 10, 1897; Vol. XXVI, No. 11, p. 358.

The Country Maid, Rondeau; *LAW*; September 10, 1897; Vol. XXVI, No. 11, p. 371.

"September Mornin's"; with sketch; *LAW*; September 17, 1897; Vol. XXVI, No. 12, p. 381.
    (This last issue marks the first appearance of Lincoln's name in the masthead as an associate editor.)

"Lover's Pond"; with sketch; *LAW*; October 1, 1897; Vol. XXVI, No. 14, p. 429.

Through the Fog; with sketch; *LAW*; October 1, 1897; Vol. XXVI, No. 14, p. 432.

Life Paths; *LAW*; October 8, 1897; Vol. XXVI, No. 15, p. 453.

Listenin' to the Wind; with sketch; *LAW*; October 8, 1897; Vol. XXVI, No. 15, p. 457.

A Chippewa Fall; with sketch; *LAW*; October 8, 1897; Vol. XXVI, No. 15, p. 458.

The Old Carryall; with sketch; *LAW*; October 15, 1897; Vol. XXVI, No. 16, p. 477.

A College Training; with sketch; *LAW*; October 15, 1897; Vol. XXVI, No. 15, p. 482.

Lute Hawkin's Wife; with sketch; *LAW*; October 22, 1897; Vol. XXVI, No. 17, p. 504.

Laying the Wires; *LAW*; October 22, 1897; Vol. XXVI, No. 17, p. 506. (Lincoln's name appears as a misprint: "by 'oe Lincoln".)

The Fisherman's Home; with sketch; *LAW*; October 29, 1897; Vol. XXVI, No. 18, p. 528.

The Rivals, A Department Store Ballad; with sketch; *LAW*; October 29, 1897; Vol. XXVI, No. 18, p. 531.

A Song of the Every-Days; *LAW*; November 5, 1897; Vol. XXVI, No. 19, p. 550.

The Village Oracle; with sketch; *LAW*; November 5, 1897; Vol. XXVI, No. 19, p. 553.

A True Bohemian; with sketch; *LAW*; November 12, 1897; Vol. XXVI, No. 20, p. 575.

"The Widder Clark"; with sketch; *LAW*; November 12, 1897; Vol. XXVI, No. 20, p. 577.

A Cold Reality; with sketch; *LAW*; November 19, 1897; Vol. XXVI, No. 21, p. 598.

November's Come; with sketch; *LAW*; November 19, 1897; Vol. XXVI, No. 21, p. 603.

Jim; with photo of a cat; *LAW*; November 26, 1897; Vol. XXVI, No. 22, p. 621.

A Crushed Hero; with sketch; *LAW*; November 26, 1897; Vol. XXVI, No. 22, p. 627.

An Old Boy; with sketch; *LAW*; December 3, 1897; Vol. XXVI, No. 23, p. 651.

The Ant and the Grasshopper; with sketch; *LAW*; December 10, 1897; Vol. XXVI, No. 24, p. 675.

Our Christmas Present; with sketch; *LAW*; December 17, 1897; Vol. XXVI, No. 25, p. 697.

The Lightkeeper; with sketch; *LAW*; December 24, 1897; Vol. XXVI, No. 26, p. 719. Page 731, see below.

(This issue of the *Bulletin* contains Daniel B. Latimer's tribute to Joe Lincoln, "Ludicrous Agreeable Writings — Joe's", one of the first if not the first comment on Joe Lincoln's writings.)

A New Year's Wish; *LAW*; December 31, 1897; Vol. XXVI, No. 27, p. 736.

"Walkin' Home with Mary"; with sketch; *LAW*; December 31, 1897; Vol. XXVI, No. 27, p. 742.

The Angel's Robe; *LAW*; February 11, 1898; Vol. XXVI, No. 6, p. 133.

The Croaker; with sketch; *LAW*; April 8, 1898; Vol. XXVII, No. 14, p. 350.

A Mission Fulfilled; with sketch; *LAW*; April 15, 1898; Vol. XXVII, No. 14, p. 381.

In Mother's Room; *LAW*; April 22, 1898; Vol. XXVII, No. 16, p. 403.

Uncle Eben Objects; with sketch; *LAW*; April 22, 1898; Vol. XXVII, No. 16, p. 414.

The Morning after The Storm; *LAW*; April 29, 1898; Vol. XXVII, No. 17, p. 435.

The Old Tune; with sketch; *LAW*; April 29, 1898; Vol. XXVII, No. 17, p. 445.

The Boys in Blue; with sketch; *LAW*; May 6, 1898; Vol. XXVII, No. 18, p. 478.

(The first of several poems on the Spanish-American War.)

The Biter Bit; with sketch; *LAW*; May 13, 1898; Vol. XXVII, No. 19, p. 509.

A Ballade of Blue-Jackets; *LAW*; May 20, 1898; Vol. XXVII, No 20, p. 539.

May Memories; with sketch; *LAW*; May 27, 1898; Vol. XXVII, No. 21, p. 564.

"Eb Small's Preaching"; with sketch; June 3, 1898; Vol. XXVII, No. 22, p. 591.

Ye Poet Carrolleth of Ye Glad Summer Time; full page sketch; *LAW*; June 3, 1898; Vol. XXVII, No. 22, p. 594.

Summer Nights at Grandpa's; with sketch; *LAW*; June 10, 1898; Vol. XXVII; No. 23, p. 621.

War & Mud; full page with sketch; *LAW*; June 17, 1898; Vol. XXVII, No. 24, p. 646.

Practical Politics; with sketch; *LAW*; June 24, 1898; Vol. XXVII, No. 25, p. 668.

A Glorious Fourth; with sketch; *LAW*; July 1, 1898; Vol. XXVIII, No. 1, p. 4.

A Cold Bite; with sketch; *LAW*; July 8, 1898; Vol. XXVIII, No. 2, p. 34.

At Eventide; *LAW*; July 8, 1898; Vol. XXVIII, No. 2, p. 39.

How the Deacon Drove the Calf; with sketch; *LAW*; July 15, 1898; Vol. XXVIII, No. 3, p. 57.

Ode to G. Washington Johnson, Errand Gent; with sketch; *LAW*; July 22, 1898; Vol. XXVIII, No. 4, p. 79.

The Sins of the Fathers; with sketch; *LAW*; July 29, 1898; Vol. XXVIII, No. 5, p. 98.

The Reg'lar Army Man; with sketch; *LAW*; August 5, 1898; Vol. XXVIII, No. 6, p. 117.

The Pickerel Pond; with sketch; *LAW*; August 19, 1898; Vol. XXVIII; No. 8, p. 162.

A Self-Sacrificing Pauper; with sketch; *LAW*; August 26, 1898; Vol. XXVIII, No. 9, p. 180.

The Miser; with sketch; *LAW*; September 2, 1898; Vol. XXVIII; No. 10, p. 198.

The Army Hardtack; with sketch; *LAW*; September 9, 1898; Vol. XXVIII, No. 11, p. 217.

The Four Legged Man; with sketch; *LAW*; September 16, 1898; Vol. XXVIII, No. 12, p. 232.

The Watchers; with sketch; *LAW*; September 23, 1898; Vol. XXVIII; No. 13, p. 247.

When Papa's Sick; with sketch; *LAW*; October 21, 1898; Vol. XXVIII, No. 17, p. 313.

Our Country's Dead; with sketch; *LAW*; October 28, 1898; Vol. XXVIII, No. 18, p. 330.

As Uncle Jabez Sees It; with sketch; *LAW*; November 25, 1898; Vol. XXVIII, No. 22, p. 393.

The Life Savers; with sketch; *LAW*; December 23, 1898; Vol. XXVIII, No. 26, p. 454.

A Snow Song; with sketch; *LAW*; December 30, 1898; Vol. XXVIII, No. 27, p. 473.

The Veteran's Tale of the Race; *Elliott's Magazine*; August, 1899, p. 62

"The Evening Hymn"; mss. typed and dated August 26, 1899.

Old Fashioned Posies; *Saturday Evening Post*; September 16, 1899.

Old Thanksgivin'; *Saturday Evening Post*; November 25, 1899, illustrated by Fanny T. Cory.

The Fate of Poor Rutherford; *Saturday Evening Post*; November 18, 1899.

The Old Daguerreotypes; mss. dated January 27, 1900.

The Winter Nights at Home; *Saturday Evening Post*; February 24, 1900, illustrated by Charlotte Harding.

The Cod-Fisher, A Journal of Civilization; *Harper's Weekly Magazine*; July 7, 1900; Vol. 64, p. 624.

A Thanksgiving Dream; American Press Association, Thanksgiving Day Page, published November, 1900, illustrated by C. W. Kannis.

"The Little Feller's Stocking"; *Saturday Evening Post*; December 8, 1900, illustrated by Fanny Y. Cory.

Uncle Ezra's New Year Reverie; American Press Association, December, 1900, "for use December 8, 1900."

Carrier's Address 1901; American Press Association, December, 1900. "Must Not Be Used Before December 15, 1900. Sold to but one paper in a Town."

On Her Account; *Century Illustrated Monthly Magazine*; February, 1901; Vol. 61, p. 640.

Columbia's Valentine; American Press Association; Valentine's Day Page, February 14, 1901.

The Ballad of McCarty's Trombone; American Press Association, St. Patrick's Day Page, March 1901, illustrated by Heyer.

Sunday Afternoons; *Current Literature*; May, 1901; Vol. 30, p. 577, originally published in *Saturday Evening Post.*

The Old Sword on the Wall; *Current Literature;* August, 1901; Vol. 31, p. 209; published from the *Saturday Evening Post.*

Christmas at the Windward Light; *Saturday Evening Post;* December 7, 1901; illustrated by F. R. Gruger and James Preston.

Thankful Jimmie; mss. typed and dated November 22, 1902.

Kekwan, A Poem; printed for private publication, November 29, 1902, 9 pgs., 7 x 5½ inches.

The Sweet Fern Cigarette; *Saturday Evening Post;* April 11, 1903, p. 39.

Sunday Clothes; *Saturday Evening Post;* October 31, 1903; p. 2.

Susan Van Doozen; sheet music, music by Henry Shepherd, c. 1903 by W. Hutchins.

Coming Home; *Saturday Evening Post;* November 21, 1903, p. 14.

A Voice for Santa Claus; *Ainslee's Magazine;* December, 1903; Vol. 12, p. 137.

The Parlor; *Saturday Evening Post;* January 23, 1904, p. 2.

Dennis to His Valentine; *Saturday Evening Post;* February 13, 1904; p. 7; illustrated by Emlen McConnell.

Driftin'; *Saturday Evening Post;* February 20, 1904; p. 4.

A Brother's Complaint; *Ainslee's Magazine;* March, 1904; Vol. 13, p. 49.

The Lady's Book; *Saturday Evening Post;* April 16, 1904; p. 10.

The Cooky Jar; *Saturday Evening Post;* June 18, 1904; p. 7; illustrated by James Preston.

The Dark Closet; *Saturday Evening Post;* September 10, 1904, p. 14, illustrated by James Preston.

Eatin' Day; *Saturday Evening Post;* November 19, 1904.

The Woodbox; *Saturday Evening Post;* December 3, 1904; p. 21, illustrated by J. J. Gould.

Tin-Roof Band; *Woman's Home Companion;* April, 1905; Vol. 32, p. 7.

"Fusts"; *Ainslee's Magazine;* February, 1906; Vol. 17, p. 44.

The Age of Wisdom; *Ainslee's Magazine;* March, 1906; Vol. 17, p. 78.

The Longest Night; *Everybody's Magazine;* December, 1908; Vol. 19, p. 771ff, illustrated by Eugenie Wireman.

"Spring - A Real Sonnet"; *Official Bulletin and Scrap Book of the League of American Wheelmen;* May, 1921.

Short Stories

The Studio Puzzle; with Howard Reynolds; *The Owl;* July, 1896; p. 35ff.

Mrs. Phidgit's System; *Harper's Bazaar;* January 13, 1900; Vol. 33, p. 43ff.

Josiah and the Seventh Son; *Saturday Evening Post;* June 23, 1900.

A Matter of Twenty Thousand; *Ainslee's Magazine;* October, 1900; Vol. 6, p. 247ff, illustrated by George Kerr.

The Woman from Nantucket; *Ainslee's Magazine;* November, 1900; Vol. 6, p. 347ff, illustrated by W. M. Burgher.

'Enry 'Iggins 'Eart Story; *Saturday Evening Post;* November 10, 1900.

Solon Pepper's Courtship; *Saturday Evening Post;* November 24, 1900.

When Santy Claus Went Wooing; *Ainslee's Magazine;* December, 1900; Vol. 6, p. 459ff, illustrated by W. M. Burgher.

In the Name of the Late Captain Kidd; *Saturday Evening Post;* January 26, 1901.

Blackbeard and the Emperor; *Ainslee's Magazine;* February, 1901; Vol. 7, p. 27ff, illustrated by Louis F. Grant.

Potank Sanitarium; *Saturday Evening Post;* February 23, 1901.

Through Fire and Water; *Ainslee's Magazine;* April, 1901; Vol. 7, p. 221ff, illustrated by W. A. Burgher.

The Fourth at Sebogan Light; American Press Association; Fourth of July Page, June, 1901.

The Red Drum; *Ainslee's Magazine;* July, 1901; Vol. 7, p. 509ff, illustrated by C. D. Williams.

The Committee of One; *Saturday Evening Post;* July 27, 1901.

The Revenge of Oaklegs; *Ainslee's Magazine;* August, 1901; Vol. 8, p. 31ff.

A Man and His Price; *Ainslee's Magazine;* September, 1901; Vol. 8, p. 131ff.

The House of Moffett; *New England Magazine;* September, 1901; Vol. 25, 81ff, illustrated by N. B. Greene.

Dusenberry's Birthday; *Ainslee's Magazine;* December, 1901; Vol. 8, p. 464ff, illustrated by C. D. Williams.

The Unexpectedness of Uncle D'rius; *Ainslee's Magazine;* January, 1902; Vol. 8, p. 539ff, illustrated by C. D. Williams.

Melissa Mayo's Special Providence; *Ainslee's Magazine;* May, 1902; Vol. 9, p. 539ff, illustrated by E. Hering.

The Strategy of General Minerva Small; *Ainslee's Magazine;* July, 1902; Vol. 9, p. 495ff, illustrated by C. D. Williams.

The Long-Lost Son; *Ainslee's Magazine;* November, 1902; Vol. 10, p. 48ff.

The Love of Lobelia 'Ankins; *Ainslee's Magazine;* February, 1903; Vol. 11, p. 140ff.

The Heroism of Surrender Peaslove; *Saturday Evening Post;* March 28, 1903; p. 18-19.

The Perils and Pitfalls; *Ainslee's Magazine;* July, 1903; Vol. 11, p. 129ff.

The Cruise of the "Dora Bassett"; *Ainslee's Magazine;* September, 1903; Vol. 12, p. 80ff.

A Pig and A Prodigal; *Ainslee's Magazine;* November, 1903; Vol. 12, p. 56ff.

The Will of Mr. Titcomb; *Ainslee's Magazine;* January 1904; Vol. 12, p. 77ff.

Moral 'Suasion and The Able Seaman; *Woman's Home Companion;* March 31, 1904; Vol. 31, p. 9-10.

The Montague-Fitzmaurice Letters; *Ainslee's Magazine;* April, 1904; Vol. 13, p. 56ff.

The Obligations of a Gentleman; *Ainslee's Magazine;* June, 1904; Vol. 13, p. 89ff.

Peleg Myrick's Piano; *Ainslee's Magazine;* July, 1904; Vol. 13, p. 36ff.

Love and the Locksmiths; *Saturday Evening Post;* August 27, 1904.

The Boojoo Man; *Ainslee's Magazine;* September, 1904; Vol. 14, p. 65ff.

In Friendship's Name; *Ainslee's Magazine;* October, 1904; Vol. 14 p. 111ff.

The Count and the Manager; *Ainslee's Magazine;* November, 1904 Vol. 14, p. 70ff.

A Prodigal Santa Claus; *Ainslee's Magazine;* December, 1904; Vol. 14, p. 113ff.

The Best Laid Plans; *Ainslee's Magazine;* January, 1905; Vol. 14, p. 94ff.

The South Shore Weather Bureau; *Everybody's Magazine;* February 1905; Vol. 12, p. 157ff.

An Assisted Backslider; *Ainslee's Magazine;* May, 1905; Vol. 15, p. 88ff.

The Simplicity of It; *Everybody's Magazine;* August, 1905; Vol. 13 p. 208ff, illustrated by Martin Justice.

The Dog Star; *Ainslee's Magazine;* September, 1905; Vol. 16, p. 81

The Mare and the Motor; *Ainslee's Magazine;* October, 1905; Vol. 16, p. 114ff.

His Native Heath; *Ainslee's Magazine;* November, 1905; Vol. 16, p. 116ff.

The Antiquers; *The American Magazine;* January, 1906; Vol. 61, p. 254ff.

The Mark on the Door; *Ainslee's Magazine;* February, 1906; Vol. 1 p. 75ff.

Heights of Art; *Everybody's Magazine;* April, 1906; Vol. 14, p. 445

Two Pairs of Shoes; *McClure's Magazine;* April, 1906; Vol. 26, p. 623ff, illustrated by Martin F. Justice.

The Reincarnation of Captain Strabo; *Ainslee's Magazine;* April, 1906; Vol. 17, p. 97ff.

Idella and the White Plague; *McClure's Magazine;* May, 1906; Vol. 27, p. 104ff, illustrated by John Sloan.

A Tarnished Star; *Everybody's Magazine;* May, 1906; Vol. 14, p. 631ff, illustrated by Rollin Kirby.

Ward and Reward; *Ainslee's Magazine;* August, 1906; Vol. 18, p. 75ff.

The Meanness of Rosy; *Everybody's Magazine;* September, 1906; Vol. 15, p. 377ff.

The Changing Years; *Ainslee's Magazine;* October, 1906; Vol. 18, p. 105ff.

"Jonesy"; *Everybody's Magazine;* October, 1906; Vol. 15, p. 539ff, illustrated by John Wolcott Adams.

The Chariot of Fate; *Ainslee's Magazine;* December, 1906; Vol. 18, p. 111ff.

An Old Fashioned Boy's Christmas; *Country Life in America;* December, 1906; Vol. 11, p. 177ff, illustrated with photos by Frances and Mary Allen.

Issy and the Other; *Everybody's Magazine;* January, 1907; Vol. 16, p. 71ff, illustrated by J. M. Flagg.

Theophilus the Diplomat; *Ainslee's Magazine;* February 1907; Vol. 19, p. 121ff.

The Jewel of Consistency; *Ainslee's Magazine;* April, 1907; Vol. 19, p. 84ff.

Esteemed Contemporaries; *Everybody's Magazine;* June, 1907; Vol. 6, p. 800ff, illustrated by Fletcher R. Ransom.

Cape Cod Clambake; *Good Housekeeping;* July 1907; Vol. 14, p. 3ff, illustrated by Martin F. Justice.

A Case of Trouble; *Ainslee's Magazine;* July, 1907; Vol. 19, p. 82ff.

Pride of Craft; *Ainslee's Magazine;* September, 1907; Vol. 20, p. 95ff.

The Inside Facts; *Collier's Weekly;* September 21, 1907; Vol. 39, p. 21ff, illustrated by A. B. Frost.

Legitimate Transaction; *American Magazine;* October, 1907; Vol. 64, p. 651ff, illustrated by Will Crawford.

The Moral Tone; *Ainslee's Magazine;* November, 1907; Vol. 20, p. 135ff.

The Cruise of the Red Car; *Munsey's;* November, 1907; p. 235ff.

Our House; *Colliers Weekly;* November 23, 1907; Vol. 40, p. 16, illustrated by Clara Elsene Peck.

Making a Man of Him; *Everybody's Magazine;* January, 1908; Vol. 18, p. 15ff.

Invention and Investment; *Ainslee's Magazine;* January, 1908; Vol. 20, p. 96-106.

An Inherited Eden; *Ainslee's Magazine;* March, 1908; Vol. 21, p. 124ff.

The Old Maids; *Collier's Weekly;* May 2, 1908; Vol. 41, p. 20ff, illustrated by Clifford Carleton.

Our Oldest Inhabitant; *Collier's Weekly;* August 29, 1908; Vol. 41, p. 41ff.

The Petticoat Cruise; *Everybody's Magazine;* September, 1908; Vol. 19, p. 400ff, illustrated by H. G. Williamson.

Teacher; *Collier's Weekly;* September 12, 1908; Vol. 41, p. 20ff.

Cupid and Clam Fritters; *Ainslee's Magazine;* November, 1908; Vol. 22, p. 43ff.

The Back Bedroom; *Ainslee's Magazine;* December, 1908; Vol. 22, p. 45ff.

Seer and Serpent; *Everybody's Magazine;* January, 1909; Vol. 20; p. 14ff, illustrated by Frederick R. Gruger.

The School Picnic; *Success Magazine;* January, 1909; p. 87.

The Valuable Christopher; *Munsey's Magazine;* February, 1909; p. 718ff, illustrated by George Wright.

Willie; *Ainslee's Magazine;* April, 1909; Vol. 23, p. 126ff.

As He Thinketh; *Everybody's Magazine;* May, 1909; Vol. 20, p. 599ff, illustrated by Martin F. Justice.

The Cure; *Ainslee's Magazine;* May, 1909; Vol. 23, p. 20ff.

A Vision Sent; *Everybody's Magazine;* July, 1909; Vol 21, p. 13ff, illustrated by Rollin Kirby.

The Transit of Venus; *Success Magazine;* July 4, 1909; p. 437ff, illustrated by Hanson Booth.

The "Pinks" and the "Jonquils"; *Ainslee's Magazine;* August, 1909; Vol. 24, p. 113ff.

The Deep Sea and the Dog; *Ainslee's Magazine;* November, 1909; Vol. 24, p. 99ff.

Way of Business; *Everybody's Magazine;* January, 1910; Vol. 22, p. 60ff, illustrated by Martin F. Justice.

Tinker the Tar; *Ainslee's Magazine;* February, 1910; Vol. 25, p. 23ff.

The Mountain and Mahomet; *Everybody's Magazine;* March, 1910; Vol. 22, p. 380ff.

The Debut of the Delanceys; *Ainslee's Magazine;* March, 1910; Vol. 25, p. 20ff.

The Pocketbook; *Ainslee's Magazine;* June, 1910; Vol. 25, p. 43ff.

Deborah and the Wizard; *Munsey's Magazine;* July, 1910; Vol. 43, p. 457ff.

Dancing Billows; *Saturday Evening Post;* February 4, 1911; Vol. 183, p. 22ff.

The Woman Haters; *Ainslee's Magazine;* May, 1911; Vol. 27, p. 1ff.

Pendlebury Tree; *Saturday Evening Post;* August 12, 1911; Vol. 184, p. 13ff, illustrated by Chase Emerson.

Ostable Postmastership; *Saturday Evening Post;* August 26, 1911; Vol. 184, p. 10ff, illustrated by May Wilson Preston.

Sign of the Windmill; *Saturday Evening Post;* January 27, 1912; Vol. 184, p. 5ff.

The Force and the Object; *Everybody's Magazine;* March, 1912; Vol. 26, 360ff, illustrated by Martin F. Justice.

A Question of Birthdays: A Cape Cod Romance; *Good Housekeeping;* May, 1912; Vol. 54, p. 603ff, illustrated by Henry Hutt.

Bethuel Nose's Nephew; *Good Housekeeping;* January, 1913; Vol. 56, p. 14ff, illustrated by Thomas J. Fogarty.

Guest from Samaria; *Everybody's Magazine;* May, 1915; Vol. 32, p. 543ff, illustrated by Harold Brett.

The Safe and the Sane; *Red Book Magazine;* July, 1919; Vol. 33, p. 83ff, illustrated by Rea Irvin.

Peacock's Feathers; *Red Book Magazine;* Vol. not known, 1919.

Injun Control; *Cosmopolitan;* November, 1920.

The Realist; *The Ladies Home Journal;* July, 1923; Vol. 40, p. 8ff, illustrated by Harold Brett.

Independence for Two; *The Ladies Home Journal;* November, 1923; Vol. 40; p. 16ff, illustrated by Gale Hoskins.

By the Airline; *The Ladies Home Journal;* December, 1923; Vol. 40, p. 24ff, illustrated by Clark Foy.

The Owl and the Mermaid; *Pictorial Review;* June, 1926; Vol. 27, p. 7ff, illustrated by Clarence Row.

Vigorine and the Missing Papers; *Saturday Evening Post;* September 18, 1926; Vol. 199, p. 8ff.

The Luck Piece; *The Ladies Home Journal;* December, 1926; Vol. 43; p. 3ff, illustrated by Thomas Fogarty.

An Honest Man's Business; *Saturday Evening Post;* July 23, 1927; Vol. 200, p. 10ff.

A Question of Title; *Ladies Home Journal;* November, 1927; Vol.
44, p. 6ff, illustrated by Grattan Condon.

The Middleman; *The Ladies Home Journal;* January, 1928; Vol.
45, p. 8ff, illustrated by Arthur Edrop.

Sandwich Overlay; *The Country Gentleman;* Issue unknown, 1928.

Limits; *Saturday Evening Post;* November 24, 1928; Vol. 201,
p. 12ff.

The Cure; *The Ladies Home Journal;* December, 1928; Vol. 45,
p. 12ff, illustrated by Herbert M. Stoops.

The Cog that Slipped; *Saturday Evening Post;* August 10, 1929;
Vol. 202, p. 16ff.

Payment Deferred; *Ladies Home Journal;* October, 1929; Vol. 46,
p. 8ff, illustrated by Harold Brett.

The Old Hooker; *Saturday Evening Post;* October 19, 1929; Vol.
202, p. 18ff, illustrated by Harold Brett.

The Castaway; *Good Housekeeping;* November, 1930; Vol. 91;
p. 18ff, illustrated by Jules Gotlieb.

The Soft Snap; *Hearst's International-Cosmopolitan;* November,
1931; Vol. 91, p. 44ff, illustrated by James Montgomery Flagg.

Two of the issues of the *League of American Wheelmen Bulletin* in which
Joe published his poetry. The left hand issue is from 1898, the right
from 1896.   *Courtesy Mrs. Percy F. Rex.*

Several magazine covers of the era. *Courtesy Mrs. Chamberlin and Mrs. Titcomb.*

Lifting Fog; *The Ladies Home Journal;* July, 1932; Vol. 49; p. 11ff, illustrated by Anton Otto Fischer.

Shale-Bastable Roots; *The Ladies Home Journal;* November, 1935; Vol. 52, p. 23ff, illustrated by Rico Tomaso.

Mr. Expert; *American Magazine;* March, 1937; Vol. 123, 52ff, illustrated by Gilbert Bundy.

CAPE COD BALLADS

AND OTHER VERSE

BY JOE LINCOLN
(Joseph Crosby Lincoln)

WITH DRAWINGS BY EDWARD W. KEMBLE

ALBERT BRANDT: PUBLISHER
TRENTON, NEW JERSEY
1902

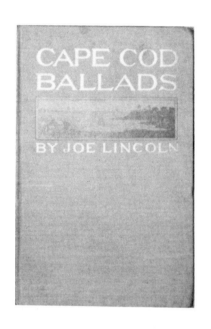

The first printing of *Cape Cod Ballads and Other Verse.*
Courtesy Ralph and Nancy Titcomb

202

The Books

CAPE COD BALLADS — 1902

CAPE COD BALLADS / AND OTHER VERSE / BY JOE
LINCOLN / (JOSEPH CROSBY LINCOLN) / WITH DRAWINGS
BY EDWARD W. KEMBLE / (publisher's logo) /ALBERT
BRANDT: PUBLISHER / TRENTON, NEW JERSEY / 1902

Copyright, 1902, by Albert Brandt / All rights reserved / Printed at THE
BRANDT PRESS, Trenton, N.J., U.S.A.

Half-title; two blank pages; frontispiece as full-page illustration; title-page;
verso; dedication page; blank page; untitled acknowledgments; blank page;
contents in three pages; list of illustrations in two pages; blank page; 17-
198; two pages of Brandt advertising.

Twenty three black and white line illustrations by Edward W. Kemble,
including frontispiece as a full-page illustration and full-page illustrations
on numbered pages 45, 54, 68, 87, 99, 114, 143, 165 and 175, with accompanying illustrations on pages 27, 31, 38, 61, 77, 105, 118, 128, 137, 152,
158, 182 and 186. The full-page frontispiece has a tissue tip-in between
it and the title-page to prevent offsetting of ink.

19½ x 12½ cm.

Yellow cloth on boards, stamped in gold lettering front and spine, with
brown printed illustration signed by artist Mira Burr Edson on front, suggestion of mast, spar and rigging on spine in brown, and seagull in brown on
back upper left corner. Unprinted endpapers. Dustwrapper is buff, printed
in brown lettering, with on front a line illustration of an inlet with light-
houses and a house, 3 x 10.5 cm., with on back a seagull in the upper left
corner. Front and back inside flaps have advertising for three Brandt books.

Acknowledgments page by author explains the sources for the contents and
gives the names of the original magazines they were published in.

Dedication is To My Wife / THIS BOOK IS AFFECTIONATELY / DED—
DEDICATED

Contents: Seventy nine poems, published previously in magazines and gathered here for publication in book form.

This is the first printing of this title, and the author's first published book.

CAPE COD BALLADS — Appleton 1st

CAPE COD BALLADS / AND OTHER VERSE / BY / JOSEPH
C. LINCOLN / WITH DRAWINGS BY EDWARD W. KEMBLE /
(publisher's logo) / D. APPLETON AND COMPANY / NEW YORK
AND LONDON / 1910

COPYRIGHT, 1910, BY / D. APPLETON AND COMPANY / (short rule) /
COPYRIGHT, 1902, BY ALBERT BRANDT / (short rule)

Half-title; two blank pages; frontispiece; title-page; verso; dedication page;
blank page; untitled acknowledgments; blank page; contents in three pages;
list of illustrations in two pages; blank page; 17-198; two blank pages.

Twenty three black and white line illustrations by Edward W. Kemble in
the same locations as the original edition of Cape Cod Ballads.

19 x 12 cm.

Green cloth on boards, stamped in gold on cover and spine, with on front
a design stamped in slightly darker green of a ship in a circle between two
pairs of fish. Green spine stamping has heart-shaped rope knot design. Unprinted endpapers.

Acknowledgments and dedication as in the original edition.

Contents remain the same from the original edition.

This is known as the "Appleton first" printing.

CAPE COD BALLADS

AND OTHER VERSE

BY
JOSEPH C. LINCOLN

WITH DRAWINGS BY EDWARD W. KEMBLE

D. APPLETON AND COMPANY
NEW YORK AND LONDON
1910

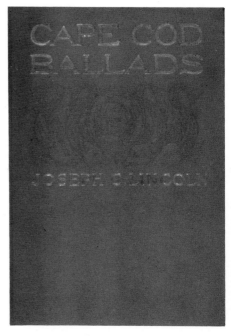

Courtesy Mrs. Mildred C. Chamberlin

204

CAP'N ERI / A Story of the Coast / BY / JOSEPH C. LINCOLN / (line illustration in double-rule box, 2.3 x 2.3 cm.) / ILLUSTRATED BY / CHARLOTTE WEBER / NEW YORK / A. S. BARNES & COMPANY / MCMIV / (all above copy enclosed in a box-rule, with stylized scallop design border outside the box-rule.)

Copyright, 1904, / By A. S. BARNES & CO. / All rights reserved / (single scallop design) / February

Half-title; blank page; title page; verso; dedication page; blank page; contents in two pages; list of illustrations; blank page; (1)-397; blank page; eight pages advertising.

Four black and white tipped-in plates, including frontispiece, and facing pages 14, 108, and 391. Red color overprinted on frontispiece.

19 x 13 cm.

Blue cloth on boards, lettering and designs in black and yellow (black geese over white-rimmed moon at top, black schooner sails with white lantern overprinted with white title at bottom; black goose with white title on top spine, publisher in white at bottom.) Endpapers unprinted.

Dedication: "Dedicated / to the memory of / my Mother"

Contents: Twenty-one chapters in which Cap'n Eri Hedge, Cap'n Perez Ryder and Cap'n Jeremiah Burgess seek a housekeeper for their home in Orham.

First book of prose fiction by Joseph C. Lincoln. This is the first printing of this title.

Courtesy Mrs. Mildred C. Chamberlin

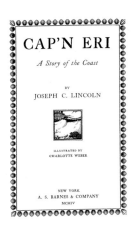

Partners of the / Tide / By / Joseph C. Lincoln / Author of "Cap'n Eri" / Frontispiece in colors by / Charlotte Weber / Decorations by John Rae / (small line illustration in a "frame") / New York / A. S. Barnes & Co. / 1905 / (the entire print-page enclosed in a decorative border composed of "scalloped" ropes and two crabs.)

Copyright, 1905 / BY / A. S. BARNES & CO. / Published April, 1905

Half-title; advertising page; title-page; verso; contents page; blank page; half-title; blank page; 1-400; seven advertising pages; blank page.

One black and white tipped-in plate as frontispiece by Charlotte Weber, chapter headings have line drawings by John Rae.

18 x 12½ cm.

Grey cloth on boards, lettering in black on front and spine, with on front illustration of mast-top with sails in black, white and yellow with white seagulls, and on spine, one white seagull.

Twenty-two chapters in which Cap'n Ezra Titcomb and Bradley Nickerson, orphan, use the tide for success in the wrecking business.

This is the first printing of Partners of the Tide. No number appears on the last printed novel-page, which is customary with the Barnes editions of Lincoln's works.

Courtesy Mrs. Mildred C. Chamberlin

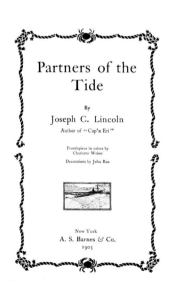

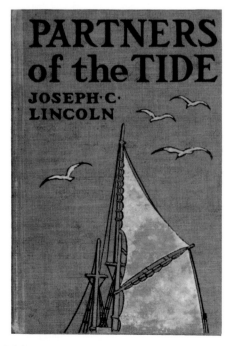

MR. PRATT / A NOVEL / BY / JOSEPH C. LINCOLN / AUTHOR OF / "CAP'N ERI", "PARTNERS OF THE TIDE." / FRONTIS- PIECE BY / HORACE TAYLOR / (line illustration within a line illustrated "frame") / NEW YORK / A. S. BARNES AND COM— PANY / 1906

COPYRIGHT, 1906, BY / A. S. BARNES & COMPANY / (short rule) / Published May, 1906

Half-title; advertising page; title-page; verso; dedication page; blank page; contents page; blank page; acknowledgments or prefacing page; blank page; 1-342.

One black and white tipped-in plate as frontispiece by Horace Taylor.

18½ x 12½ cm.

Blue cloth on boards; lettering in white front and spine, with on front the black, white and red likeness of a man rowing in a black and white stamped circle, 5.2 cm. in diameter. Unprinted endpapers.

Dedication: "To / MY FRIEND / GILMAN HALL".

Nineteen chapters in which Solomon Pratt of Orham helps two New Yorkers to briefly live the "natural life".

This is the assumed first printing of Mr. Pratt. No number is present at at the end of the book, which was customary with Barnes.

Courtesy Mrs. Mildred C. Chamberlin

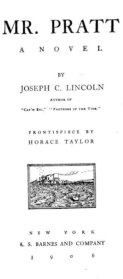

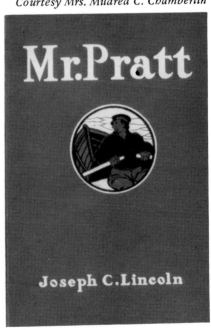

THE
"OLD HOME HOUSE"

BY
JOSEPH C. LINCOLN
Author of "MR. PRATT," "CAP'N ERI," "PARTNERS
OF THE TIDE," ETC., ETC.

NEW YORK
A. S. BARNES & COMPANY
1907

The first Barnes printing of *The Old Home House.* The Barnes editions of Lincoln's works seem to have been issued without dustwrappers.
Courtesy Mrs. Mildred C. Chamberlin

208

THE OLD HOME HOUSE — 1907

THE / "OLD HOME HOUSE" / BY / JOSEPH C. LINCOLN / Author of "MR. PRATT," "CAP'N ERI," "PARTNERS OF THE TIDE," ETC., ETC. / (line drawing of character in small boat on seas with cloud, 3 x 1.9 cm.) / NEW YORK / A. S. BARNES & COMPANY / 1907

Copyright 1907 by / A. S. BARNES & COMPANY

Half-title; publisher's advertising page for "Mr. Pratt"; title-page; verso; contents; blank page; list of illustrations; blank page; 1-291; blank page; four advertising pages. Two or three unnumbered pages separate each story but do not add to the page numbers.

One black and white tipped-in illustration as frontispiece by Martin Justice, "She Jibed, — Oh, yes — She Jibed," as originally seen with other illustrations by Justice in the magazine publication of "Two Pairs of Shoes," the first story in The Old Home House. Line illustrations throughout the book by Robert A. Graef.

18½ x 12½ cm.

Light brown cloth on boards, cover designs in light green and black with light green and black lettering front and spine. Unprinted endpapers.

Eleven short stories about the Old Home House, in which the comedy team of Barzilla Wingate, Cap'n Jonadab Wixon, and Peter Theodosius Brown "turn Wellmouth Port from a sand flea's paradise into a hospital where city dwellers could have their bank accounts amputated and not suffer more'n was necessary."

Originally published in various magazines at various times as follows:

Two Pairs of Shoes	McClure's Magazine, April, 1906
The Count and the Manager	Ainslee's Magazine, November, 1904
The South Shore Weather Bureau	Everybody's Magazine, Feb., 1905
The Dog Star	Ainslee's Magazine, September, 1905
The Mare and the Motor	Ainslee's Magazine, October, 1905
The Mark on the Door	Ainslee's Magazine, February, 1906
The Love of Lobelia 'Ankins	Ainslee's Magazine, February, 1903
The Meanness of Rosy	Everybody's Magazine, September, 1906
The Antiquers	American Magazine, January, 1906
His Native Heath	Ainslee's Magazine, November, 1905
"Jonesy"	Everybody's Magazine, October, 1906

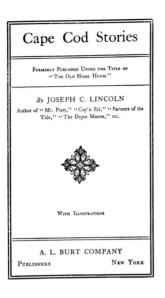

Cape Cod Stories

FORMERLY PUBLISHED UNDER THE TITLE OF
"THE OLD HOME HOUSE"

By JOSEPH C. LINCOLN
Author of "Mr. Pratt," "Cap'n Eri," "Partners of the
Tide," "The Depot Master," etc.

WITH ILLUSTRATIONS

A. L. BURT COMPANY
PUBLISHERS   NEW YORK

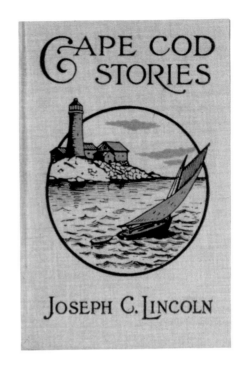

Courtesy Mrs. Mildred C. Chamberlin.

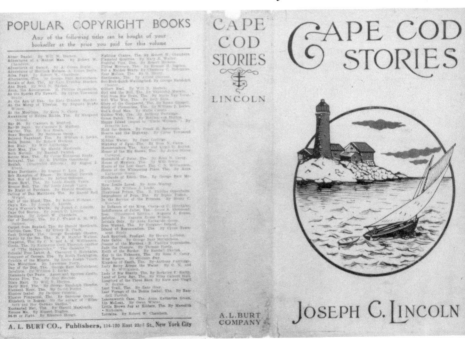

CAPE COD STORIES — (1912)

Cape Cod Stories / (double rule) / FORMERLY PUBLISHED
UNDER THE TITLE OF / "THE OLD HOME HOUSE" / (rule) /
By JOSEPH C. LINCOLN / Author of "Mr. Pratt," "Cap'n Eri,"
"Partners of the / Tide," "The Depot Master," etc. / (decorative
diamond design, 2.3 x 2.4 cm.) / WITH ILLUSTRATIONS /
(double rule) / A. L. BURT COMPANY / PUBLISHERS
NEW YORK / (the entire type-page enclosed in a double
box-rule.)

Copyright, 1907, by / A. S. BARNES & COMPANY

Two blank pages; half-title; blank page; title-page; verso; contents page;
blank page; list of illustrations; blank page; half-title; blank page; 1-291;
blank page; ten advertising pages; six blank pages.

One black and white tipped-in plate as frontispiece, "She Jibed - Oh, Yes,
- She Jibed", together with line illustrations as in the original edition of
The Old Home House.

18½ x 12½ cm.

Light olive cloth, black lettering on front and spine, with on front a pictorial printed in black with white features as a circle containing rocks, sea,
a lighthouse and a sailboat, these last two projecting slightly beyond the
circle-border. Anchor-and-rope design in black on spine. Unprinted
endpapers. Dustwrapper is white paper with black lettering on front and
spine, with on front an orange and black lighthouse on a cliff, with a sailboat in the foreground printed in white and orange with black outlines de-
lineating all of the objects. Back of the dustwrapper is a list of Burt books,
which continues on the inside front and back flaps.

Contents are the same as for the Old Home House.

This edition has (1) printed on the last novel-page, indicating that this
is the first printing of this title as Cape Cod Stories.

CY WHITTAKER'S
PLACE

By

JOSEPH C. LINCOLN

Author of
"Cap'n Eri," "Mr. Pratt," etc.

WITH ILLUSTRATIONS BY
WALLACE MORGAN

D. APPLETON AND COMPANY
NEW YORK   MCMVIII

"'Isn't it a truly bell? Didn't it ought to ring?'"
[Page 91]

The first printing of *Cy Whittaker's Place. Courtesy Mrs. Mildred C. Chamberlin*

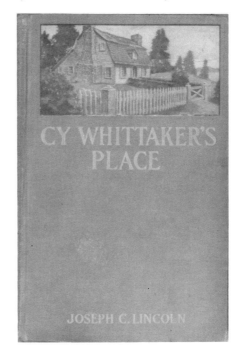

CY WHITTAKER'S PLACE — 1908

CY WHITTAKER'S / PLACE / By / JOSEPH C. LINCOLN / Author of / "Cap'n Eri," "Mr. Pratt," etc. / (publisher's logo) / WITH ILLUSTRATIONS BY / WALLACE MORGAN / D. APPLETON AND COMPANY / NEW YORK   MCMVIII

Copyright, 1908, BY / D. APPLETON AND COMPANY / [flush left] Published, September, 1908.

Half-title; two blank pages; frontispiece; title-page; verso; dedication page; blank page; contents in two pages; list of illustrations in two pages; 1-(403); three blank pages; with the exception of plates as listed below.

Twenty seven black and white line illustrations by Wallace Morgan, including frontispiece and full-page illustrations facing pages 24, 46, 110, 134, 152, 166, 250, 258, 270, 302, 344, 352, 362, 382 and 396. Other illustrations occur on pages 14, 33, 73, 107, 123, 164, 208, 225, 231 and 245.

19 x 12½ cm.

Light green cloth on boards, white lettering on front cover and spine, paper label illustrated with full-color cottage with white picket fence, 5½ x 11 cm., pasted within blind-stamped rectangle slightly larger than label. Unprinted endpapers.

Dedication: "TO / F. S. L." (His wife, Florence Sargent Lincoln)

Twenty one chapters, in which Cap'n Cyrus M. Whittaker adopts and raises the almost orphan, Emily Richards Thomas, with the help of Bailey Bangs and Asaph Tiditt in Bayport.

This is the first printing of this title, although no number appears on the last printed novel-page.

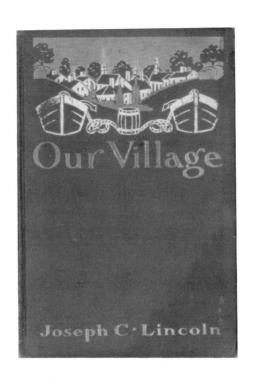

OUR VILLAGE

BY

JOSEPH C. LINCOLN
Author of "Cy Whittaker's Place,"
"Cap'n Eri," etc.

ILLUSTRATED

D. APPLETON AND COMPANY
NEW YORK
1909

"'Good morning, Pashy. How d'ye do, Huldy? Nice seasonable
weather we're having.'"

[Page 67.]

The first printing of *Our Village*.　*Courtesy Ralph and Nancy Titcomb*

214

OUR VILLAGE — 1909

OUR VILLAGE / BY / JOSEPH C. LINCOLN / Author of "Cy Whittaker's Place," / "Cap'n Eri," etc. / (line illustration, 3.9 x 2.9 cm.) / ILLUSTRATED / D. APPLETON AND COMPANY / NEW YORK / 1909

COPYRIGHT, 1909, BY / D. APPLETON AND COMPANY / (short rule) / Copyright, 1906, by Doubleday, Page & Company / Copyright, 1907, by The Phelps Publishing Company / Copyright, 1908, by P. F. Collier & Son / Copyright, 1909, by The Success Company. / [flush right] Published, April, 1909

Half-title; list of books by Joseph C. Lincoln; title-page; verso; acknowledgments page; blank page; list of illustrations; blank page; half-title; 3-(183); blank page; four advertising pages.

Olive cloth on boards stamped in gold with on front, two dories in white, with rope and a barrel in between them. Spine stamped in gold with a white anchor-and-dory design. Fore- and bottom edges are untrimmed, top edge is imitation gold leaf. Unprinted endpapers.

Four black and white tipped-in plates by C. Carleton, including frontispiece and facing pages 52, 120 and 182.

Dedication: TO / S.E.H. / WHO KNEW AND LOVED / "OUR HOUSE" / AND THOSE WHO DWELT THEREIN

Acknowledgments gives original sources for the contents of Our Village and thanks the editors of the various magazines for their permission to reprint.

Contents are seven sketches of life in a small Cape Cod village in the 19th Century, previously published in various magazines at various times, as follows:

Our House	Collier's Weekly, November 23, 1907
A Cape Cod Clambake	Good Housekeeping, July, 1907
The Old Maids	Collier's Weekly, May 2, 1908
The School Picnic	Success Magazine
Our Oldest Inhabitant	Collier's Weekly, August 29, 1908
Teacher	Collier's Weekly, September 12, 1908
A Christmas Memory	An Old Fashioned Boy's Christmas, Country Life in America, December, 1906

This edition has a (1) printed on the last page of the book, and is the first printing of this title.

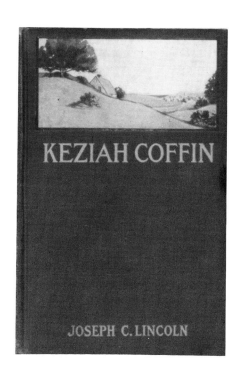

The first printing of *Keziah Coffin. Courtesy Ralph and Nancy Titcomb*

"'All right,' she said; 'then I suppose I shall have to take it.'"
[Page 88.]

KEZIAH COFFIN

BY

JOSEPH C. LINCOLN
AUTHOR OF "CY WHITTAKER'S PLACE,"
"CAP'N ERI," ETC.

WITH ILLUSTRATIONS BY
WALLACE MORGAN

D. APPLETON AND COMPANY
NEW YORK AND LONDON: MCMIX

216

KEZIAH COFFIN — 1909

KEZIAH COFFIN / BY / JOSEPH C. LINCOLN / AUTHOR OF "CY WHITTAKER'S PLACE," / "CAP'N ERI," ETC. / (publisher's logo) / WITH ILLUSTRATIONS BY / WALLACE MORGAN / D. APPLETON AND COMPANY / NEW YORK AND LONDON: MCMIX

COPYRIGHT, 1909, BY / D. APPLETON AND COMPANY / [flush left] Published September, 1909

Two blank pages; half-title; list of books by Joseph C. Lincoln; blank page; frontispiece; title-page; verso; contents in two pages; list of illustrations; blank page; 1-(387); blank page; two advertising pages. Exceptions to the pagination are noted below as full-page illustrations.

Eight black and white full-page illustrations by Wallace Morgan on unnumbered pages with blank pages backing them including the frontispiece and facing pages 18, 38, 120, 178, 220, 308 and 320.

19 x 12½ cm.

Olive green cloth on boards with white stamping on front and spine, red- and green-tinted paper label, 5.5 x 11.1 cm., on front top illustrating a cottage behind a hill, with a tree on the hill and a cottage in the distance with the ocean beyond. A blind-stamped area slightly larger than the label to accomodate the same. Unprinted endpapers.

Twenty two chapters in which the Reverend John Ellery and his house-keeper, Mrs. Keziah Hall Coffin, attempt Christian unity in Trumet.

This edition has a (1) printed on the last novel-page, (387), and is the first printing of this title.

"Sim, . . . have you heard anything about Williams buying
the Smalley house?"

[Page 13]

THE
DEPOT MASTER

BY

JOSEPH C. LINCOLN

AUTHOR OF "CY WHITTAKER'S PLACE,"
"KEZIAH COFFIN," ETC.

ILLUSTRATED

D. APPLETON AND COMPANY
NEW YORK AND LONDON: 1910

The first printing of *The Depot Master. Courtesy Mrs. Mildred C. Chamberlin*

THE DEPOT MASTER — 1910

THE / DEPOT MASTER / BY / JOSEPH C. LINCOLN / AUTHOR
OF "CY WHITTAKER'S PLACE," / "KEZIAH COFFIN," ETC. /
(publisher's logo) / ILLUSTRATED / D. APPLETON AND COM-
PANY / NEW YORK AND LONDON: 1910

COPYRIGHT, 1910, BY / D. APPLETON AND COMPANY / [flush left]
Published May, 1910 / Copyright, 1907, by the Phillips Publishing Company /
Copyright, 1901, 1904, 1907, 1909, by Ainslee Magazine Company /
Copyright, 1907, by P.F. Collier and Son / Copyright, 1907, 1909, 1910,
by the Ridgway Company / Copyright, 1907, by The Frank A. Munsey
Company.

Half-title; list of books by Joseph C. Lincoln; title-page; verso; contents
page; blank page; list of illustrations; blank page; 1-(380).

Four black and white tipped-in plates by Howard Heath including frontispiece and facing pages 180, 276 and 372.

19 x 12½ cm.

Reddish-brown cloth on boards with white lettering on front and spine.
Oval-shaped two color printed label on front depicting the Depot Master
with pipe, hat and mittens. Unprinted endpapers.

Eighteen short stories, some originally published separately in magazines,
in which Cap'n Solomon Berry, the depot master, is in the center of village
life in East Harniss.

This printing has a (1) on the last novel-page, (380), and is the first printing
of this title. Some of the material was originally published as short stories
in magazines. Previous publication was as follows:

Supply and Demand	Ogden Williams and the Johnny Cake,
A Baby and a Robbery	Willie, Ainslee's Magazine, April, 1909
Aviation and Avarice	The Inside Facts, Collier's Weekly, September 21, 1907
The Obligations of a Gentleman	Ainslee's Magazine, June, 1904
A Vision Sent	Everybody's Magazine, July, 1909
Dusenberry's Birthday	Ainslee's Magazine, December, 1901
Effie's Fate	Seer and Serpent, Everybody's Magazine, January, 1909
The Cruise of the Red Car	Munsey's Magazine, November, 1907
Issy's Revenge	Issy and "the Other", Everybody's Magazine, January, 1907
The Mountain and Mahomet	Everybody's Magazine, March, 1910

The first printing of *The Woman Haters.* *Courtesy Mrs. Mildred C. Chamberlin.*

"'Who said I'd done anything? It's a lie.'"
[Page 44.]

THE

WOMAN-HATERS

A YARN OF EASTBORO TWIN-LIGHTS

BY

JOSEPH C. LINCOLN

AUTHOR OF

"CAP'N ERI," "CY WHITTAKER'S PLACE,"
"KEZIAH COFFIN," ETC.

ILLUSTRATED

NEW YORK AND LONDON
D. APPLETON AND COMPANY
1911

220

THE WOMAN-HATERS — 1911

THE / WOMAN-HATERS / A YARN OF EASTBORO TWIN-LIGHTS / BY / JOSEPH C. LINCOLN / AUTHOR OF / "CAP'N ERI," "CY WHITTAKER'S PLACE," / "KEZIAH COFFIN," ETC. / (publisher's logo) / ILLUSTRATED / NEW YORK AND LONDON / D. APPLETON AND COMPANY / 1911

COPYRIGHT, 1911, BY / D. APPLETON AND COMPANY / (short rule) / Copyright, 1904, 1906, 1911, by Ainslee Magazine Company / [flush left] Published June, 1911

Half-title; list of books by Joseph C. Lincoln; title-page; verso; dedication page; blank page; Foreword in two pages; contents page; blank page; list of illustrations; blank page; 1-(339); blank page.

Four black and white tipped-in plates by Howard Heath including frontispiece and facing pages 12, 168 and 336.

18½ x 12½ cm.

Reddish-brown cloth on boards, stamped in white on front and spine with paper label on front, oval shaped, 11 x 8.2 cm., printed in two colors, by Howard Heath. The front is blind stamped with a perimeter rule and an oval shaped area to accomodate the label. Unprinted endpapers.

"Foreword / (By Way of Explanation)" is a whimsical explanation of how the novel grew from a short story of the same name previously published in magazine form.

Dedication: TO / J. FREEMAN LINCOLN

Seventeen chapters in which Seth Atkins and John Brown (assumed names) try to be woman haters at Eastboro Twin-lights.

This edition has a (1) printed on the last novel-page, (339), and is the first printing of this title.

"Captain Warren had risen from his chair and was facing her."
[Page 48.]

CAP'N WARREN'S WARDS

BY

JOSEPH C. LINCOLN

AUTHOR OF

"CY WHITTAKER'S PLACE," "KEZIAH COFFIN," "THE
DEPOT MASTER," "THE WOMAN-HATERS," ETC.

ILLUSTRATED BY
EDMUND FREDERICK

D. APPLETON AND COMPANY
NEW YORK AND LONDON: 1911

The first printing of *Cap'n Warren's Wards. Courtesy Ralph and Nancy Titcomb*

CAP'N WARREN'S WARDS — 1911

CAP'N WARREN'S WARDS / BY / JOSEPH C. LINCOLN /
AUTHOR OF / "CY WHITTAKER'S PLACE," "KEZIAH
COFFIN," "THE / DEPOT MASTER," "THE WOMAN-HATERS,"
ETC. / (publisher's logo) / ILLUSTRATED BY / EDMUND
FREDERICK / D. APPLETON AND COMPANY / NEW YORK
AND LONDON: 1911

COPYRIGHT, 1911, BY / D. APPLETON AND COMPANY / [flush left]
Published October, 1911

Half-title; list of books by Joseph C. Lincoln; title-page; verso; list of illustrations; blank page; 1-(380); two blank pages.

Four black and white tipped-in plates by Edmund Frederick including frontispiece and facing pages 60, 194 and 358.

19 x 12.5 cm.

Olive green cloth on boards, blind stamped with brick wall pattern on front, with title area at top front as blind stamped decorative border area; stamped in white front and spine; spine has a blind stamped anchor design. Unprinted endpapers.

Twenty two chapters in which Cap'n Elisha Warren "rescues" a niece and nephew from New York City "society" and brings them to South Denboro.

This edition has a (1) printed on the last novel-page, (380), and is the first printing of this title.

THE

POSTMASTER

BY

JOSEPH C. LINCOLN

AUTHOR OF

"CY WHITTAKER'S PLACE," "THE DEPOT MASTER,"
"CAP'N WARREN'S WARDS," ETC.

ILLUSTRATED

D. APPLETON AND COMPANY
NEW YORK AND LONDON: 1912

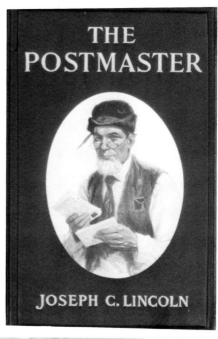

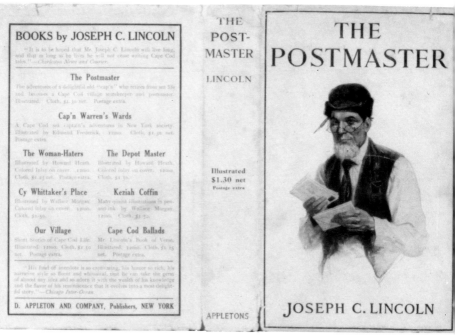

The first printing of *The Postmaster. Courtesy Mrs. Mildred C. Chamberlin*

224

THE POSTMASTER — 1912

THE / POSTMASTER / BY / JOSEPH C. LINCOLN / AUTHOR OF / "CY WHITTAKER'S PLACE," "THE DEPOT MASTER," / "CAP'N WARREN'S WARDS," ETC. / (publisher's logo) / ILLUSTRATED / D. APPLETON AND COMPANY / NEW YORK AND LONDON: 1912

COPYRIGHT, 1912, BY / D. APPLETON AND COMPANY / (short rule) / Copyright, 1911, 1912, by the Curtis Publishing Company / Copyright, 1911, 1912, by the Ainslee Magazine Company / Copyright, 1912, by the Ridgway Company / [flush left] Published, April, 1912

Half-title; blank page; title-page; verso; contents page; blank page; list of illustrations; blank page; 1-(317); three blank pages.

Four black and white tipped-in plates by Howard Heath including frontispiece and facing pages 14, 90 and 264.

18½ x 12½ cm.

Reddish-brown cloth, stamped with white lettering front and spine, oval label on front by Howard Heath, 10.9 x 8.4 cm., printed in two colors. Front blind-stamped with perimeter rule and oval-shaped area to receive label. Unprinted endpapers. Dustwrapper is printed black on white with on front, lettering in black and an illustration of the Postmaster by Howard Heath, tinted in red, all with an enclosing black box rule. The spine and back are in black, together with a list and short description of Lincoln's books. The front and back inside flaps are synopses of Cap'n Warren's Wards and The Woman-Haters, respectively.

Sixteen chapters in which Cap'n Zebulon Snow, Ostable Postmaster, is involved in village life and politics.

This edition has a (1) printed on the last novel-page, (317). It is printed flush left rather than the usual flush right. This is the first printing of this title. Some of the chapters were originally published as short stories, as follows:

I Get Into Politics	Ostable Postmastership, Saturday Evening Post, August 26, 1911
The Force and the Object	Everybody's Magazine, March, 1912
The Sign of the Windmill	Saturday Evening Post, January 27, 1912.

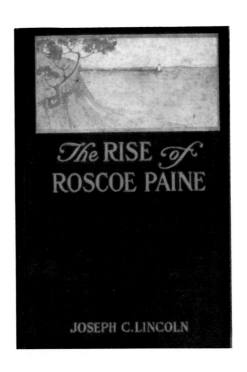

"'Proud to see you amongst us, sir,' said Sim."

[Page 128]

THE RISE OF
ROSCOE PAINE

BY

JOSEPH C. LINCOLN

AUTHOR OF

"THE POSTMASTER," "CAP'N WARREN'S WARDS,"
"KEZIAH COFFIN," ETC.

ILLUSTRATED

NEW YORK AND LONDON
D. APPLETON AND COMPANY
1912

The first printing of *The Rise of Roscoe Paine*.

Courtesy Ralph and Nancy Titcomb

226

THE RISE OF ROSCOE PAINE — 1912

THE RISE OF / ROSCOE PAINE / BY / JOSEPH C. LINCOLN / AUTHOR OF / "THE POSTMASTER," "CAP'N WARREN'S WARDS," / "KEZIAH COFFIN," ETC. / (publisher's logo) / ILLUSTRATED / NEW YORK AND LONDON / D. APPLETON AND COMPANY / 1912

COPYRIGHT, 1912, BY / D. APPLETON AND COMPANY

Half-title; list of books by Joseph C. Lincoln; title-page; verso; list of illustrations; blank page; 1-(469); three blank pages.

Four black and white tipped-in plates by Edmund Frederick including frontispiece and facing pages 82, 200 and 290.

19 x 12.5 cm.

Green cloth on boards with yellow lettering on front and spine; paper label on front printed in light blue and yellow depicting sand dune with scrub pine, bay and point of land with lighthouse, 5.7 x 11.2 cm. Label area blind stamped to receive label. Heart-shaped knotted-rope design on spine. Unprinted endpapers.

Twenty three chapters in which Roscoe Paine learns to forget the past with Mabel Colton and her father James Colton in Denboro.

This edition has a (1) printed on the last novel-page, (469), and is the first printing of this title.

MR. PRATT'S
PATIENTS

BY

JOSEPH C. LINCOLN

AUTHOR OF

"THE RISE OF ROSCOE PAINE," "CAP'N WARREN'S WARDS,"
"MR. PRATT," ETC.

ILLUSTRATED

NEW YORK AND LONDON
D. APPLETON AND COMPANY
1913

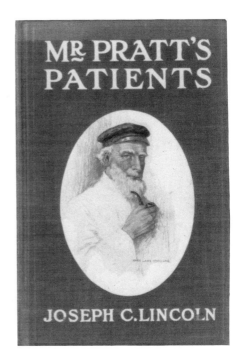

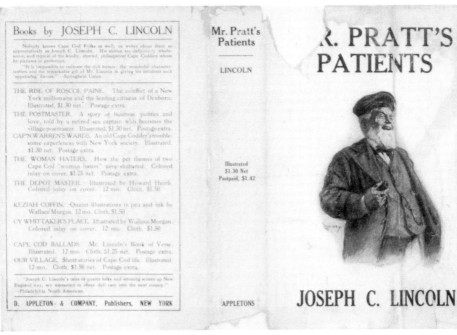

The first printing of *Mr. Pratt's Patients.* *Courtesy Mrs. Mildred C. Chamberlin*

228

MR. PRATT'S PATIENTS — 1913

MR. PRATT'S / PATIENTS / BY / JOSEPH C. LINCOLN /
AUTHOR OF / "THE RISE OF ROSCOE PAINE," "CAP'N
WARREN'S WARDS," / "MR. PRATT," ETC. / (publisher's
logo) / ILLUSTRATED / NEW YORK AND LONDON / D.
APPLETON AND COMPANY / 1913

COPYRIGHT, 1913, BY / D. APPLETON AND COMPANY

Half-title, list of books by Joseph C. Lincoln; title-page; verso; list of
illustrations; blank page; 1-(345); blank page.

Four black and white tipped-in plates by Howard Heath, including frontispiece and facing pages 110, 248, and 320.

19 x 12½ cm.

Light red cloth on boards, with white lettering on front and spine, oval
portrait of Mr. Pratt by Mary Lane MacMillan in black with red tint on
front cover as a paper label, 11 x 8.2 cm., cloth blind stamped to receive
the label. Unprinted endpapers. Dustwrapper has color character portrait
by J. Henry in black with red tint, with on back a list of books by Joseph
Lincoln. Front and back inside flaps bear synopses of Mr. Pratt's Patients
and The Rise of Roscoe Paine, respectively.

Fourteen chapters, in which Solomon Pratt and Eureka Sparrow set in
order Dr. Lysander P. Wool's Sea Breeze Bluff Sanitarium in Wapatomac.

This edition has a (1) printed on the last novel-page, and is the first
printing of this title.

CAP'N DAN'S
DAUGHTER

BY

JOSEPH C. LINCOLN

AUTHOR OF "MR. PRATT'S PATIENTS," "THE RISE OF ROSCOE
PAINE," "THE POSTMASTER," ETC.

ILLUSTRATED

NEW YORK AND LONDON
D. APPLETON AND COMPANY
1914

The first printing of *Cap'n Dan's Daughter.   Courtesy Mrs. Mildred C. Chamberlin.*

230

CAP'N DAN'S DAUGHTER — 1914

CAP'N DAN'S / DAUGHTER / BY / JOSEPH C. LINCOLN / AUTHOR OF "MR. PRATT'S PATIENTS," "THE RISE OF ROSCOE / PAINE," "THE POSTMASTER," ETC. / (publisher's logo) / ILLUSTRATED / NEW YORK AND LONDON / D. APPLETON AND COMPANY / 1914

COPYRIGHT, 1914, BY / D. APPLETON AND COMPANY

Half-title; list of books by Joseph C. Lincoln; title-page; verso; list of illustrations; blank page; 1-(390); four blank pages.

Three black and white tipped-in plates by J. Henry, including frontispiece and facing pages 258, and 354.

19 x 12½ cm.

Dark blue cloth on boards, white lettering front and spine, illustrated label on left side of front printed in black and red, 18 x 5.1 cm., enclosed in a white box-rule, the lettering adjoining it boxed by a continuation of this white box-rule, which in turn forms a larger box framing the entire cover. Label illustration by Edmund Frederick. Unprinted endpapers. The dustwrapper contains the same elements as the front cover on a lighter background, with a notice on the right-hand blue panel in red and white, "This Novel Has not been Serialized." Spine and back are lettered in black, with on back a list of books by Joseph C. Lincoln in black. Front and back inside flaps contain synopses of Cap'n Dan's Daughter and Mr. Pratt's Patients, respectively.

Sixteen chapters in which Miss Gertrude Dott saves her father, Cap'n Daniel Dott, by rescuing her mother from the Scarford Guild of the Ladies of Honor in Trumet.

This edition has a (1) printed on the last novel-page, and is the first printing of this title.

KENT KNOWLES:
QUAHAUG

BY
JOSEPH C. LINCOLN
AUTHOR OF "MR. PRATT'S PATIENTS," "THE RISE
OF ROSCOE PAINE," ETC.

ILLUSTRATED BY
J. N. MARCHAND

NEW YORK AND LONDON
D. APPLETON AND COMPANY
1914

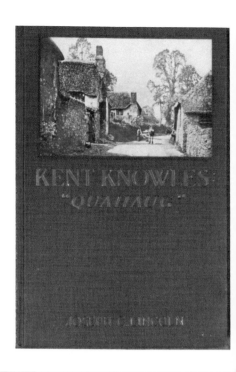

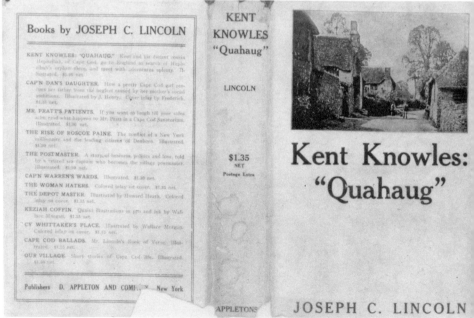

The first printing of *Kent Knowles: "Quahaug"*. *Courtesy Ralph and Nancy Titcomb*

232

KENT KNOWLES: "QUAHAUG" — 1914

KENT KNOWLES: / QUAHAUG / BY / JOSEPH C. LINCOLN / AUTHOR OF "MR. PRATT'S PATIENTS," "THE RISE / OF ROSCOE PAINE," ETC. / (publisher's logo) / ILLUSTRATED BY / J. N. MARCHAND / NEW YORK AND LONDON / D. APPLETON AND COMPANY / 1914

COPYRIGHT, 1914, BY / D. APPLETON AND COMPANY

Half-title; list of books by Joseph C. Lincoln; title-page; verso; contents in two pages; list of illustrations; blank page; 1-(451); blank page.

Four black and white tipped-in plates by J. N. Marchand, including frontispiece and facing pages 152, 250, and 274.

18½ x 12½ cm.

Green cloth on boards, gold stamping on front and spine, paper label at top of front, 7 x 10.5 cm., sepia-toned photograph tinted green and red of an English village scene, with a blind-stamped rectangle for label slightly larger than the same. Unprinted endpapers.

Twenty-nine chapters in which Hosea Kent Knowles, son of Captain Philander Kent Knowles, searches for a lost child and discovers himself.

This edition has a (1) printed on the last novel-page, and is the first printing of this title.

THANKFUL'S INHERITANCE

BY

JOSEPH C. LINCOLN

AUTHOR OF "KENT KNOWLES, QUAHAUG,"
"CAP'N DAN'S DAUGHTER," ETC.

ILLUSTRATED BY
H. M. BRETT

NEW YORK AND LONDON
D. APPLETON AND COMPANY
1915

The first printing of *Thankful's Inheritance.* *Courtesy Jeremy Morritt*

THANKFUL'S INHERITANCE — 1915

THANKFUL'S / INHERITANCE / BY / JOSEPH C. LINCOLN /
AUTHOR OF "KENT KNOWLES, QUAHAUG," / "CAP'N
DAN'S DAUGHTER," ETC. / (publisher's logo) / ILLUSTRATED
BY / H. M. BRETT / NEW YORK AND LONDON / D. APPLETON
AND COMPANY / 1915

COPYRIGHT, 1915, BY / D. APPLETON AND COMPANY

Half-title; list of books by Joseph C. Lincoln; title-page; verso; list of illustrations; blank page; 1-(383); three blank pages.

Four black and white tipped-in plates by Harold Brett, including frontispiece and facing pages 24, 214 and 380.

18½ x 12½ cm.

Light green cloth on boards, stamped in gold front and spine, with on top front, a gold and white stamped representation of a village street, and on the spine a representation of several small houses stamped in white. Unprinted endpapers.

Eighteen chapters in which Thankful Cahoon Barnes turns her inherited home into "High Cliff House" for boarders in East Wellmouth.

This edition has a (1) printed on the last novel-page, and is the first printing of this title. It is also the first book by Joseph C. Lincoln to be illustrated by Harold M. Brett.

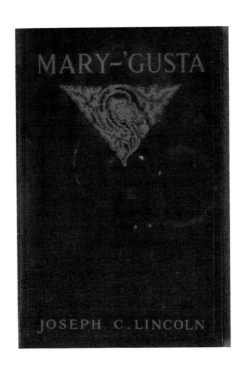

MARY-'GUSTA

BY

JOSEPH C. LINCOLN

AUTHOR OF "THANKFUL'S INHERITANCE," "KENT KNOWLES: 'QUAHAUG,'" ETC.

ILLUSTRATED BY
H. M. BRETT

D. APPLETON AND COMPANY
NEW YORK   LONDON
1916

"There he stood stock still, staring"
[PAGE 398.]

The first printing of *Mary-'Gusta. Courtesy Ralph and Nancy Titcomb*

MARY-'GUSTA — 1916

MARY-'GUSTA / BY / JOSEPH C. LINCOLN / AUTHOR OF
"THANKFUL'S INHERITANCE," "KENT KNOWLES:
'QUAHAUG,' " ETC. / (publisher's logo) / ILLUSTRATED BY /
H. M. BRETT / D. APPLETON AND COMPANY / NEW YORK
  LONDON / 1916

COPYRIGHT, 1916, BY / D. APPLETON AND COMPANY

Half-title; blank page; title-page; verso; list of illustrations; blank page;
1-(411); three blank pages.

Four black and white tipped-in plates by Harold M. Brett, including frontispiece and facing pages 52, 130 and 232.

19 x 12½ cm.

Coral cloth on boards, stamped in gold front and spine, with on front, a
gold-stamped inverted triangular floral design below the title, 4.9 x 7.4
cm. Blind-stamped box-rule around perimeter of front. Unprinted
endpapers.

Thirty chapters in which Mary Augusta Lathrop, an orphan, is willed to
and brought up by Cap'n Shadrack Gould and Zoeth Hamilton in South
Harniss.

This edition has a (1) printed on the last novel-page, and is the first
printing of this title.

EXTRICATING
OBADIAH

BY

JOSEPH C. LINCOLN

AUTHOR OF "MARY-'GUSTA," "THANKFUL'S INHERITANCE,"
"KENT KNOWLES: 'QUAHAUG,'" ETC.

ILLUSTRATED BY
WALT LOUDERBACK

D. APPLETON AND COMPANY
NEW YORK   LONDON
1917

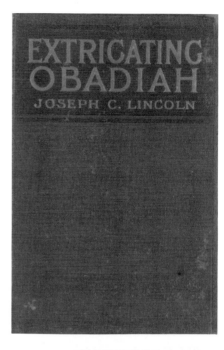

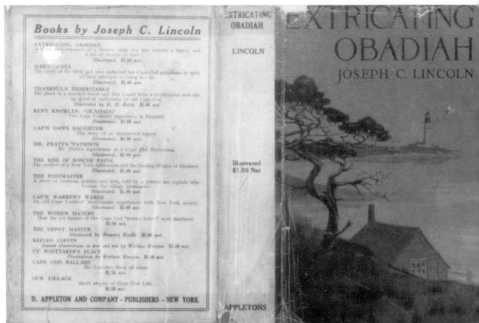

The first printing of *Extricating Obadiah.* *Courtesy Mrs. Mildred C. Chamberlin*

238

EXTRICATING OBADIAH – 1917

EXTRICATING / OBADIAH / BY / JOSEPH C. LINCOLN / AUTHOR OF "MARY-'GUSTA," "THANKFUL'S INHERI- TANCE," / "KENT KNOWLES: 'QUAHAUG,' " ETC. / (pub- lisher's logo) / ILLUSTRATED BY / WALT LOUDERBACK / D. APPLETON AND COMPANY / NEW YORK   LONDON / 1917

COPYRIGHT, 1917, BY / D. APPLETON AND COMPANY

Half-title; list of books by Joseph C. Lincoln; title-page; verso; list of illustrations; blank page; 1-(381); blank page.

Four black and white tipped-in plates by Walt Louderback, including frontispiece and facing pages 52, 116, and 242.

18½ x 12½ cm.

Reddish- deep brown cloth on boards, gold stamping on front and spine, blind stamped double rules top and bottom of front copy and upper spine copy. Unprinted endpapers. Dustwrapper has gold and blue printed on front as an illustration of a cottage and stunted pine with a lighthouse on a spit of land across the water in background. Lettering on front, spine and back in black, with on back, books by Joseph C. Lincoln. Front and back inside flaps contain synopses of Extricating Obadiah and Mary-'Gusta, respectively.

Twenty two chapters in which Cap'n Noah Newcomb rescues his former ship's cook, Obadiah Burgess, from the perils of inherited property in Trumet.

This edition has a (1) printed on the last novel-page of the book, and is the first printing of this title.

"SHAVINGS"

A NOVEL

BY
JOSEPH C. LINCOLN
AUTHOR OF
"EXTRICATING OBADIAH," "MARY-'GUSTA," ETC., ETC.

ILLUSTRATED BY
H. M. BRETT

D. APPLETON AND COMPANY
NEW YORK   LONDON
1918

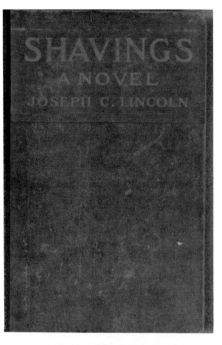

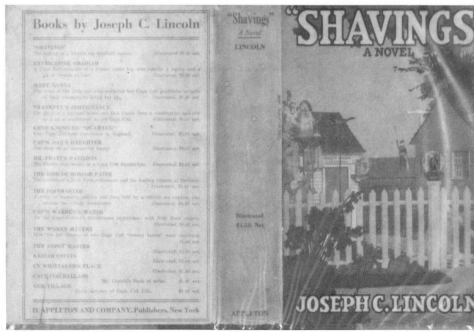

The first printing of *Shavings. Courtesy Ralph and Nancy Titcomb*

"SHAVINGS" — 1918

"SHAVINGS" / A NOVEL / BY / JOSEPH C. LINCOLN /
AUTHOR OF / "EXTRICATING OBADIAH," "MARY-
'GUSTA," ETC., ETC. / (publisher's logo) / ILLUSTRATED
BY / H. M. BRETT / D. APPLETON AND COMPANY /
NEW YORK   LONDON / 1918

COPYRIGHT, 1918. BY / D. APPLETON AND COMPANY

Two blank pages; half-title; list of books by Joseph C. Lincoln; title-page;
verso; list of illustrations; blank page; 1-382; two blank pages.

Four black and white tipped-in plates by Harold Brett, including
frontispiece and facing pages 50, 122 and 292.

18½ x 12½ cm.

Boards bound in light brown paper, with spine and hinge area in a
dark brown cloth. Front and spine lettering is in yellow, front lett-
ering-panel is blind stamped. Unprinted endpapers. Dustwrapper is
a full-color painting of two cottages with white picket fence, with
lettering in white outlined in blue. Spine and back are printed in
blue, the back bearing a listing of Joseph C. Lincoln's books.
Front inside flap is a synopsis of "Shavings," and back flap is a short
biography of Joseph Lincoln accompanied with a picture. Front inside
flap has notice that the book has not been serialized.

Twenty two chapters in which Jedidah Edgar Wilfred Winslow lives
a life of "give-ups" and makes toy windmills in Orham.

This edition has a (1) printed on the last novel-page, and is
the first printing of this title.

THE PORTYGEE

A NOVEL

BY

JOSEPH C. LINCOLN

AUTHOR OF

"SHAVINGS," "EXTRICATING OBADIAH,"
"MARY 'GUSTA," ETC.

FRONTISPIECE BY
H. M. BRETT

D. APPLETON AND COMPANY
NEW YORK   LONDON
1920

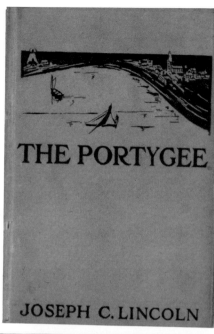

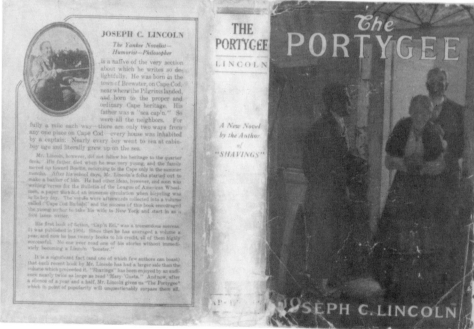

The first printing of *The Portygee*. The rare stamping as described had the top of the black area to the top perimeter of the cover. *Courtesy Jeremy Morritt*

242

THE PORTYGEE — 1920

THE PORTYGEE / A NOVEL / BY / JOSEPH C. LINCOLN
/ AUTHOR OF / "SHAVINGS," "EXTRICATING OBAD-
IAH," / "MARY-'GUSTA," ETC. / (publisher's logo) / FRON-
TISPIECE BY / H. M. BRETT / D. APPLETON AND COM-
PANY / NEW YORK   LONDON / 1920

COPYRIGHT, 1920, BY / D. APPLETON AND COMPANY / Copyright, 1919, 1920, by THE BUTTERICK PUBLISHING CO.

Half-title; blank page; title-page; verso; half-title; blank page; 1-361;
blank page.

Frontispiece plate, tipped-in, a reproduction of a full-color Harold
Brett painting.

18½ x 12½ cm.

Pale blue cloth on boards with on front light green overstamping on
a black line illustration. Lettering in black front and spine, with a
small illustration in black on spine. Some first printings do not have
the green coloring for clouds on front and are rare. Dustwrapper is a full-
color reproduction of the main character in the story at the door of an
elderly couple at night. Lettering on front is white outlined in dark blue,
spine and back are printed in black, with on back a short biographical piece
on Joseph C. Lincoln. Front and back inside flaps are a synopsis of The
Portygee and a list of books by Joseph C. Lincoln, respectively.

Twenty chapters in which Albert Miguel Carlos Speranza, an orphan
and grandson of Cap'n Zelotes Albert Snow, comes to live in South
Harniss, and finds mutual respect in business and war.

This edition has a (1) printed on the last novel-page, and is the first
printing of this title. It is the first of the novels to be serialized in magazine
publication, in the Delineator, October, 1919 to June, 1920.

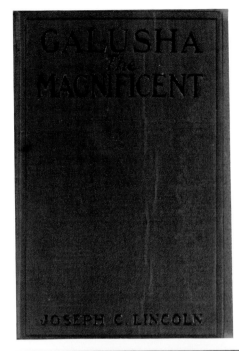

GALUSHA THE
MAGNIFICENT
A NOVEL

BY
JOSEPH C. LINCOLN
AUTHOR OF "SHAVINGS," "THE PORTYGEE,"
"EXTRICATING OBADIAH," "MARY 'GUSTA," ETC.

D. APPLETON AND COMPANY
NEW YORK : : 1921 : : LONDON

The first printing of *Galusha the Magnificent. Courtesy Mrs. Mildred C. Chamberlin*

GALUSHA THE MAGNIFICENT — 1921

GALUSHA THE / MAGNIFICENT / A NOVEL / BY / JOSEPH C. LINCOLN / AUTHOR OF "SHAVINGS," "THE PORTYGEE," / "EXTRICATING OBADIAH," "MARY-'GUSTA," ETC. / (publisher's logo) / D. APPLETON AND COMPANY / NEW YORK : : 1921 : : LONDON

COPYRIGHT, 1921, BY / D. APPLETON AND COMPANY / Copyright, 1921, by The Pictorial Review, Inc.

Half-title; list of books by Joseph C. Lincoln; title-page; verso; dedication; blank page; 1-(407); blank page; two advertising pages.

19 x 12½ cm.

Red cloth on boards, black stamping on front and spine with blind stamped perimeter rule on front. Unprinted endpapers. Dustwrapper is full color depiction of large house with brown picket fence with lighthouse to right and tree to left. Lettering is in white outlined in blue, with spine and back printed in blue, with on back a list of Joseph C. Lincoln's works and his portrait, together with a short biographical piece. Front and back inside flaps are synopses of Galusha the Magnificent and The Portygee, respectively. Inside of dustwrapper is advertising.

Dedication: TO / JAMES A. FAIRLEY

Twenty four chapters in which Galusha Bangs, an inoffensive archaeologist, proves his worth to the doubting inhabitants of East Wellmouth.

This edition is not numbered, but is considered to be the first printing of this title.

FAIR HARBOR

A NOVEL

BY

JOSEPH C. LINCOLN

AUTHOR OF "GALUSHA THE MAGNIFICENT,"
"SHAVINGS," "MARY 'GUSTA," "MR. PRATT,"
"CAP'N ERI," ETC.

D. APPLETON AND COMPANY
NEW YORK :: 1922 :: LONDON

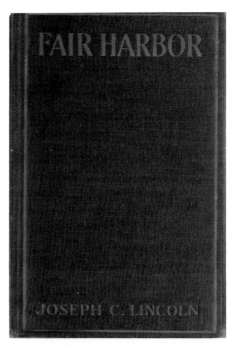

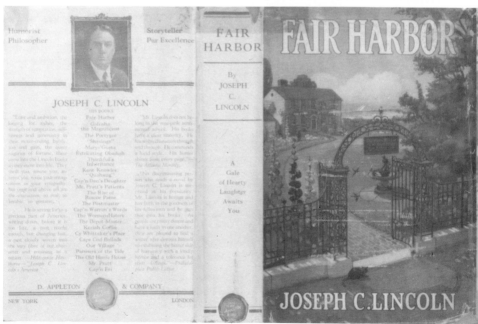

The first printing of *Fair Harbor. Courtesy Mrs. Mildred C. Chamberlin*

246

FAIR HARBOR – 1922

FAIR HARBOR / A NOVEL / BY / JOSEPH C. LINCOLN /
AUTHOR OF "GALUSHA THE MAGNIFICENT," /
"SHAVINGS," "MARY-'GUSTA," "MR. PRATT," / "CAP'N
ERI," ETC. / (publisher's logo) / D. APPLETON AND COM-
PANY / NEW YORK : : 1922 : : LONDON

COPYRIGHT, 1922, BY / D. APPLETON AND COMPANY / Copyright,
1922, by the Curtis Publishing Company

Half-title; list of books by Joseph C. Lincoln; title-page; verso; half-
title; blank page; 1-(379); blank page; two advertising pages.

There are no plates or illustrations in this edition.

19 x 12½ cm.

Bright red cloth on boards, with gold stamping on front and spine,
with on front a perimeter box-rule, stamped in gold. Unprinted endpapers.
Dustwrapper is on front a full-color illustration of Fair Harbor with iron
fence and gate as decoration in black, with lettering in white outlined in
blue. Spine has blue lettering, as well as back, with on back a portrait of
Joseph C. Lincoln and a listing of his works, a short biography, with on
front and back inside flaps synopses of Fair Harbor and Galusha the
Magnificent, respectively. The inside of the jacket contains advertising
for Joseph C. Lincoln, with listings of the books by him published by
Appleton.

Twenty chapters in which Cap'n Sears Kendrick and his ship's cook,
Judah Cahoon, change things at Fair Harbor, a home for mariners'
women, in Bayport.

This edition has a (1) printed on the last novel-page, and is the first
printing of this title. The contents of the book had been serialized
in Ladies Home Journal, June through November, 1922.

DOCTOR NYE
OF NORTH OSTABLE

A NOVEL

BY

JOSEPH C. LINCOLN

AUTHOR OF "FAIR HARBOR," "GALUSHA THE MAGNIFICENT,"
"SHAVINGS," "MARY-'GUSTA," ETC.

D. APPLETON AND COMPANY
NEW YORK :: 1923 :: LONDON

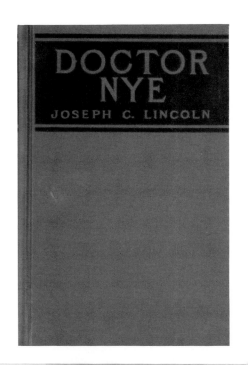

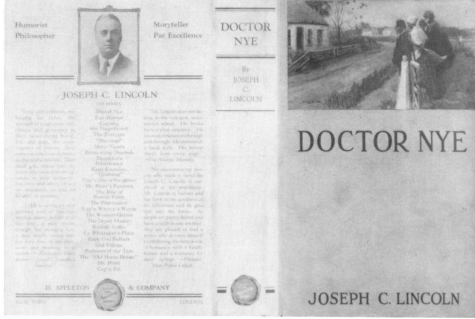

The first printing of *Dr. Nye of North Ostable.* *Courtesy Ralph and Nancy Titcomb*

248

DOCTOR NYE OF NORTH OSTABLE — 1923

DOCTOR NYE / OF NORTH OSTABLE / A NOVEL / BY / JOSEPH C. LINCOLN / AUTHOR OF "FAIR HARBOR," "GALUSHA THE MAGNIFICENT," / "SHAVINGS," "MARY-'GUSTA," ETC. / (publisher's logo) / D. APPLETON AND COMPANY / NEW YORK : : 1923 : : LONDON

COPYRIGHT, 1923, BY / D. APPLETON AND COMPANY / Copyright, 1923, by the Pictorial Review Company

Half-title; list of books by Joseph C. Lincoln; title-page; verso; half-title; blank page; 1-423; blank page; two advertising pages.

18½ x 13 cm.

Light brown cloth on boards, title and author stamped as reverse embossing, of a reddish-brown color on front and spine. Unprinted endpapers. Dustwrapper has author and title, as "Doctor Nye", with full-color Harold Brett painting reproduced, 6.4 x 11.6 cm. Spine and back are in blue ink, with on back a list of Lincoln's books and his portrait, together with book notices. Front and back inside flaps are synopses as advertising for Dr. Nye of North Ostable and Fair Harbor, respectively. Inside of jacket contains Appleton advertising.

Twenty fiye chapters in which Doctor Ephraim Basset Nye returns from jail to fight polluted water and heal ex-friends in North Ostable.

This edition has a (1) on the last printed novel-page, and is the first printing of this title. The contents of the book had been serialized in 1923 in Pictorial Review.

RUGGED WATER

BY

JOSEPH C. LINCOLN

AUTHOR OF "DOCTOR NYE," "SHAVINGS," ETC.

D. APPLETON AND COMPANY
NEW YORK :: 1924 :: LONDON

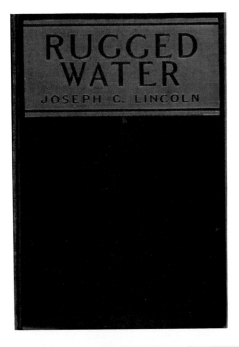

The first printing of *Rugged Water. Courtesy Mrs. Mildred C. Chamberlin*

250

RUGGED WATER — 1924

RUGGED WATER / BY / JOSEPH C. LINCOLN / AUTHOR
OF "DOCTOR NYE," "SHAVINGS," ETC. / (publisher's
logo) / D. APPLETON AND COMPANY / NEW YORK : :
1924 : : LONDON

COPYRIGHT, 1924, BY / D. APPLETON AND COMPANY / Copyright, 1924, by the Curtis Publishing Company

Half-title; list of books by Joseph C. Lincoln; title-page; verso; half-
title; blank page; 1-385; blank page.

19 x 13 cm.

Dark green cloth on boards, gold stamping front and spine as panels
with lettering in reverse. Unprinted endpapers. Dustwrapper has a two-
color illustration of a girl on a dock, lettered in black, with brown
lettering on the spine, and on the back reviews and a listing of Joseph
Lincoln's books together with his portrait, also in brown. Inside
front and back flaps have synopses of Rugged Water and Doctor Nye
of North Ostable, respectively. Inside jacket are publisher's advertisements for Joseph C. Lincoln's books and one book by Grant
Overton.

Nineteen chapters in which Calvin Homer and Seleucus Gammon
live and work at the Setuckit Life Saving Station.

This edition has a (1) printed on the last novel-page, and is the
first printing of this title. The contents of the book had been serialized
by the Curtis Publishing Company.

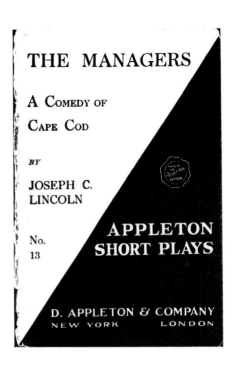

THE MANAGERS
A COMEDY OF CAPE COD

BY
JOSEPH C. LINCOLN

D. APPLETON AND COMPANY
NEW YORK ✹ LONDON ✹ MCMXXV

The first printing of *The Managers. Courtesy Mrs. Mildred C. Chamberlin.*

252

THE MANAGERS – 1925

THE MANAGERS / A COMEDY OF CAPE COD / BY / JOSEPH
C. LINCOLN / (publisher's logo) / D. APPLETON AND COM-
PANY / NEW YORK (design) LONDON (design) MCMXXV

COPYRIGHT, 1925, BY / D. APPLETON AND COMPANY / (short
rule) / All Rights Reserved / [there follows a statement of reservation
of rights as to printing and play production] / Copyright, 1925, by
Joseph C. Lincoln

Half-title; blank page; title-page; verso; dedication; stage layout for
play; 1-(35); blank page; two advertising pages.

18½ x 12½ cm.

Pamphlet with heavier stock saddle-bound to book as cover, printed
deep blue on white, with on cover, deep blue panel covers half of
front, ending at a line from upper right corner to lower left. The
blue panel has, in reverse, APPLETON / SHORT PLAYS / D. APPLE-
TON & COMPANY / NEW YORK   LONDON. Upper unprinted
panel has No. / 13 printed in blue at bottom. The back cover has,
printed in blue, the Appleton logo. The inside front cover has lists
of Appleton Little Theatre Plays and Appleton Short Plays.

Dedication: TO / B. B. WELLS / THE FIRST "TIMOTHY TIDDITT,"
AND / MY COMRADE IN THIS AND SO MANY / OTHER DRAMA-
TIC ADVENTURES. FROM / HIS FRIEND OF TWENTY YEARS, /
JOSEPH C. LINCOLN

A one-act play in which Hiram Salters, bachelor, and Timothy Tidditt,
bachelor, are "managed" by Gertrude Salters, their niece, even though
they think they are the managers themselves.

This edition has a (1) printed on the last printed play page of the pamphlet, and is the first known printing of this title.

QUEER JUDSON

BY

JOSEPH C. LINCOLN

AUTHOR OF "RUGGED WATER," "SHAVINGS,"
"CAP'N ERI," ETC.

D. APPLETON AND COMPANY
NEW YORK :: 1925 :: LONDON

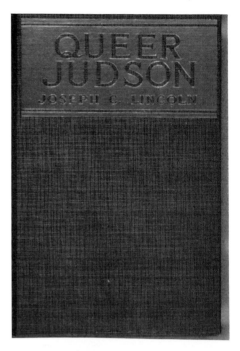

The first printing of *Queer Judson.* *Courtesy Mrs. Mildred C. Chamberlin*

254

QUEER JUDSON — 1925

QUEER JUDSON / BY / JOSEPH C. LINCOLN / AUTHOR
OF "RUGGED WATER," "SHAVINGS," / "CAP'N ERI,"
ETC. / (publisher's logo) / D. APPLETON AND COMPANY /
NEW YORK : : 1925 : : LONDON

COPYRIGHT, 1925, BY / D. APPLETON AND COMPANY / Copyright, 1925, by The Curtis Publishing Company

Half-title; list of books by Joseph C. Lincoln; title-page; verso; half-title; blank page; 1-362.

18½ x 12½ cm.

Dark brown cloth on boards; gold stamping front and spine as solid panels with title and author in reverse on each. Endpapers unprinted. Dustwrapper has full-color illustration by Harold Brett, depicting James Carey Judson, with lettering in black on front, blue on spine and back, with on back a photograph of Lincoln and reviewer's quotes. Front and back inside flaps have synopses of Queer Judson and Rugged Water, respectively. Inside of jacket is publisher's advertising, featuring a portrait and short history of Daniel Appleton, the founder.

Eighteen chapters in which James Carey Judson, Jr. returns to Wellmouth as a financial failure, and carves birds and a new life for himself in his native village.

This edition has a (1) printed on the last novel-page, and is the first printing of this title. The contents had been serialized in the Ladies Home Journal, July through October 1925.

The Big Mogul

by

Joseph C. Lincoln

Author of "Queer Judson," "Rugged Water,"
"Shavings," etc.

D. Appleton and Company
New York   1926   London

The first printing of *The Big Mogul. Courtesy Mrs. Mildred C. Chamberlin*

THE BIG MOGUL — 1926

The Big Mogul / by / Joseph C. Lincoln / Author of "Queer Judson," "Rugged Water," / "Shavings," etc. / (rule) / (publisher's logo) / (rule) / D. APPLETON AND COMPANY / NEW YORK   1926   LONDON

COPYRIGHT, 1926, BY / D. APPLETON AND COMPANY / Copyright, 1926, by the Crowell Publishing Company

Half-title; list of books by Joseph C. Lincoln; title-page; verso; half-title; blank page; 1-386; blank page; seven advertising pages.

19 x 13 cm.

Red cloth on boards, gold stamping front and spine, stamped double rules front and spine between title and author, with on front a perimeter box rule. Unprinted endpapers. Dustwrapper is white, printed in black and red with black lettering, with on front an illustration by Harold Brett in black and red. Back has a picture of Joseph Lincoln with a short biography. Front and back inside flaps are synopses of The Big Mogul and Queer Judson, respectively.

Twenty five chapters in which Cap'n Foster Bailey Townsend, "The Big Mogul," and Miss Reliance Clark, postmistress and milliner, share in raising Esther Townsend, the Captain's orphan niece, in Harniss.

This edition has a (1) printed on the last novel-page, and is the first printing of this title. The contents had been serialized in Colliers Weekly, May 1 through July 10, 1926.

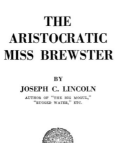

THE
ARISTOCRATIC
MISS BREWSTER

BY

JOSEPH C. LINCOLN

AUTHOR OF "THE BIG MOGUL,"
"RUGGED WATER," ETC.

NEW YORK ✠ LONDON
D. APPLETON & COMPANY
MCMXXVII

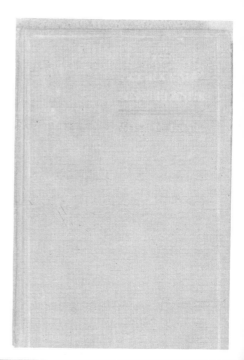

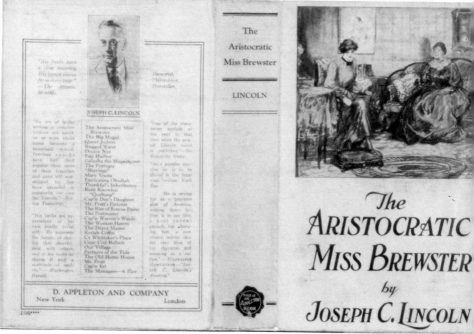

The first printing of *The Aristocratic Miss Brewster. Courtesy Mrs. Mildred C. Chamberlin*

258

THE ARISTOCRATIC MISS BREWSTER — 1927

THE / ARISTOCRATIC / MISS BREWSTER / BY / JOSEPH C. LINCOLN / AUTHOR OF "THE BIG MOGUL," / "RUGGED WATER," ETC. / (publisher's logo) / NEW YORK   (design)   LONDON / D. APPLETON & COMPANY / MCMXXVII / (entire type-page enclosed in a box-rule)

(rule) / COPYRIGHT — 1927 — BY / D. APPLETON AND COMPANY / PRINTED IN THE UNITED STATES OF AMERICA / (rule) / Copyright, 1927, by The Pictorial Review Company

Half-title; list of books by Joseph C. Lincoln; title-page; verso; half-title; blank page; 1-(404); blank page; two advertising pages; three blank pages.

19 x 13 cm.

Green cloth on boards, gold stamping front cover and spine, copy on front cover is in upper left hand corner, with on front, a gold stamped perimeter rule. Unprinted endpapers. Dustwrapper is white, printed in black lettering, with on front a black and red illustration of Mary Brewster and other principals, by George Wright. Back has newspaper reviews, a list of Joseph Lincoln's books, and his portrait. Inside of jacket is advertisements for publisher.

Twenty one chapters in which Mary Brewster astounds her housekeeper, Mrs. Azure Crisp, by becoming a bookkeeper in the Wapatomac National Bank.

This edition has a (1) printed on the last novel-page, and is the first printing of this title. The contents had been serialized in Pictorial Review, June through November, 1927.

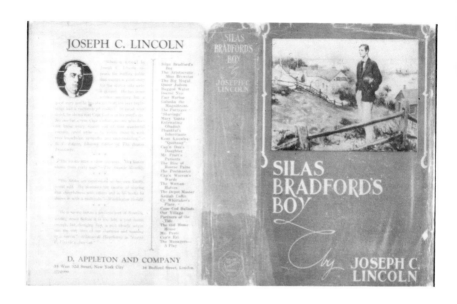

The first printing of *Silas Bradford's Boy*. *Courtesy Mrs. Mildred C. Chamberlin*

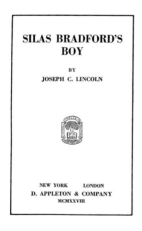

SILAS BRADFORD'S
BOY

BY

JOSEPH C. LINCOLN

NEW YORK   LONDON
D. APPLETON & COMPANY
MCMXXVIII

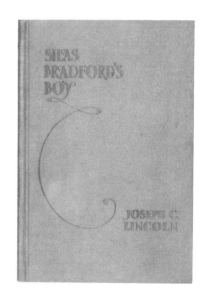

260

SILAS BRADFORD'S BOY — 1928

SILAS BRADFORD'S / BOY / BY / JOSEPH C. LINCOLN /
(publisher's logo) / NEW YORK   LONDON / D. APPLETON
& COMPANY / MCMXXVIII / (entire type-page enclosed in
a box-rule)

(rule); COPYRIGHT — 1928 — BY / D. APPLETON AND COMPANY
/ (rule) / Copyright, 1928 by Curtis Publishing Company

Half-title; list of books by Joseph C. Lincoln; title-page; verso; half-
title; blank page; 1-(377); blank page.

19 x 13 cm.

Blue cloth on boards, gold stamping front cover and spine. Unprinted
endpapers. Dustwrapper printed solid blue on front with black and red
illustration by Harold Brett with white lettering. Book reviews with
booklist and portrait of Joseph Lincoln on back, portrait as a line
drawing. Front and back inside flaps are synopses of Silas Bradford's
Boy and The Aristocratic Miss Brewster, respectively. This edition
has rough-cut fore- and bottom-edges.

Twenty five chapters in which Silas Banks Bradford comes home to
Denboro to practice law, and finds a strange inheritance.

This edition has a (1) on the last novel-page, and is the first printing
of this title. The contents had been serialized in the Ladies Home
Journal, June through October, 1928, and illustrated by Harold Brett.

The first printing of *Blair's Attic.* *Courtesy Mrs. Mildred C. Chamberlin.*

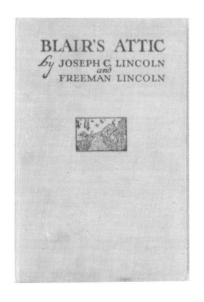

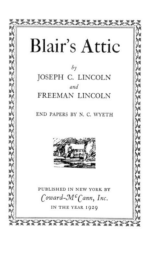

BLAIR'S ATTIC — 1929

Blair's Attic / by / JOSEPH C. LINCOLN / and / FREEMAN
LINCOLN / END PAPERS BY N. C. WYETH / (green line drawing
of house, trees and fence in front, 2.2 x 3.2 cm.) / PUBLISHED
IN NEW YORK BY / [in green] Coward-McCann, Inc. / IN THE
YEAR 1929 / (green floral border outside double box-rule in
green encloses entire type-page)

COPYRIGHT, 1929, BY / COWARD-McCANN, INC. / (rule) / All rights
reserved / (publisher's trademark, "C" and "M" with ribbon connecting
them)

Two blank pages; half-title; list of books by Joseph C. Lincoln; title-page;
verso; contents page; blank page; half-title; blank page; 3-369; seven blank
pages.

19 x 13 cm.

Light blue cloth on boards, stamping in black on spine and black and yellow
on front, line illustration stamped on front, 2.7 x 4.2 cm. Endpapers printed
in blue ink as reverse in which gulls and sea-foam appear as white, design by
N. C. Wyeth. Dustwrapper is full-color painting by N. C. Wyeth which extends to the back of the jacket with lettering in black and red outlined in
white, with black lettering on spine. Front and back flaps contain a synopsis of Blair's Attic and a short biographical note on Joseph Lincoln, respectively.

Five parts in which Miss Iantha Beasley Hallett and Jonas Cahoon Jones
seek Cap'n George Crossley's mysterious "thing" in East Orham.

The Coward-McCann trademark on the verso of this edition is the best
indication that this is the first printing of this title.

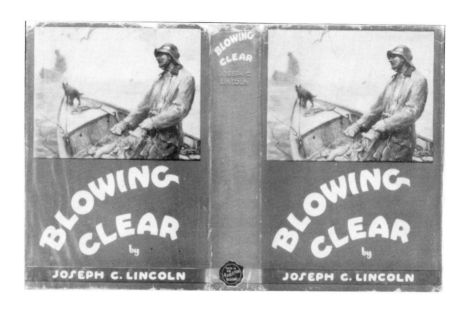

The first printing of *Blowing Clear*. *Courtesy Mrs. Mildred C. Chamberlin*

BLOWING CLEAR

BY
JOSEPH C. LINCOLN

D. APPLETON AND COMPANY
NEW YORK   LONDON
1930

BLOWING CLEAR — 1930

BLOWING CLEAR / BY / JOSEPH C. LINCOLN / (publisher's logo) / D. APPLETON AND COMPANY / NEW YORK   LONDON / 1930

COPYRIGHT — 1930 — BY / D. APPLETON AND COMPANY / (statement of reservation of rights in two lines) / Copyright, 1930, by the Curtis Publishing Co.

Half-title; list of books by Joseph C. Lincoln; title-page; verso; half-title; blank page; 1-(333); blank page.

19 x 13½ cm.

Blue cloth on boards, stamped in gold front and spine with stamping designs and rules front and spine, respectively. Unprinted endpapers. Dustwrapper is solid blue with white lettering and an orange stripe at the bottom that often fades to yellow on the spine, with author printed in orange. Back and front has same Harold Brett drawing in sepia tones of fisherman in skiff with dog at bow, and another fisherman in a boat in fog at upper left, 9.6 x 12.6 cm. Front and back inside flaps are a synopsis of Blowing Clear and a short biography of Joseph C. Lincoln, respectively.

Nineteen chapters in which "Hi" Heath, "Lo" Weeks, and the dog "Jack" bring up the orphan Ralph Raymond Condon at "Seven Up" in Nanticook.

This edition has a (1) printed on the last novel-page, and is the first printing of this title. The contents had been serialized in the Ladies Home Journal, July through October, 1930.

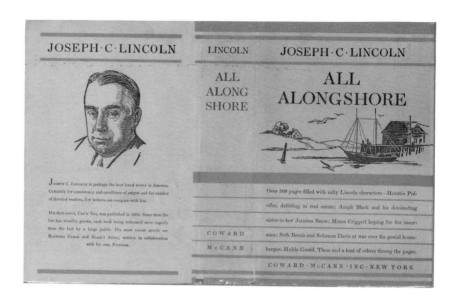

The first printing of *All Alongshore. Courtesy Mrs. Mildred C. Chamberlin*

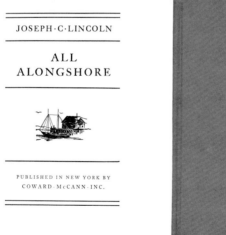

ALL ALONGSHORE — 1931

(double blue rule) / JOSEPH · C · LINCOLN / (blue rule) / ALL/
ALONGSHORE / (blue rule) / (line drawing of a boat with dock
and dock-house, 2.6 x 4.5 cm.) / (blue rule) / PUBLISHED IN
NEW YORK BY / COWARD · McCANN · INC. / (double blue
rule)

COPYRIGHT, 1931, / COWARD-McCANN, INC. / (short rule) / All
Rights Reserved / (C-M trademark)

Half-title; blank page; title-page; verso; contents in two pages; acknowledgments; blank page; half-title; blank page; 1-532; two blank pages.
20 x 14 cm.

Light green cloth on boards, front has same line illustration as title-
page, but in light blue ink. Spine has lettering in light blue and rules in
light blue and dark green. Unprinted endpapers. Dustwrapper is tan
printed in blue and green, with lettering in blue and illustration from
title-page extended and printed in blue, with green horizontal stripes
and rules separating each line of type. Line drawing of Joseph C. Lincoln and short biography on back, with on front and back inside flaps,
synopses of All Alongshore and Freeman Lincoln's novel, Sam, respectively.

Acknowledgments refer to the original published sources for the short
stories that comprise the book.

Eighteen short stories, originally published in magazines as follows:

Payment Deferred	Ladies Home Journal, October, 1929
An Honest Man's Business	Saturday Evening Post, July 23, 1927
The Missing Papers	Saturday Evening Post, September 18, 1926
The Owl and the Mermaid	Pictorial Review, June, 1926
The Luck Piece	Ladies Home Journal, December, 1926
Limits	Saturday Evening Post, November 24, 1928
A Question of Title	Ladies Home Journal, November, 1927
The Castaway	Good Housekeeping, November, 1930
The Cog that Slipped	Saturday Evening Post, August 10, 1929
The Old Hooker	Saturday Evening Post, October 19, 1929
The Cure	Ladies Home Journal, December, 1928
Sandwich Overlay	The Country Gentleman
The Middleman	Ladies Home Journal, January, 1928
By the Air Line	Ladies Home Journal, December, 1923
Independence for Two	Ladies Home Journal, November, 1923
The Realist	Ladies Home Journal, July, 1923
The Safe and the Sane	Redbook Magazine, July, 1919
Peacock's Feathers	Redbook Magazine, 1919

Because of the Coward-McCann trademark on the verso of this edition, this is
the assumed first printing of this title.

The first printing of *Cape Cod Characters.*

Courtesy Mrs. Mildred C. Chamberlin

ALL ALONGSHORE

CAPE COD
CHARACTERS

JOSEPH C. LINCOLN

BLUE RIBBON BOOKS·NEW YORK

ALL ALONGSHORE: CAPE COD CHARACTERS – (1941)

ALL ALONGSHORE / CAPE COD / CHARACTERS / JOSEPH
C. LINCOLN / (rule) / (illustration, 2.6 x 4.5 cm., same as in
All Alongshore) / (rule) / BLUE RIBBON BOOKS · NEW YORK

1941 / BLUE RIBBON BOOKS / 14 WEST 49TH STREET, NEW YORK,
N.Y. / COPYRIGHT, 1931 / COWARD-McCANN, INC. / (short rule) /
ALL RIGHTS RESERVED / ORIGINALLY PUBLISHED UNDER THE /
TITLE All Alongshore / CL / PRINTED IN THE U.S.A.

Half-title; blank page; title-page; verso; contents in two pages; acknowledgments; blank page; half-title; blank page; 1-532; two blank pages.

20 x 14 cm.

Blue cloth on boards, black lettering on spine only. Dustwrapper has
Harold Brett full-color illustration, "Cutting and Heading", at top of
front, 9.9 x 11.8 cm., with title in large red italic letters below it.
Back has printed message headed "Have you been missing something?"
Front and back inside flaps have synopses of Cape Cod Characters and
Cape Cod Yesterdays, respectively. Inside of jacket is promotional advertising for other books.

Acknowledgments is as in earlier printings/editions.

Contents are the same as in the original edition.

All running heads on left-hand pages state "All Alongshore" rather than
"Cape Cod Characters", indicating the probability that the plates were
used intact from the printing(s) of All Alongshore.

JOSEPH · C · LINCOLN

PAYMENT
DEFERRED

PRINTED FOR
THE BOOKSELLERS OF AMERICA BY
COWARD · McCANN · INC.

The special edition of *Payment Deferred. Courtesy Mrs. Mildred C. Chamberlin*

PAYMENT DEFERRED — 1931

(double rule) / JOSEPH·C·LINCOLN / (rule) / PAYMENT / DEFERRED / (rule) / (same illustration as on the title-page of All Alongshore) / (rule) / PRINTED FOR / THE BOOK-SELLERS OF AMERICA BY / COWARD · McCANN · INC · / (double rule)

COPYRIGHT, 1929, / LADIES' HOME JOURNAL / CURTIS PUB-LISHING CO. / COPYRIGHT, 1931, BY / COWARD-McCANN, INC. / (short rule) / All Rights Reserved / (C and M trademark)

Half-title; blank page; limited edition notice page with author's signature as tip-in sewn in with book signature; title-page; verso; 1-32.

Half-bound in light blue cloth on boards, dark blue cloth on spine, with a deep blue vertical stripe printed where the binding cloths meet front and back. Blue illustration on front is the same as the title-page, spine and back are otherwise unprinted. Unprinted endpapers.

Special limited edition, so stated on page above indicated as follows: THIS COPY OF / PAYMENT DEFERRED / IS ONE OF 500 / PRINTED SOLELY FOR THE MEMBERS / OF THE AMERICAN BOOK TRADE / WITH THE COMPLIMENTS OF / (author's hand-written signature)

The contents are the same as appeared in All Alongshore under the short story of the same name, and in the Ladies Home Journal.

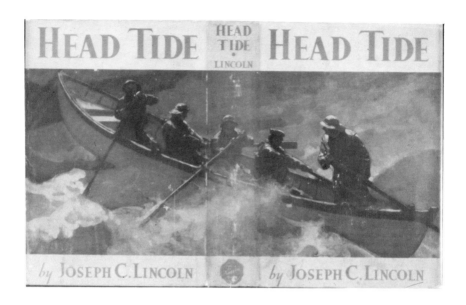

The first printing of *Head Tide*. *Courtesy Mrs. Mildred C. Chamberlin*

HEAD TIDE

BY
JOSEPH C. LINCOLN

NEW YORK AND LONDON
D. APPLETON AND COMPANY
MCMXXXII

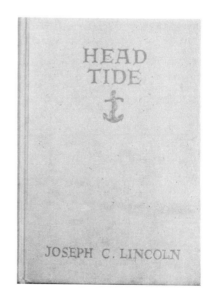

HEAD TIDE — 1932

HEAD TIDE / BY / JOSEPH C. LINCOLN / (publisher's logo) / NEW YORK AND LONDON / D. APPLETON AND COMPANY / MCMXXXII

COPYRIGHT, 1932, BY / D. APPLETON AND COMPANY / (statement of reservation of rights) / COPYRIGHT, 1932, BY JOSEPH C. LINCOLN

Half-title; list of books by Joseph C. Lincoln; title-page; verso; half-title; blank page; 1-(388); two blank pages.

19 x 14 cm.

Bright blue cloth on boards, stamped in gold front and spine, anchor design and short rope design as rule on front and spine, respectively. Unprinted endpapers. Dustwrapper has full-color illustration by N.C. Wyeth wraps around to back, with on front and back light blue areas top and bottom with title in blue repeated on front and back. Front and back inside flaps are synopses of Head Tide and of Joseph C. Lincoln, respectively.

Twenty seven chapters in which Franklin Cobb and Elisha Napoleon Bonaparte Dodson publish the deceased Beriah Higham's newspaper, "The Eagle", in Wellmouth.

This edition has a (1) printed on the last novel-page, and is the first printing of this title.

The first printing of *Back Numbers. Courtesy Mrs. Mildred C. Chamberlin*

JOSEPH · C · LINCOLN

BACK NUMBERS

PUBLISHED IN NEW YORK BY
COWARD · McCANN · Inc.

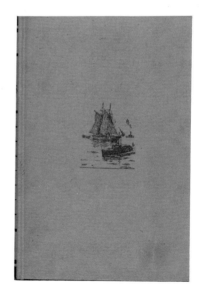

(double rule) / JOSEPH · C · LINCOLN / (rule) / BACK NUMBERS / (rule) / (line illustration by John D. Whiting) / (rule) / PUBLISHED IN NEW YORK BY / COWARD · McCANN · INC. / (double rule)

LINCOLN · BACK NUMBERS / COPYRIGHT · 1933 · BY JOSEPH C. LINCOLN / ALL RIGHTS RESERVED / FIRST EDITION

Half-title; blank page; title-page; verso; Foreword in two pages; contents page; blank page; acknowledgments; blank page; half-title; blank page; 1-371; blank page.

20 x 14 cm.

Light green cloth on boards, illustrated by J. D. Whiting, stamped in light blue on front, 5.1 x 4.4 cm., spine as follows from top; double dark green rule, LINCOLN in light blue, dark green rule, seven light blue rules, dark green rule, COWARD / McCANN / double dark green rule. Unprinted endpapers. Dustwrapper is printed in light blue and yellow on white paper, lettering in front in white and blue, back is black printed advertising for Coward McCann, front and back inside flaps are synopses of Back Numbers and Nod by Freeman Lincoln, respectively.

Foreword: by J. C. Lincoln, "Chatham, Mass., June 24, 1933"; summarizes the Cape Cod of 25-30 years before. Explains some of the reasons why the present work saw publication.

Acknowledgments are to the original magazine publishers of the stories in Back Numbers.

Contains eighteen short stories originally published in Hearst's International Cosmopolitan, Ainslee's and Everybody's magazines, as follows:

As He Thinketh	Everybody's Magazine, May, 1909
The Boojoo Man	Ainslee's Magazine, September, 1904
An Inherited Eden	Ainslee's Magazine, March, 1908
The Soft Snap	Cosmopolitan, November, 1931
A Matter of Twenty Thousand	Ainslee's Magazine, October, 1900
Making A Man of Him	Everybody's Magazine, January, 1908
In Friendship's Name	Ainslee's Magazine, October, 1904
Esteemed Contemporaries	Everybody's Magazine, June, 1907
His Native Heath	Ainslee's Magazine, November, 1905
A Tarnished Star	Everybody's Magazine, May, 1906
The Pocketbook	Ainslee's Magazine, June, 1910
The Petticoat Cruise	Everybody's Magazine, September, 1908
The Moral Tone	Ainslee's Magazine, November, 1907
Dusenberry's Birthday	Ainslee's Magazine, December, 1901
Tinker the Tar	Ainslee's Magazine, February, 1910
Cupid and Clam Fritters	Ainslee's Magazine, November, 1908
The Deep Sea and the Dog	Ainslee's Magazine, November, 1909
Issy and "The Other"	Everybody's Magazine, January, 1907

The first printing of *The Peel Trait. Courtesy Mrs. Mildred C. Chamberlin*

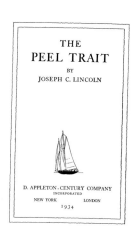

THE
PEEL TRAIT
BY
JOSEPH C. LINCOLN

D. APPLETON - CENTURY COMPANY
INCORPORATED
NEW YORK   LONDON
1934

THE PEEL TRAIT — 1934

THE / PEEL TRAIT / BY / JOSEPH C. LINCOLN / (line drawing of ship, 3.3 x 2.3 cm.) / D. APPLETON-CENTURY COMPANY / INCORPORATED / NEW YORK   LONDON / 1934 / (the entire type-page enclosed in a double box-rule of wavy lines)

COPYRIGHT, 1934, BY / D. APPLETON-CENTURY COMPANY, INC. / (statement of reservation of rights in three lines) / Copyright, 1925, by the Butterick Company

Two blank pages; half-title; list of books by Joseph C. Lincoln; title-page; verso; half-title; blank; 1-309; three blank pages.

19 x 13 cm.

Bright blue cloth, gold stamped front and spine. Endpapers are buff, printed in brown with marine animals, zodiac signs, ships, a windmill, and "The ABC Houses of Wapatomac". Dustwrapper has full-color illustration of girl and old man in front of house, with lettering in black on buff background top and bottom which extends to the spine and back of jacket. Illustrations on spine and back differ from front, with lighthouse and stunted pine on spine, and dories on beach on back. Front and back inside flaps bear synopses of The Peel Trait and a short biography of Joseph C. Lincoln, respectively.

Twenty two chapters in the life of Lettice Peel, the child of her father, Cap'n Cyrenus Peel, and of her Peel ancestors in Wapatomac.

This edition has a (1) printed on the last novel-page, and is the first printing of this title. Originally published serially in The Delineator, March through June, 1925.

The first printing of *Storm Signals. Courtesy Mrs. Mildred C. Chamberlin*

STORM SIGNALS

By

JOSEPH C. LINCOLN

D. APPLETON - CENTURY COMPANY
INCORPORATED
NEW YORK   LONDON
1935

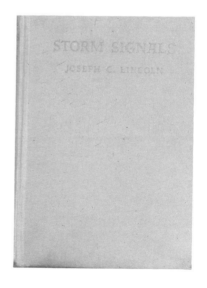

278

STORM SIGNALS — 1935

STORM SIGNALS / By / JOSEPH C. LINCOLN / (publisher's logo) / D. APPLETON-CENTURY COMPANY / INCORPOR-ATED / NEW YORK   LONDON / 1935

COPYRIGHT, 1935, BY / D. APPLETON-CENTURY CO., INC. / (statement of reservation of rights) / Copyright, 1934, 1935, by Joseph C. Lincoln

Half-title; list of books by Joseph C. Lincoln; title-page; verso; half-title; blank page; 1-337; blank page.

19 x 14 cm.

Bright blue cloth on boards, gold stamping front and spine. Unprinted endpapers. Dustwrapper has full color illustration by Matt Clark that wraps from front to back, in black and red, with black and red lettering. Front and back inside flaps are a synopsis of Storm Signals and an article on Joseph C. Lincoln, respectively.

Twenty five chapters in which Cap'n Benjamin A. Snow returns crippled from a shipwreck off Cape Hatteras to Bayport at the beginning of the Civil War.

This edition has a (1) printed on the last novel-page, and is the first printing of this title.

CAPE COD
YESTERDAYS

By

JOSEPH C. LINCOLN

§ *Paintings and Drawings by* §
HAROLD BRETT

BOSTON
LITTLE, BROWN, AND COMPANY · 1935

Title pages from the Little, Brown editions of *Cape Cod Yesterdays.* On left is the Chatham edition and on right the later pictorial title-page edition. Compare this with the original painting on page 122.

Courtesy Mrs. Mildred C. Chamberlin

CAPE COD YESTERDAYS — 1935

CAPE COD / YESTERDAYS / By / JOSEPH C. LINCOLN / (line drawing on oval buff overprint, 4.8 x 3.9 cm.) / Paintings and Drawings by / HAROLD BRETT (this and the preceeding line with finial designs at their ends) / BOSTON / LITTLE, BROWN, AND COMPANY · 1935

Copyright, 1935, / BY JOSEPH C. LINCOLN and HAROLD BRETT / All rights reserved · Published August, 1935

Two blank pages; half-title; four blank pages; title page; verso; THE PREFACE / A Warning and an Invitation in eleven pages; blank page; (special edition notice and autograph page is here inserted as tipped- and sewn-in page); contents page as "THE STORIES"; blank page; list of illustrations in two pages as "THE PICTURES"; half-title; blank page; (3)-286, with addition of plates at designated places as indicated below.

Plates for this edition are as tipped-in sheets with printed illustrations in full color by Harold Brett as tipped-on to the leaves and opposite numbered pages as follows:

Cutting and Heading   Frontispiece

Untrimmed except for top edge, approximately 24 x 17 cm., deckled fore-edge.

Blue and white calico cloth on boards, half-bound natural linen back. Tan paper label printed in dark blue on spine. Slipcase covered in buff paper with light blue label on spine, printed in dark blue.

PREFACE, "A Warning and an Invitation", invites the reader to visit the Cape Cod of "not so long ago as one generation," with the "warning" that this will be a remembering of simple proportions.

Sixteen parts or chapters in which the author remembers various places and happenings of his childhood on Cape Cod. The reasons for their publication may be found in the PREFACE.

This is the Chatham edition, limited to 1075 copies numbered and signed by the author and artist.

CAPE COD YESTERDAYS — 1st Little, Brown

[in green] CAPE COD / [in green] YESTERDAYS / (the first two lines within a light green pictorial ribbon-banner) / (full-color reproduction of the Harold Brett painting) / · The Road to the Harbor · / (the line preceeding within a similar, smaller banner in light green, and below the painting) / [in green] by [in red] JOSEPH C. LINCOLN / [in green] · WITH PICTURES BY · / [in green] HAROLD BRETT / (the above two lines within a ribbon-banner

in light green) / [in red] LITTLE, BROWN & / [in red] COM-
PANY, BOSTON / (the above two lines within a pink banner, this
with no ribbon-tails) / (the entire page, banners and illustrations,
on a background of light blue)

Copyright, 1935, / BY JOSEPH C. LINCOLN and HAROLD BRETT / All
rights reserved / Published October, 1935

Two blank pages; half-title; blank page; two tipped-in leaves, as blank,
frontispiece; the second the title-page, verso (both tipped-in); THE PREFACE
/A Warning and an Invitation in eleven pages; blank page; contents page as
"THE STORIES"; blank page; lists of illustrations in two pages as "THE
PICTURES"; half-title; blank; (3)-286; two blank pages.

Plates are as in the original edition and are tipped-in as full pages.

22 x 14½ cm.

Coral cloth on boards with dark blue printed lettering front and spine, with
on front a windmill and decorations, and decorations front and spine. Endpapers are printed in blue and deep yellow on light blue paper, from
a painting by Harold Brett of twin lighthouses on a bluff with three dories
on the beach and seagulls in the foreground. Dustwrapper is tan or buff
paper printed with full color Harold Brett painting of "A Cape Cod
Clam Digger" with his rake and box, a cottage and the ocean in the background at what appears to be the dawn of the day. Lettering is in red and
dark brown on an "antiqued" reddish background.

Preface and dedication are the same as in the original edition.

Contents the same as the original edition.

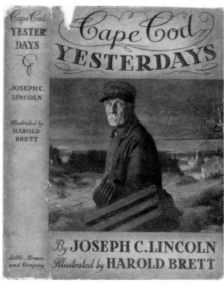
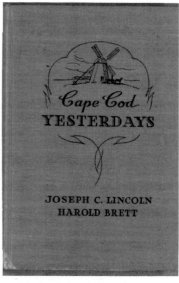

The dustwrapper and front cover of *Cape Cod Yesterdays,* the Little, Brown
pictorial title-page edition.   *Courtesy Mrs. Mildred C. Chamberlin*

Dustwrapper for the Blue Ribbon edition of *Cape Cod Yesterdays,* with advertising message on the back cover. Previous jackets for Little, Brown were blank on the back. *Courtesy Mrs. Mildred C. Chamberlin*

CAPE COD YESTERDAYS — (Blue Ribbon Edition)

CAPE COD / YESTERDAYS / By / JOSEPH C. LINCOLN / (illustration same as the original on the title-page of the Chatham edition, but without yellow background) / Paintings and Drawings by / HAROLD BRETT / (the last two lines with finial decorations covering their ends) / (Blue Ribbon Books logo) / BLUE RIBBON BOOKS · NEW YORK

Copyright, 1935, / BY JOSEPH C. LINCOLN and HAROLD BRETT / All rights reserved / BLUE RIBBON BOOKS EDITION, APRIL, 1939 / PRINTED AND BOUND BY THE CORNWALL PRESS, INC., FOR / BLUE RIBBON BOOKS, INC., 386 FOURTH AVE., NEW YORK CITY

Half-title; blank page; title-page; verso; THE PREFACE (as before) in eleven pages; blank page; contents as THE STORIES; blank page; list of illustrations in two pages as THE PICTURES; half-title; blank page; (3)-286; two blank pages.

Plates are printed as in other editions as tip-ins, but for this printing back one another up, with the exception of the frontispiece, and are found in differing places from the other printings, as follows:

    Frontispiece, Captain Hunter, An Old Scallop Fisherman
    The Herring Run, facing page xiv
    The General Store, facing page xv

Thursday Night Prayer Meeting, facing page 60
"Would You Like for Any" , facing page 61
The Old Chatham-Harwich Stage, facing page 76
Cranberry Time, facing page 77
Gathering Seaweed for the Winter, facing page 140
Gunning on the Marshes, facing page 141
Cutting and Heading, facing page 156
The Fish Weirs on Brewster Shores at Twilight, facing page 157
A Wreck Off Monomoy, facing page 236
Heaving and Hauling on Old Monomoy, facing page 237
The Old Brewster Packet Leaving for Boston City, facing page 252
The Old Windmill at Stage Harbor, facing page 253

20 x 14 cm.

Blue cloth on boards, same lettering as on cloth of tan cloth editions, but
in black. Endpapers unprinted. Dustwrapper is the same as the earlier Little,
Brown with illustration by Brett of "A Cape Cod Clam Digger", with lettering
same as the earlier edition, with on back in black and red a general advertising statement for Blue Ribbon Books. Front and back inside flaps are
synopses of Cape Cod Yesterdays and Cape Cod Characters, respectively.

Preface remains the same from earlier editions.

Contents are the same.

This is the first of five known printings, all within the month of April, 1939

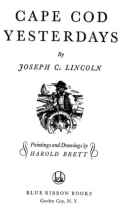

CAPTAIN HUNTER, AN OLD SCALLOP FISHERMAN

Tipped-in Brett frontispiece and title-page for the Blue Ribbon edition of
Cape Cod Yesterdays.   *Courtesy Mrs. Mildred C. Chamberlin*

CAPE COD YESTERDAYS — (Vacation Edition)

CAPE COD / YESTERDAYS / By / JOSEPH C. LINCOLN / (line drawing as in original, except without buff background) / VACATION EDITION / Paintings and Drawings by / HAROLD BRETT (this line and preceeding one with finial designs enclosing their ends) / BOSTON / LITTLE, BROWN, AND COMPANY · 1937

Copyright, 1935, / BY JOSEPH C. LINCOLN and HAROLD BRETT / All rights reserved · Published October, 1935 / Reprinted October, 1935 / Vacation Edition / Published June, 1937

Pagination for this edition remains the same except that the page following the illustrations page is blank.

This edition contains eight of the original Brett tipped-in plates, facing pages as follows:

Cutting and Heading	Frontispiece
The Old Brewster Packet Leaving for Boston City	44
Captain Hunter, An Old Scallop Fisherman	58
Gathering Seaweed for the Winter	100
Gunning on the Marshes	136
Heaving and Hauling on Old Monomoy	184
The Old Windmill at Stage Harbor	220
A Wreck Off Monomoy	240

20½ x 14 cm.

Tan cloth on boards with dark blue stamping for lettering and illustration on front and spine. Unprinted endpapers. Dustwrapper is exactly the same as the full-color Little, Brown title pages with Brett's "The Road to the Harbor", except on a white rather than light blue background. Spine copy is in black, with on back advertising for A. W. Tarbell's "Cape Cod Ahoy" and S.C. Gruber's "The Cape Cod Cookbook", printed in black and red. Both inside flaps are devoted to a synopsis of Cape Cod Yesterdays.

Contents remain the same for this edition.

The first printing of *Great-Aunt Lavinia*.   *Courtesy Mrs. Mildred C. Chamberlin*

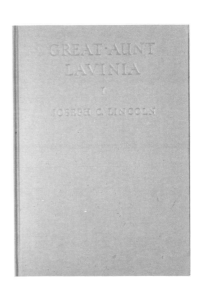

GREAT-AUNT LAVINIA

By

JOSEPH C. LINCOLN

D. APPLETON-CENTURY COMPANY
INCORPORATED
NEW YORK   1936   LONDON

GREAT-AUNT LAVINIA — 1936

GREAT-AUNT LAVINIA / By / JOSEPH C. LINCOLN / (publisher's logo) / D. APPLETON-CENTURY COMPANY / INCORPORATED / NEW YORK   1936   LONDON / (above copy enclosed in box-rule)

COPYRIGHT, 1936, BY / D. APPLETON-CENTURY COMPANY, INC. / (statement of reservation of rights) / COPYRIGHT, 1936, BY HEARST MAGAZINES, INC.

Two blank pages; half-title; list of books by Joseph C. Lincoln; title-page; verso; half-title; blank page; 1-339; five blank pages.

19 x 14 cm.

Bright blue cloth on boards, stamped in gold front and spine. Unprinted endpapers. Dustwrapper has illustration by Meade Schaeffer in black and white with yellow tint. Front and spine have yellow lettering on a deep red or maroon background. Back has reviews, a list of books by Lincoln and his portrait, all in black. The front and back inside flaps are a synopsis of Great-Aunt Lavinia and a short biography of Joseph C. Lincoln, respectively.

Twenty five chapters in which Lavinia Holt Badger shows her business sense in Wapatomac.

This edition has a (1) printed on the last novel-page, and is the first printing of this title. It was published originally as a serial in Good Housekeeping, July through December, 1936.

The first printing of *Storm Girl.* *Courtesy Mrs. Mildred C. Chamberlin.*

STORM GIRL

By

JOSEPH C. LINCOLN

D. APPLETON-CENTURY COMPANY
INCORPORATED
NEW YORK   LONDON
1937

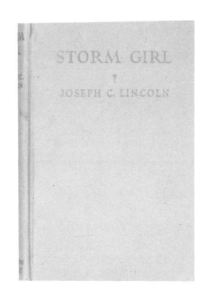

STORM GIRL — 1937

STORM GIRL / By / JOSEPH C. LINCOLN / (publisher's logo) /
D. APPLETON-CENTURY COMPANY / INCORPORATED /
NEW YORK   LONDON / 1937

COPYRIGHT, 1937, BY / D. APPLETON-CENTURY COMPANY, INC. /
(statement of reservation of rights) / COPYRIGHT, 1937, BY HEARST
MAGAZINES, INC.

Two blank pages; half-title; list of books by Joseph C. Lincoln; title-page;
verso; half-title; blank page; 3-278; four blank pages.

18½ x 12½ cm.

Blue cloth on boards, gold stamping front and spine. Unprinted endpapers.
Dustwrapper is a full-color illustration by John O'Hara Cosgrave II with
lettering in yellow and white, the illustration wrapping around the spine to
the back. Front and back inside flaps are a synopsis of Storm Girl and a
short biography of Joseph C. Lincoln, respectively.

Seventeen chapters in which events in the life of Emily Blanchard occur
in storms in East Trumet.

This edition has a (1) printed on the last novel-page, and is the first printing
of this title.

The first printing of *A. Hall & Co.* *Courtesy Mrs. Mildred C. Chamberlin.*

A. HALL & CO.

BY

JOSEPH C. LINCOLN

D. APPLETON-CENTURY COMPANY
INCORPORATED
NEW YORK   1938   LONDON

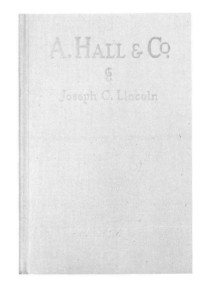

290

A. HALL & CO. — 1938

A. HALL & CO. / BY / JOSEPH C. LINCOLN / (publisher's logo) / D. APPLETON-CENTURY COMPANY / INCORPOR-ATED / NEW YORK   1938   LONDON

COPYRIGT, [correct spelling!] 1938, BY / D. APPLETON-CENTURY COMPANY, INC. / (statement of reservation of rights.

Half-title; list of books by Joseph C. Lincoln; title-page; verso; half-title; blank page; 1-336; two blank pages.

19 x 13 cm.

Bright blue cloth on boards, stamped in gold front and spine, endpapers unprinted. Dustwrapper has a full color painting of a young woman on a dock with inlet and house on a point of land, by John O'Hara Cosgrave II, with title in white lettering as a reverse, author in black lettering, same on spine. Illustration extends to the back of the jacket. Front and back inside flaps are a synopsis of A. Hall & Co., and a short biographical piece on Joseph C. Lincoln, respectively. These flaps are larger than for other books, about 11 and 10.5 cm. wide, respectively.

Twenty five chapters in which Carver Hall returns to West Orham to become involved in a proposed real estate development.

This edition has a (1) printed on the last novel-page, and is the first printing of this title. The word "COPYRIGHT" appearing first on verso has the "h" left out.

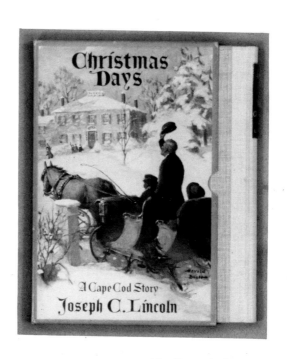

The first printing of *Christmas Days* in its boxed, half-bound special edition. *Courtesy Ralph and Nancy Titcomb.*

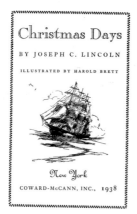

Christmas Days

BY JOSEPH C. LINCOLN

ILLUSTRATED BY HAROLD BRETT

New York

COWARD-McCANN, INC., 1938

CHRISTMAS DAYS — 1938

Christmas Days / BY JOSEPH C. LINCOLN / ILLUSTRATED BY HAROLD BRETT / (line drawing of square-rigged ship) / New York / COWARD McCANN, INC., 1938 / (all copy and the illustration enclosed in a wavy blue border)

COPYRIGHT, 1938, BY COWARD-McCANN, INC. / (notice of reservation of rights) / Typography by Robert Josephy / MANUFACTURED IN THE UNITED STATES OF AMERICA / VAN REES PRESS · NEW YORK

Notice of limited edition page; blank page; half-title; list of books by Joseph C. Lincoln; title-page; verso; contents page; blank page; half-title, Part I; (8)-62; 63 a half-title for Part II; (64)-(114); 115 a half-title for Part III; (116)-(158); blank page. Exceptions as blanks, not numbered, are (29-30), (39-40); (57-8); (71-2); (105-6); (123-4) and (127-8).

Full-page black and white illustrations on page 8 and facing pages 28, 38, 56, 70, 104, 122 and 126. Illustrations on pages 65, 75, 77, 79, 87-8, 97, 140, 141 and (158). All illustrations are line illustrations. Full color tipped-in frontispiece by Harold Brett of the same painting as in the later edition.

19 x 14 cm.

Half-bound in bright blue cloth on boards with spine in tan cloth with black block printed and overstamped in gold with ship's design, title and author. Publisher's name at bottom in gold stamping. The whole in a clear glasseine wrapper within a slipcase covered in blue paper with the Brett full-color painting as in the book as a label on front with black lettering.

Limited edition page is as follows: THIS EDITION OF CHRISTMAS DAYS IS / LIMITED TO ONE THOUSAND COPIES / SIGNED BY THE AUTHOR AND ARTIST. / THIS COPY IS NUMBER _____ . [the number of the particular copy is here recorded] / [Signatures of author and artist follow]

The regular edition of *Christmas Days* with Brett jacket, printed cloth and title page. Note the slight difference in the wavy title-page border between this and the boxed edition.

Courtesy Ralph and Nancy Titcomb

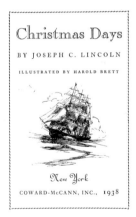

294

CHRISTMAS DAYS — (Regular Edition)

Christmas Days / BY JOSEPH C. LINCOLN / ILLUSTRATED BY HAROLD BRETT / (line drawing of a square-rigged ship) / New York / COWARD-McCANN, INC., 1938 / (all copy and the illustration enclosed in a wavy border)

COPYRIGHT, 1938, BY COWARD-McCANN, INC. / (notice of reservation of rights) / Typography by Robert Josephy / MANUFACTURED IN THE UNITED STATES OF AMERICA / VAN REES PRESS · NEW YORK

Pagination is the same as the earlier edition, with the exception that there is no special editon page in the front part of the book.

Illustrations remain the same from the earlier work, and include the Harold Brett full-color painting as a tipped-in frontispiece that runs off the edge of the page.

21 x 14 cm.

Tan cloth on boards, with on front, a line illustration of a ship in black with title in blue and author in black beneath it, all enclosed in a blue box-rule. Endpapers are glossy paper printed with a full-color painting by Harold Brett of sleigh drawing up to a yellow, hip-roofed house, with a man standing up in the sleigh and waving to others near the house, the whole in the snow. Dustwrapper is the same Harold Brett full-color painting as the endpapers, with lettering in black. The front and back inside flaps are synopses of "Christmas Days" and Marjorie Bayley's "In Friends We Trust," respectively.

This is the regular edition of Christmas Days after the special, limited edition described above.

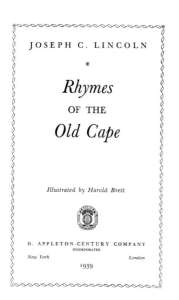

JOSEPH C. LINCOLN

*

Rhymes

OF THE

Old Cape

Illustrated by Harold Brett

D. APPLETON-CENTURY COMPANY
INCORPORATED
New York   London
1939

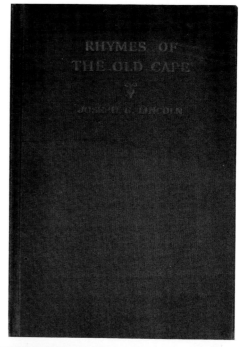

The first printing of *Rhymes of the Old Cape*, with the Brett jacket painting.
Courtesy Mrs. Mildred C. Chamberlin

296

RHYMES OF THE OLD CAPE — 1939

JOSEPH C. LINCOLN / (ornament) / Rhymes / OF THE / Old
Cape / Illustrated by Harold Brett / (publisher's logo) / D. APPLE-
TON-CENTURY COMPANY / INCORPORATED / New York
London / 1939 / (above copy enclosed in a decorative border
rule.)

COPYRIGHT, 1939, BY / D. APPLETON-CENTURY COMPANY, INC. /
(statement of reservation of rights) / Copyright, 1902, by Albert Brandt /
Copyright, 1910, by D. Appleton and Company / Copyright, 1929, 1938,
by Joseph C. Lincoln

Illustrated half-title; list of books by Joseph C. Lincoln; title-page; verso;
illustrated dedication page; blank page; foreword in two pages; contents in
four pages; illustrated half-title; blank page; 1-258.

Full-color painting by Harold Brett as tipped-in frontispiece, accompanied
by the first three lines of the last stanza of Lincoln's poem, "The Surf Along
the Shore."

19½ x 13 cm.

Dark blue cloth on boards, gold stamping on front and spine. Unprinted
endpapers. Dustwrapper has full-color painting by Harold Brett, same as
the color frontispiece, of horse and surrey on sand road with on left a
carriage house and houses and the ocean in the background. Yellow
and white lettering on black background front and spine. Back has black
and white portrait of Joseph C. Lincoln with a short biographical piece.
Front flap is a synopsis of the book, and the back flap lists the author's
works.

Foreword in two pages comments on customs and scenes of the Cape,
with the addition that some of the poems are newly in print [ie., not included in the earlier "Cape Cod Ballads"] .

Dedication page has line illustration, 5.5 x 7.8 cm., with below it the following: On the fly-leaf of my first book, CAPE COD BALLADS, / published
in 1902, were printed these words: / TO MY WIFE / THIS BOOK IS AFFEC-
TIONATELY DEDICATED. / Now, thirty-seven years later, I still do not /
see how that dedication could be improved.

One hundred and nine poems in five sections as follows: The Old Fash-
ioned Boy; Old Fashioned People; Memories; Here and There and The Sea.
Rhymes of the Old Cape contains seventy-one poems from the earlier
Cape Cod Ballads and Other Verse, rearranged, with the addition of thirty-
eight new poems which had seen magazine publication, omitting the "off-
Cape" poems from the earlier Ballads.

Published in 1939 as distinct from the earlier Cape Cod Ballads and Other
Verse. This edition has a (1) printed on the last book-page, (258).

The first printing of *The Ownley Inn.   Courtesy Mrs. Mildred C. Chamberlin*

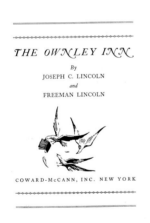

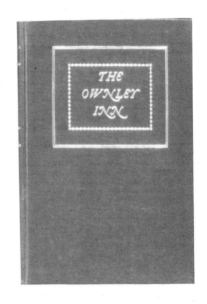

THE OWNLEY INN — 1939

(double rule) / (decorative rule) / THE OWNLEY INN / By / JOSEPH C. LINCOLN / and / FREEMAN LINCOLN / (line drawing of three birds and a book, 5.2 x 5.6 cm.) / COWARD-McCANN, INC., NEW YORK / (decorative rule) / (double rule)

COPYRIGHT, 1939, BY COWARD-McCANN, INC. / (statement of reservation of rights) / Manufactured in the United States of America / Van Rees Press, New York

Half-title; lists of books by Joseph C. and Freeman Lincoln; title-page; verso; contents in two pages; half-title for first part; Prologue; blank page; 3-311; three blank pages. Each of the parts of the book are preceeded by a half-title for that part followed by a blank page, these two forming in all cases a leaf.

20½ x 13½ cm.

Shiny finished blue cloth on boards, stamped in silver front and spine , with on front a decorative border box-rule and outside it a double-box-rule enclosing the copy, and on the spine, publisher, title, and decorative and plain rules in silver. Endpapers are light blue paper printed in black, with two life savers carrying a body onto a beach from a beached boat, with high seas in the offing and rain in the skies. The dustwrapper is a full-color painting of the Ownley Inn on its island, as though seen from an airplane, with the scene extending to a small village with harbor on the back, where a storm is brewing behind the island. Lettering in black on the spine and front. Front and back inside flaps are a synopsis of The Ownley Inn and reviews and a line drawing from Christmas Days, respectively.

Nine parts, including Prologue, in which Seth Hammond Ownley, the owner of the Ownley Inn on Sepatonk Island, seeks the thief who has stolen a copy of the New England Primer.

This is the original edition of this title.

The first printing of *Out of the Fog. Courtesy Mrs. Mildred C. Chamberlin*

OUT OF THE FOG

By

JOSEPH C. LINCOLN

D. APPLETON-CENTURY COMPANY
INCORPORATED
New York   *1940*   *London*

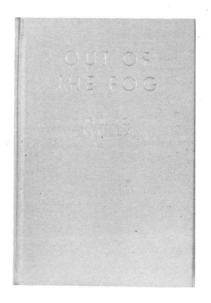

OUT OF THE FOG — 1940

OUT OF THE FOG / By / JOSEPH C. LINCOLN / (Publisher's logo) / (dotted rule) / D. APPLETON-CENTURY COMPANY / INCORPORATED / New York   1940   London

Copyright, 1940, by / D. APPLETON-CENTURY COMPANY, INC. / (statement of reservation of rights and disclaimer of fictitious nature of characters.

Half-title; list of books by Joseph C. Lincoln; title-page; verso; half-title; blank page; 3-360; one blank page.

19½ x 13 cm.

Light blue cloth on boards with gold stamping front cover and spine. Dustwrapper is full-color reproduction of a town with fog in the distance and a car with road. Lettering in white, with the picture wrapping around to a grey panel on the back, with on the panel, an advertising phrase about Joseph Lincoln. Front and back inside flaps are a synopsis of Out of the Fog and a piece about the books of the author, respectively.

Seventeen chapters in which Myra Simpson Crusit becomes a sleuth to solve a mystery plaguing her boss, Cap'n Mark Hanson, bank president, in Wellmouth.

This edition has a (1) on the last novel-page, and is the first printing of this title.

The first printing of *The New Hope*. *Courtesy Ralph and Nancy Titcomb*.

The New Hope

JOSEPH C. LINCOLN
and
FREEMAN LINCOLN

COWARD-McCANN, INC.
◆◆◆
NEW YORK

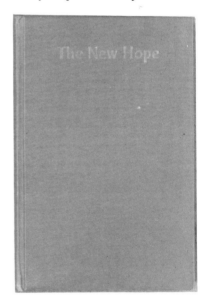

THE NEW HOPE — 1941

The New Hope / JOSEPH C. LINCOLN / and / FREEMAN
LINCOLN / (line illustration of sailing ship, 4.8 x 7.9 cm.) /
COWARD-McCANN, INC. / (decorative rule) / NEW YORK

COPYRIGHT, 1941, BY COWARD-McCANN, INC. / (statement of reservation of rights.)

Two blank pages; half-title; lists of books by Joseph C. and Freeman
Lincoln; title-page; verso; Foreword in two pages; contents; blank page;
half-title for chapter one; blank page; 1-498; four blank pages; with half-
title pages for each of the chapters followed by a blank page in each case.

21 x 14 cm.

Green cloth on boards, gold stamping cover and spine. Endpapers are
printed black and red on buff paper with a map of Trumet during the
summer of 1814 showing houses, features, etc., from the novel, designed
by J. P. Sims. Dustwrapper is a full-color reproduction of a painting of
the village with a red stagecoach in the foreground and the sea and a ship
as the scene wraps around to the back of the book. Lettering is in black
on front and spine. Inside front and back flaps are a synopsis of the book.

Foreword by the authors, inscribed "Chatham, Massachusetts / July, 1941",
stating that the locals and events of the story may be similar to locals and
events known and recorded, but are actually entirely fictional.

Nine chapters or parts in which Cap'n Isaiah Hamilton Dole, master of the
New Hope, and his first mate, Jonathan Bangs, engage in a Trumet community enterprise in the War of 1812.

This is the first printing of this title.

The first printing of *The Bradshaws of Harniss.*
Courtesy Mrs. Mildred C. Chamberlin.

THE BRADSHAWS
OF HARNISS

BY

JOSEPH C. LINCOLN

D. Appleton-Century Company
INCORPORATED
New York   London
1943

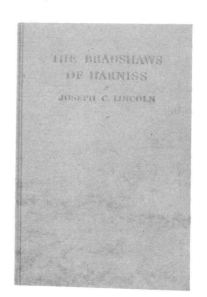

THE BRADSHAWS OF HARNISS — 1943

THE BRADSHAWS / OF HARNISS / BY / JOSEPH C. LINCOLN / (publisher's logo) / D. Appleton-Century Company / INCOR-PORATED / New York   London / 1943

Copyright, 1943, by / D. Appleton-Century Company, Inc. / (statements of reservation of rights and of compliance with War Production Board regulations follow)

Half-title; list of books by Joseph C. Lincoln; title-page; verso; 1-(380).

19½ x 13½ cm.

Blue cloth on boards, gold stamping on front cover and spine. Unprinted endpapers. Dustwrapper has full-color illustration by John O'Hara Cosgrave II, as scene from inside a shop window of the street outside with a man and girl on the street, with a ships' model among other articles in the window. Lettering in black and red on a cream background, with picture of young soldier and girl on spine and on back, a portrait of Joseph C. Lincoln on the front lawn at his home, Crosstrees. (An additional jacket has Lincoln in John Emery's candle factory). Front and back inside flaps are a synopsis of The Bradshaws of Harniss and a list of Joseph C. Lincoln's books, respectively.

Eighteen chapters in which Zenas Bradshaw II, with the help of Emily Thacher Bradshaw, keeps the Bradshaw family store going in Harniss.

This edition has a (1) printed on the last novel-page, and is the first printing of this title. This is the last original novel by Joseph C. Lincoln.

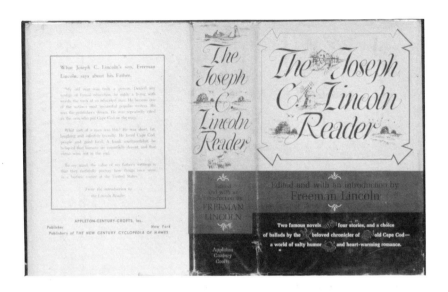

Although not an original book by Joseph C. Lincoln, this item is quite rare
and sought after by collectors.

Courtesy Ralph and Nancy Titcomb

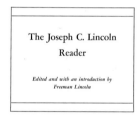

The Joseph C. Lincoln
Reader

Edited and with an introduction by
Freeman Lincoln

Appleton-Century-Crofts, Inc.
New York

THE JOSEPH C. LINCOLN READER — 1959

The Joseph C. Lincoln / Reader / Edited and with an introduction by/ Freeman Lincoln / (the above enclosed in a box-rule, with a second set of rules top and bottom within the box.) / (publisher's logo) / Appleton-Century-Crofts, Inc. / New York

Copyright © 1959 by Freeman Lincoln / (There follows in four sections the sources, with publishing dates, for the contents) / (statement of reservation of rights in three lines) / (disclaimer regarding the fictional nature of the contents) / Library of Congress Card Number: 59-6739 / 539-1 / PRINTED IN THE UNITED STATES OF AMERICA.

Half-title; blank page; title-page; verso; contents page; blank page; Introduction in two pages; half-title for Partners of the Tide; blank page; 3-220; half-title for Galusha the Magnificent; blank page; 223-495; blank page; half-title for Stories From The Old Home House; blank page; 499-549; blank page; half-title for Ballads from Rhymes of the Old Cape; blank page; 553-562; six blank pages.

21 x 14 cm.

Half-bound with tan cloth on boards and lighter tan cloth on back and hinge area, with brown lettering on spine only. Bottom and fore-edges are rough-trimmed, top edge is stained orange. Unprinted endpapers. Dustwrapper is white paper printed in orange and black with on front lettering in black and as white on black, as follows; title in black with orange dock, windmill and haystack designs, all enclosed by a decorative orange border; an orange horizontal stripe with notice of editor and white finial designs top and bottom, and below a black stripe with orange shellfish and shell designs together with white type describing the book. Spine is similar in arrangement with varying, orange designs on top and publisher's name in orange on black at bottom. Back is black printed on white, an excerpt from the editor's introduction, with around it an orange border, and orange publisher's name and blurb at bottom. Front and back inside flaps are a synopsis of the book.

Introduction by Joseph Freeman Lincoln, the author's son, is an appreciation of his father's contribution as an author and a remembrance of him.

Contents are the complete novels Partners of the Tide and Galusha the Magnificent, four selected stories from The Old Home House, and eight "Ballads" from Rhymes of the Old Cape.

This is not an original work by Joseph C. Lincoln, but is important to collectors and dealers in Lincoln material.

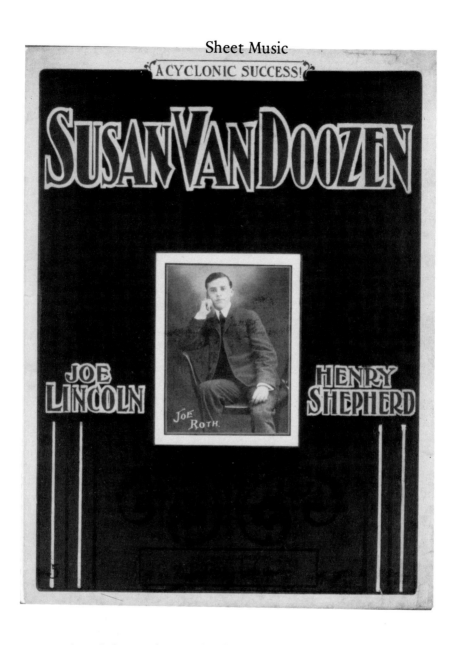

The only known sheet music whose words were written by Joseph C.
Lincoln. The music was written by Henry Shepherd.

SUSAN VAN DOOZEN.

Words by JOE LINCOLN.

Music by HENRY SHEPHERD.

The first music page of Susan Van Doozen.
This and preceeding page courtesy of Ralph and Nancy Titcomb.

309

Plays

This represents the known plays produced or in manuscript form that were actually authored by Joseph C. Lincoln, in whole or in part.

Cy Whittaker's Place: a play in four acts by Joseph Crosby Lincoln and William Danforth; copyrighted in manuscript form but never published; 114 pages.

Uncle Tom's Cabin: a play by Sewall Ford and Joseph Crosby Lincoln, produced by the Unitarian Dramatic Club with Joseph C. Lincoln in the title role; played at the Lyric Theatre, Hackensack, N.J., April 19, 1915.

Gladys of the Brick Yards, or Plinkity Plunk on the Plank Road: a play, based on places in Hackensack. Produced by the Unitarian Dramatic Club.

The Mortgage, the Minister and The Million, or "Gracious Heaven What a Night": a play by Joseph Crosby Lincoln, produced by the Unitarian Club with Joseph C. Lincoln in the title role, April 10 and 11, 1917.

Grandpa: a play by Joseph Crosby Lincoln, produced with Joseph Lincoln in the title role for the benefit of the Cape Cod Red Cross Chapter in several towns, produced at the Unitarian Church, Hackensack, May 2, 3, and 5, 1919. Originally seen in Cape Cod towns in the summer of 1918. In mm mss. form, 28 pages, available through the Library of Congress.

Suppressed Desires: a farce in two acts by Joseph Crosby Lincoln, produced by the Unitarian Dramatic Club, January 14, 1922.

Commodore Peters, a Character Sketch: The Rest Cure, a one-act Farce: [and] Dust of the Road, A Dramatic Allegory: three plays by Joseph C. Lincoln produced by the Unitarian Dramatic Club, March 2 and 3, 1922.

The Managers, a Comedy of Cape Cod: 1925 by D. Appleton & Co., in their series Appleton Short Plays, this being number 13 (see also The Managers in the book section for a physical description of the pamphlet).

Several books were later to be dramatised, among them Shavings and Galusha the Magnificent.

Movies

These are the known movies fashioned from the novels of Joseph C. Lincoln. Interestingly enough, only one, Rugged Water, ever paid anything in royalties to the author.

Partners of the Tide: Eastern Film Corporation, Providence, Rhode Island, 1916. Filmed in the Providence-Newport area, this movie starred a Mr. O'Neill and a Mr. Swenson.

Petticoat Pilot (based on *Mary-'Gusta*): Paramount Pictures, February 20, 1918, five reels, starring Vivian Martin and Theodore Roberts.

Partners of the Tide: Irvin V. Willat Productions, distributed by the W.W. Hodkinson Corp., March, 1921, 35mm., in seven reels, starring Jack Perrin and Marion Faducha, Gordon Mullen, Daisy Robinson, and J.P. Lockney.

Rugged Waters: Famous Players-Lasky Corp., distributed by Paramount Pictures, August, 17, 1925, 35 mm., six reels, starring Lois Wilson, Wallace Beery, Warner Baxter, and Phyllis Haver.

No Trespassing (based on *The Rise of Roscoe Paine*): Holtre Productions, distributed by W.W. Hodkinson Corp., June 11, 1922, 35 mm., seven reels, starring Irene Castle, Ward Crane, Howard Truesdale, Eleanor Barry and Emily Fitzroy.

Idle Tongues (based on *Doctor Nye of North Ostable*): Thomas H. Ince Corp., distributed by First National Pictures, December 21, 1924, 35 mm., six reels, starring Percy Marmont, Doris Kenyon, Claude Gillingwater, Lucille Ricksen, and David Torrence

(see also pages 87-89 for further information)

311

The movie poster for the Paramount release of Rugged Water, 1925.

Courtesy Ralph and Nancy Titcomb

Index

314

318

Mrs. Nancy May Abel
Charles and Ethyl Adams
Madeleine F. Allen
B. Albert Anderson
Henry A. Anderson
Wayne E. Anderson
Marie E. Andrews
Edmund D. Ashley
Anne Austill
Harry O. Austin
Mrs. Harold W. Austin
Walter E. Babbitt
George F. Ballentine, Jr.
Richard Bannister
Mr. and Mrs. Harry E. Barber
Barbara & William D. Barrington Jr.
Allan G. Barrows, Jr.
Mrs. Helen M. Bayes-Harris
Mr. & Mrs. Edward P. Bearse
Mrs. Edward D. Bement
Colonel Kenneth R. Benjamin
Eleanor A. Bennett
Ralph R. Bennett
Richard J. Besciak
Elizabeth S. Beveridge
Mrs. Bernice R. Bigelow
James W. Blackburn
Ruth E. Blackmer
BON-HO-MIE
Mr. & Mrs. Herbert M. Borden
Katherine Border
Bourne High School Library
John F. Bowen
Boyden Library
Lt. Col. & Mrs. Edward Brady
Mrs. Ross Bridgeman
Brooks Free Library
I. Thomas Buckley
William Brewster Bunnell, Jr.
Deborah M. Burgess
Howard B. Burgess
Mr. & Mrs. Leon A. Burgess
Edward D. & Frances L. Busby
Mr. Archie H. Cahoon
Miss Elsie A. Cahoon
Oscar J. Cahoon

Cape Cod Community College
Library-Learning Resources Center
Mr. & Mrs. Drenon Carlyle
Gordon A. Carpenter
Priscilla L. Cash
Centerville Library
Mr. & Mrs. Ralph L. Chamberlin
Ralph L. Chamberlin, Jr.
Mr. & Mrs. Eldon Seely Chapman
Mrs. C. Earl Chase
Christopher W. Chute
Edward H. Chute
Grace M. Clark
Mrs. John S. Cobb
Mrs. Carroll P. Cobleigh
Arthur III & Barbara Colburn
Ann C. Collins
Earl S. & Lillian L. Collins
Eleanor Wright Collins
Thelma & Sidney A. Collins
Margaret A. Connelly
Mr. Maxwell S. Conover
Mr. & Mrs. Allison R. Cook
Elizabeth K. Cook
Helen Livings Cook
Mr. & Mrs. William A. Cook
Mrs. John O'Hara Cosgrave II
Mrs. Lura B. Crump
Raymond F. Cunniff
Richard A. & Carole D. Curry
Mr. & Mrs. James F. Curtis
Priscilla Alden Daggett
Jane Dalton
Mr. & Mrs. Frank D'Amico
Dorothy Robertson Davis
George H. Davis
Edward F. & Margaret H. Day
Edward F. Dean Jr.
Mr. & Mrs. Richard DeBoer, Jr.
L. Edward & Jane Perry DeGagne
Edna L. Demarest
Dennis Memorial Library
Harriet M. Dimmick
Frances T. Dinneen
Mrs. Albertina B. Discenza
Virginia D. & Arthur N. Doane

Edw. E. Doane
Freeman R. Dodsworth
Merton & Bernice Douglas
Elizabeth D. Draeger
Roger A. Dring
Helen A. Driscoll
Lillian P. Dunbar
Ralph L. Earle
Drs. Richard & DuRee Eaton
Richard P. Eckardt
Mr. & Mrs. Calvin B. Eldredge
Virginia E. Eldredge
Esther H. Emmons
Roger C. Engdahl
John P. English
Falmouth Public Library
Harry A. Fanning
Glen A. Fowler
F. L. Frazier
Lyell G. Galbraith
Lynn F. Galbraith
Mrs. Robert M. Galbraith
Inez Gassett
Mr. & Mrs. Henry E. Geberth
Robert M. Gibbs
Robert Gidley
Mrs. Charles F. Gilden
Arline Gilman
David & Suzanne Goehringer
Mr. & Mrs. Harry L. Goff
Lawrence E. Goley, Jr.
Florence H. Gordon
Geraldine Gould
Mr. & Mrs. Paul J. Gray
Priscilla B. Green
Laura A. Greene
Edith Hodges Griggs
Andrew Griscom
Dr. Harry T. Gumaer
Col. & Mrs. Mark R. M. Gwilliam
Judge & Mrs. Allan M. Hale
Mrs. Anna M. Hall
Miss Grace Hallein
Carl H. Handel
Arthur M. Handy
Mr. & Mrs. Carleton T. Handy
Hazel F. Handy
Mildred Harris

George F. Hatch
Carolyn Hayes
Ruth M. Henshaw
Esther & Bob Hickey
Mr. & Mrs. Robert E. Hickey
Josephine Crosby Lincoln Higgins
Beverly E. Hilferty
Margaret Thornton Hodges
Mr. & Mrs. Charles Hodgson
Donald Farrell Hollis
Winifred M. Howard
Mrs. Anson H. Howes
Mrs. Donald A. Hull
Mr. & Mrs. Joseph F. Hunter
Mrs. Arthur Hyoslef
Josephine Buck Ivanoff
Richard F. Irwin
Robert B. & Josephine H. Irwin
Donald & Beverly Jacobs
James White Memorial Library
Trudy M. James
Dorothy H. Johnson
Esther H. Johnson
Mrs. Peter Johnson
Jonathan Bourne Library
Barbara Rex Kaemmerlen
Michele & Bruce Kaemmerlen
Susan & John Kaemmerlen
Lester B. Keedy
Betsey D. Keene (In Memoriam)
Lincoln T. Keller
Mr. & Mrs. D. Charles Kelley
Louise H. Kelley
Veronica M. S. Kennedy
Lawrence G. & Cynthia D. Kent
Harry & Mary Knickerbocker
Eliot S. Knowles
William A. Koelsch
Roland O. Laine
Helen Landers
Doris M. LaRese
Mr. & Mrs. F. T. Lawrence
Mr. & Mrs. Joseph E. Leavitt
Nelson C. Leland
Liberty Lore Antiques
Anne Sargent Lincoln
Mrs. Joseph Freeman Lincoln
Mr. & Mrs. T. P. Lindberg

320

Mrs. Herbert A. Long
Lorania's Book Shop
Mr. Russell A. Lovell, Jr.
Mr. & Mrs. Kenneth A. Luce
Mrs. L. R. Lyman Jr.
Mr. & Mrs. Thomas A. Lyons
Donalda MacGregor
Mrs. Ralph F. Macomber
Mr. & Mrs. Ernest H. Macurdy
Christopher Burgess McConnell
Robert McDowell
O. Herbert McKenney
Edward F. McLaughlin
John M. McLean
Katharine Spring McMillan
Ellen U. Magnuson
Frances J. Mague
Ann Rex Martin
Virginia Rex Martin
Joseph Maslak, Muriel M. Boyle
Mattapoisett Public Library
Mrs. Edwin Hyatt May
Robert G. Melendy
Elizabeth A. Merring
Middleboro Public Library
Millicent Library
Mr. & Mrs. Joseph A. Milner
Margaret E. Miner
Shirley I. Mollineaux
Lola G. Monbleau
Mrs. Irene Morgan
Mr. & Mrs. Jeremy W. Morritt
Florence Gunson Morse
Herbert M. Moskowitz
Albert & Julie Neilson
New Bedford Public Library
Elliott M. Newcomb
Velma L. (Bourne) Newland
Walter D. Nichols
Arthur C. Nickerson
Cora E. Nickerson
Mrs. Edward D. Nickerson
Mr. & Mrs. Herbert D. Nickerson
Mr. & Mrs. Leslie V. Nickerson
Walter S. Nutt
Mrs. Grace Swift Nye
Marie J. O'Grady
Dr. & Mrs. Warren G. Odom

Francis H. O'Donnell
Mr. & Mrs. E. Burnell Overlock
Mrs. Mildred B. Paine
Elizabeth A. Paquette
Averill S. Pappalardo
Parnassus Book Service
David C. Paul
Deborah K. Paul
Elizabeth Rex Paul
Erica S. Paul
Irving C. Paul, Jr.
Thomas R. Perkins
Mr. & Mrs. Elmer F. Perry
Elwell H. Perry
Leonard E. Perry
Mr. & Mrs. Reginald H. Perry
Mr. & Mrs. Trevor Peterson
Elizabeth B. Phinney
Lucy W. Pickett
Plainville Public Library
Elizabeth J. Porter
Mrs. Marion L. Potter
Patricia Beck Powell
Mark Alexander Preston
Bryce & Harriet B. Prindle
Ralph W. Proctor
Wayne A. Proctor
Mr. & Mrs. Kauko K. Pukki
A. T. Purseglove
Kenton E. Quint
Mrs. Olive G. & Dr. Sylvia J. Ranney
Bill & Mary Regan
Richard O. & Irene H. Rex
Richard O. Rex, Jr.
Ruth Irwin Rex
Mrs. Anna S. Rice
Mr. & Mrs. Howard L. Rich
Mrs. Mervyn E. Richards
Frederick C. Richardson
Eleanor C. Richter
Raymond A. Rider
Mr. & Mrs. Harold C. Ripley
Mertie E. Romaine
William D. Romey
Mr. & Mrs. George J. Rullo
Russell Memorial Library
Sandwich Public Library
Susan P. Sasnett

Bette Savage
Mr. & Mrs. Richard Sawyer
Mr. & Mrs. Douglas Scally
Mrs. Ernest Schofield
Sally Crowell Schumann
Elizabeth Thompson Sears
Joseph Semple
Franklin H. Senior
Frank J. Shealey
Mr. & Mrs. Daniel H. Shearer
Marie C. Sheldon
Rev. & Mrs. Allen G. Skiff
Mrs. William Slossar
Mr. & Mrs. Francis L. Smalley
Virginia B. Smith
Clara F. Smyth
Mr. & Mrs. William C. Snow
Somerset Public Library
South Yarmouth Library
Aileen Andres Sox
Dr. John A. Spargo
Frank J. Sparks, Jr.
Mrs. Joseph Steele
Mr. & Mrs. Frederic Stilmar
Stewart & Carol Strickler
Mr. & Mrs. George F. Studley
The Sturgis Library
Gustave H. Suhm
JoAnne Fisher Sullivan
Swansea Public Library
Tales of Cape Cod, Inc.
Marjorie B. Tassinari

Joan I. Taylor
Alden & Barbara Tellstrom
Muriel Thomas
Mrs. R. S. Thomas
John T. Thomson
Florence M. Tibbetts
Richard H. Tilden
Kay & Ed Towne
Douglas C. Townson
Mrs. Allen W. Tracy
Clarence E. Trudeau
Shirley Keene Tucker
Elmer F. Vandewater
Salvador R. Vasques, III
Rosamond Lombard Vondermuhll
Pierre & Marion Vuilleumier
Professor & Mrs. Lee Walp
Mrs. William W. Walsh
Mr. & Mrs. Joseph A. Watkins
D. S. Watson
Mrs. W. Arthur Watt
West Bridgewater Public Library
West Dennis Library
E. Weston Wilbur
M. Ursula Wing
Deborah J. Winkler
Mrs. Kenelm Winslow, Jr.
Gordon & Mary Wixon
Mr. & Mrs. Carl A. Wold, Jr.
Mr. & Mrs. Jack A. Wood
Rebecca S. Woodman
Donald E. & Elizabeth B. Worley